Language and Intercultural Comm[...]
the Workplace

From language classrooms to outdoor markets, the workplace is fundamental to socialization. It is not only a site of employment where money is made and institutional roles are enacted through various forms of discourse; it is also a location where people engage in social actions and practices. The workplace is an interesting research site because of advances in communication technology, cheaper and greater options for travel, and global migration and immigration. Work now requires people to travel over great geographical distances, communicate with cultural 'others' located in different time zones, relocate to different regions or countries, and conduct business in online settings. The workplace is thus changing and evolving, creating new and emerging communicative contexts.

This book provides a greater understanding of workplace cultures, particularly the ways in which working in highly interconnected and multicultural societies shape language and intercultural communication. The chapters focus on critical approaches to theory and practice, in particular how practice is used to shape theory. They also question the validity and universality of existing models. Some of the predominant models in intercultural communication have been criticized for being Eurocentric or Anglocentric, and this volume proposes alternative frameworks for analysing intercultural communication in the workplace. This book was originally published as a special issue of *Language and Intercultural Communication*.

Hans J. Ladegaard is a Professor and the Head of the Department of English at the Hong Kong Polytechnic University. He is interested in intercultural communication, language attitudes and stereotypes, language and gender, narratives of migration, pragmatics, and discourse analysis.

Christopher J. Jenks is an Assistant Professor of English at the University of South Dakota, Vermillion, SD, USA. He is interested in global Englishes, intercultural communication, race and ethnicity, national identities, critical pedagogy, and discourse analysis.

Language and Intercultural Communication in the Workplace

Critical approaches to theory and practice

Edited by
Hans J. Ladegaard and Christopher J. Jenks

Routledge
Taylor & Francis Group

LONDON AND NEW YORK

First published 2017
by Routledge

2 Park Square, Milton Park, Abingdon, Oxfordshire OX14 4RN
52 Vanderbilt Avenue, New York, NY 1007

Routledge is an imprint of the Taylor & Francis Group, an informa business

First issued in paperback 2018

Copyright © 2017 Taylor & Francis

All rights reserved. No part of this book may be reprinted or reproduced or utilised in any form or by any electronic, mechanical, or other means, now known or hereafter invented, including photocopying and recording, or in any information storage or retrieval system, without permission in writing from the publishers.

Notice:
Product or corporate names may be trademarks or registered trademarks, and are used only for identification and explanation without intent to infringe.

British Library Cataloguing in Publication Data
A catalogue record for this book is available from the British Library

ISBN 13: 978-1-138-20492-8 (hbk)
ISBN 13: 978-0-367-07777-8 (pbk)

Typeset in TimesNewRomanPS
by diacriTech, Chennai

Publisher's Note
The publisher accepts responsibility for any inconsistencies that may have arisen during the conversion of this book from journal articles to book chapters, namely the possible inclusion of journal terminology.

Disclaimer
Every effort has been made to contact copyright holders for their permission to reprint material in this book. The publishers would be grateful to hear from any copyright holder who is not here acknowledged and will undertake to rectify any errors or omissions in future editions of this book.

Contents

CONTENTS

Citation Information

The chapters in this book were originally published in *Language and Intercultural Communication*, volume 15, issue 1 (February 2015). When citing this material, please use the original page numbering for each article, as follows:

CITATION INFORMATION

Chapter 5

Preparing students for the global workplace: the impact of a semester abroad
Jane Jackson
Language and Intercultural Communication, volume 15, issue 1 (February 2015) pp. 76–91

Chapter 6

The impact of international students on the university work environment: a comparative study of a Canadian and a Danish university
Jane Vinther and Gordon Slethaug
Language and Intercultural Communication, volume 15, issue 1 (February 2015) pp. 92–108

Chapter 7

'The cultural stuff around how to talk to people': immigrants' intercultural communication during a pre-employment work-placement
Prue Holmes
Language and Intercultural Communication, volume 15, issue 1 (February 2015) pp. 109–124

Chapter 8

Virtual team management: what is causing communication breakdown?
Jane Lockwood
Language and Intercultural Communication, volume 15, issue 1 (February 2015) pp. 125–140

Chapter 9

Identities at odds: embedded and implicit language policing in the internationalized workplace
Spencer Hazel
Language and Intercultural Communication, volume 15, issue 1 (February 2015) pp. 141–160

Chapter 10

International city branding as intercultural discourse: workplace, development, and globalization
Shi-xu
Language and Intercultural Communication, volume 15, issue 1 (February 2015) pp. 161–178

For any permission-related enquiries please visit:
http://www.tandfonline.com/page/help/permissions

Notes on Contributors

Spencer Hazel is a Research Fellow in the Business Development Unit 'Linguistic Profiling for Professionals' in the School of English, University of Nottingham, UK. He has previously worked at the University of Southern Denmark, Roskilde University, and the University of Luxembourg. His research interests include workplace interaction, professional communication, internationalization, intercultural communication, embodiment, and the creative industries.

Prue Holmes is a Reader in the School of Education, Durham University, UK. She is the pathway leader of the MA Intercultural Communication and Education, and she researches and supervises doctoral students in intercultural communication and its links to education, languages, competence, and dialogue. She is co-investigator of 'Researching Multilingually at the Borders of Language, the Body, Law and the State', a research project funded by the British Arts and Humanities Research Council. She is a chair of the International Association for Languages and Intercultural Communication.

Jane Jackson is a Professor in the English Department at the Chinese University of Hong Kong. Her research interests include intercultural communication, language and identity, and education abroad. Her recent books include *Language, Identity, and Study Abroad: Sociocultural Perspectives* (2008); *Intercultural Journeys: From Study to Residence Abroad* (2010); *The Routledge Handbook of Language and Intercultural Communication* (2012); and *Introducing Language and Intercultural Communication* (2014).

Christopher J. Jenks is an Assistant Professor of English and ESL/TESOL Coordinator at the University of South Dakota, Vermillion, SD, USA. He is the author and co-editor of several books, including an edited collection on second language learning that was runner-up for the 2011 British Association for Applied Linguistics Book Award. His research interests include ICC, world Englishes, English as a lingua franca, and social identities, including race and ethnicity relations in education. He is currently working on a book that explores race in the English language teaching profession in South Korea.

Yew Lie Koo has recently retired as Professor of culture, language and literacy in multilingual contexts in the School of Language Studies and Linguistics at Universiti Kebangsaan Malaysia. She has published widely on topics in applied linguistics, cultural politics and knowledge production, language and literacy education in multilingual/cultural contexts, and the internationalization of higher education.

Hans J. Ladegaard studied at Odense University, Denmark and Cambridge University, England. Prior to his present post as a Professor and the Head of the Department of English at the Hong Kong Polytechnic University, he taught at Hong Kong Baptist University, the University of Southern Denmark, and Cambridge University. His research interests include intercultural communication, language attitudes and stereotypes, language and gender, narratives of migration, and pragmatics and discourse analysis, and he has published widely on these issues in international journals and books. He is a co-editor and review editor of *Pragmatics and Society* (John Benjamins).

Agnes Lucy Lando obtained her PhD in Social Communication from The Pontifical Gregorian University, Rome. She is an Associate Professor and Associate Head in the Department of Communication at Daystar University, Kenya. She has published articles on communication, ethics, higher education in Africa, and on the idea of a Catholic university in the 21st century. Her publications have contributed to a growing scholarship on media ethics, higher education, media studies, and new media and communication theory in Africa and beyond. She is the co-author of *Impact of Communication and the Media on Ethnic Conflict* (2016).

Sze Seau Lee is a PhD candidate in the School of Language Studies and Linguistics at Universiti Kebangsaan Malaysia. Her research focuses on enhancing learning through research-informed pedagogy in order to make English language learning more relevant and engaging to students. She is currently teaching in a private college in Malaysia in the areas of English for academic purposes and English for specific purposes.

Jane Lockwood is an Associate Professor in the Department of English at the City University of Hong Kong. She has worked in the United Kingdom, Australia, the Philippines, and Hong Kong, in the tertiary and industry sectors. Her research interests are in English communication challenges in Asian workplaces with specific reference to outsourcing in Asia and in virtual team communication. Most of her recent publications relate to communication breakdown in call centres.

Judith N. Martin is a Professor of Intercultural Communication in the School of Human Communication at Arizona State University, USA. Her principle research interests focus on the role of culture in communication competence and online communication, interethnic and interracial communication, and sojourner adaptation and reentry. She has published numerous research articles in Communication journals as well as other disciplinary journals. She has co-authored three textbooks on intercultural communication as well as co-edited books on White identity and culture and online communication.

Linda Muthuri is in her final year of MA studies in Corporate Communication at Daystar University, Kenya. She has vast work experience with Corporates, having worked with both the government and the private sector. Her ongoing thesis examines the impact of culture and intercultural communication on organizations' cohesion and service delivery.

Shanta Nair-Venugopal was most recently an Associate Fellow, and subsequently guest scholar, at the Institute of Malaysian and International Studies, National University of Malaysia (NUM). She was previously Principal Fellow in language, discourse, and intercultural communication at the Institute of Occidental Studies at NUM. Prior to this appointment, she was a Professor in the School of Language Studies and Linguistics at NUM, where she taught, supervised, and examined at undergraduate and graduate levels for more than 30 years. Her publications include *The Gaze of the West and Framings of the East* (2012) and *The Discourse of Ethics and Equity in Intercultural Communication* (2016).

Thomas K. Nakayama is a Professor of Communication Studies at Northeastern University, USA. He has also held administrative and teaching positions at several universities, including two Fulbright teaching awards at the Université de Mons, Belgium. His research addresses how racial difference functions rhetorically in society, as well as how larger economic, political, cultural, and social contexts function to structure intercultural communication and interaction in particular ways. He is widely published in both US and international journals, and is the founding editor of the *Journal of International and Intercultural Communication*.

Paul R. Odira is in the final year of his MA studies in Corporate Communication at Daystar University, Kenya. He has vast work experience with Corporates, having worked with both the government and the private sector. His ongoing thesis examines the impact of culture and intercultural communication on organizations' cohesion and service delivery.

Gordon Slethaug is a Professor of English Studies at the University of Waterloo, Canada. His research focuses on international education, globalization, rhetoric, semiotics, and American culture. He is the author of *Teaching Abroad: the Cross-Cultural Classroom and International Education* (with Janette Ryan, 2007), *International Education and the Chinese Learner* (2010), and *International Teaching and Learning at Universities: Achieving Equilibrium with Local Culture and Pedagogy* (with Jane Vinther, 2016). He has recently taught at the University of Southern Denmark, and prior to that, he taught at the University of Hong Kong and Sun Yat-sen University, China.

Jane Vinther is the Director of English Studies at the Kolding Campus of the University of Southern Denmark. She has extensive teaching and research experience in language and culture, intercultural communication, second language acquisition, and internationalization of education. She has researched and published on international teaching and learning as well as language learning from various pedagogical perspectives. Her teaching has been recognized by The Outstanding Teacher Award for the Humanities at the University of Southern Denmark.

Shi-xu is a Changjiang Distinguished Professor and the Director of the Centre for Discourse & Cultural Studies, at Hangzhou Normal University, and the Director of the Centre for Contemporary Chinese Discourse Studies at Zhejiang University, China. He has also taught in the Netherlands, Singapore, and the United Kingdom. His books in English include *Cultural Representations*, *A Cultural Approach to Discourse*, *Discourse and Culture*, *Chinese Discourse Studies*, *Discourses of the Developing World* (with Prah and Pardo), *Read the Cultural Other* (with Kienpointner and Servaes), and *Discourse as Cultural Struggle* (editor). He is the founding Editor-in-Chief of *Journal of Multicultural Discourses* and the General Editor of *Cultural Discourse Studies* (both with Routledge).

INTRODUCTION

Language and intercultural communication in the workplace: critical approaches to theory and practice

Hans J. Ladegaard[a] and Christopher J. Jenks[b]

[a]Department of English, Hong Kong Baptist University, Ho Sin Hang Campus, Kowloon Tong, Hong Kong; [b]Department of English, University of South Dakota, Vermillion, USA

In much contemporary theorising on culture and globalisation, it is argued that the emerging international network of sociopolitical systems has led to a weakening of the nation as a source of identity (*cf.* Blasco, 2004). Giddens (2002) points out that despite its sudden popularity, it is often not clear what different people mean by globalisation, although there seems to be a general consensus that it 'has something to do with the thesis that we now live in one world' (p. 7). Some scholars have taken this argument further and argued that the era of the nation state is over; concepts like nationalism and national culture have become obsolete and are being replaced by the new concept of 'global culture' which is 'tied to no place or period. It is context-less, a true mélange of disparate components drawn from everywhere and nowhere, born upon the modern chariots of global telecommunications systems' (Smith, 1990, p. 177; see also Ohmae, 1995). Global commodities and the ever-present influence of multinational business corporations have been presented as evidence that, if not now then at least as a likely scenario for the future, we shall live in 'a world of sameness' where 'growing global interconnectedness will lead to the death cultural diversity' (Hannerz, 2001, p. 57).

However, a potential problem with these predictions about the decreasing importance of culture in a globalised world is that they do not consider the interface between theory and practice. Only by looking at cultural and linguistic practices in people's lives as they work, talk, socialise and go about their everyday business do we get an insight into their orientations and dispositions in a globalised world (see Ladegaard, 2007). Another potential problem with the idea of a world of sameness and interconnectedness is that it was developed by Western scholars focusing on Western contexts (see Asante, Miike, & Yin, 2013; Shi-xu, 2009, for a critique). With rising tension and inter-ethnic and inter-religious conflicts in the Middle East, in Eastern Europe and in many parts of Asia, the idea of cultural uniformity seems purely hypothetical and a dream scenario at best. Rather than being a place of sameness and interconnectedness, the world, as Geertz (2000) points out, 'is growing both more global and more divided, more thoroughly interconnected and more intricately partitioned' (p. 246). It has become 'a scramble of differences in a field of connections' (p. 250), which makes the call for cultural awareness, tolerance and intercultural dialogue more pertinent than ever.

The workplace is a site where the notion of a connected *and* disconnected world is perhaps most evident. Every day, people around the world have to engage in unfamiliar cultural and linguistic practices in the workplace in order to solve problems, sell products or concepts, negotiate terms and prices, or simply to get the job done. More often than not, workplace practices are carried out in a second or third language and with people who not only have different cultural values and norms but also little knowledge of, and specific training to deal with, cultural, linguistic and religious diversity.

Thus, the workplace demands research on linguistic and intercultural practices; the current Special Issue of *Language and Intercultural Communication* is dedicated to this endeavour. It brings a select number of the papers that were presented at the 13th annual conference of the International Association for Languages and Intercultural Communication (IALIC), which held its second conference in Asia at Hong Kong Baptist University, 29 November–1 December 2013. The conference theme was 'Language and Intercultural Communication in the Workplace: Critical Approaches to Theory and Practice', and the papers that are published in this Special Issue will focus on various aspects of this theme.

The workplace

From multinational corporations to family-owned shops, from language classrooms to outdoor markets, the workplace is fundamental to socialisation. It is not only a site of employment where money is made and institutional roles are enacted through various forms of discourse; but it is also a location where people engage in social actions and cultural practices, from befriending or bullying a colleague to complimenting or gossiping about the boss. In other words, the workplace possesses cultural and linguistic norms and conventions for engaging in work- and non-work-related activities (see Angouri & Marra, 2011; Holmes & Stubbe, 2003).

In recent years, the workplace has attracted increasing attention from language and communication scholars for several reasons: first, because of advances in communication technology, which have radically changed the ways in which people communicate at work (see, for example, Herring, 1996, 2004; Waldvogel, 2007; see also Lockwood, 2015); second, because cheaper and greater options for travel have led to a boom in global tourism as well as in work placements and overseas exchange programmes for students and staff in secondary and tertiary education (see, for example, Jackson, 2010; Thurlow & Jaworski, 2010; see also Jackson; and Vinther & Slethaugh, 2015), and finally, because global migration and immigration have become a way of life, and for many, particularly in Asia and Africa, a necessary means for survival (see, for example, Blommaert, 2010; Ladegaard, 2012a). Work is no longer confined to a single space. It now requires people to travel over great geographical distances, communicate with cultural 'others' located in different time zones, relocate to different regions or countries and, not least, conduct business in virtual teams and other online settings. The workplace is thus constantly changing and evolving, creating new and emerging communicative contexts.

The aim of this Special Issue is to promote greater understanding of workplace cultures, particularly the ways in which working in highly interconnected and multi-cultural societies shape language and intercultural communication (ICC). The collection, which include papers from authors and regions that are under-represented in intercultural scholarship, encourages greater dialogue between researchers studying workplace issues with different theoretical and methodological frameworks (including sociolinguistics, ethnography, social psychology and communication) and between researchers and practitioners. It is vital that scholars and practitioners, businesses and NGOs, and schools and universities work together, drawing on each other's expertise to solve complex communication problems in the workplace and together propose ways to move forward. The papers in this Special Issue also take a critical approach to theory and practice, in particular how the latter is used to shape the former, and how the validity and universality of existing models may be questioned by considering new frameworks, alternative perspectives from scholars in Africa and Asia, or by studying new cultural and communicative contexts.

Critiquing Eurocentric/Anglocentric frameworks

Many Asian scholars have criticised some of the predominant models in ICC for being Eurocentric/Anglocentric and proposed alternative frameworks as the way forward in language and ICC research in non-Western contexts (see, for example, Chen & Miike, 2003; Miike, 2009, 2013; Shi-xu, 2009, 2013). More than 10 years ago, Kramsch (2002) raised the same problem. She argued:

> To realize how much intercultural communication itself is typical of a certain Anglo-Saxon culture, discourse and worldview, proponents of intercultural communication would have to confront the inequalities among cultures, the inevitability of conflict, and the tragic dimensions of human action … It might also help us [to] realize that the concept of intercultural communication as it is currently used can be easily highjacked [*sic*] by a global ideology of 'effective communication' Anglo-Saxon style, which speaks an English discourse even as it expresses itself in many different languages. (Kramsch, 2002, pp. 283–284)

Despite several notable attempts by non-Western (and Western) scholars to change this perspective (see, for example, Asante et al., 2013; Nakayama & Halualani, 2010), Eurocentric/Anglocentric frameworks still seem to weigh heavy in many workplaces and educational settings, as well as in scholarly work. Below are a couple of authentic examples from workplace contexts.

Scenario 1

A global company with subsidiaries in 38 countries across the world introduces a new set of global strategies, which should apply to all employees irrespective of where they work. These strategies stipulate that pay, status and rank in the company will be determined by the employees' ability to 'step up, utilize their resources, think outside the box, be proactive, be vocal, and challenge conventional thinking' (from the company's internal paper, released to all employees worldwide in the spring of 2013).

Scenario 2

A Hong Kong Chinese student in an ICC class writes to his professor:

> In a Western mindset, it's good to be expressive and vocal, to communicate directly, and to engage in close relationships. However, as you know, many Chinese people think the opposite … There is a contradiction between two assumptions we seem to make in class: (1) There is no such thing as 'good' and 'bad' culture; and (2) Most of the models we adopt in class are based on a Western mindset, and according to these models, our indirect approach to communication is bad. Is there any way out of this dilemma? Please correct me if I'm wrong. (Daniel, Hong Kong Chinese student, in an email to his teacher in the autumn of 2012)

What these examples illustrate is that ICC is still being hijacked by global ideologies of effective, proactive, direct, upfront communication Anglo-Saxon style, which replicates Western discourses even when the language and the context are Chinese. In the Chinese subsidiaries of the global company in Scenario 1, the employees argued that Asian employees would be severely disadvantaged compared to their European and American colleagues if these new policies were implemented because their cultural and linguistic background would work against them. Subsequently, the CEO of the Hong Kong subsidiary managed to set up a meeting between a member of the company's senior management and an ICC scholar who was asked to explain if and to what extent employees' cultural and linguistic background should be taken into account in formulating global organisational strategies. Although not without its problems, and certainly not without its critics, the discussion included references to Hofstede's (2001) work arguing that the relatively larger power distance and the greater preponderance of uncertainty avoidance that characterise many Asian workplaces may be a hindrance to individual employees' attempts to step up, be vocal and challenge conventional thinking (cf. Ladegaard, 2012b). It was also mentioned that having to step up, be vocal and negotiate important issues in a foreign language is significantly more difficult for some than for others, and this may also disadvantage Chinese and other Asian employees. The company paper was later modified in the attempt to address these problems.

Daniel's email to his professor is typical for many Chinese students' experience. They were brought up in families and in a school system that favour an indirect approach to communication, where respect for authorities is of paramount importance, and where being (excessively) vocal and expressive is a common negative stereotype of a *gweilo* ('white ghost' in Cantonese but commonly used as a term for a white person in Hong Kong) more than something a Chinese person should strive towards. Thus, the university experience may be a dilemma for Chinese students who struggle to become more vocal, upfront and expressive, and yet, feel that this would require them to adopt a new and alien identity (see Ladegaard, 2015). Daniel's final comment – a request to be corrected in case he is wrong – is also typical of the respect and deference many Asian students and employees might prefer in conversations with their superiors, and again, not something that would give bonus points if the aim is to be upfront, critical and expressive. What these two examples have made pertinent is that by allowing students and employees to express themselves in ways that are 'natural' to them, and thus aligned with their cultural expectations, we also allow them to align their discourse with their identity, and this may be a possible way out of Daniel's – and many other Asian students' and employees' – dilemma (see Scollon, Scollon, & Jones, 2011).

When it comes to ICC research, it is still a fact that Western paradigms dominate, even when non-Western contexts are being analysed. Despite extensive criticism arguing that these models do not adequately encompass the Asian experience, Hofstede's (2001) taxonomies and Brown and Levinson's (1987) Politeness Theory, for example, are still widely applied to ICC research in Asian workplaces (see Bond, Zegarac, & Spencer-Oatey, 2000; Matsumoto, 1988 for a critique). In the attempt to propose non-Eurocentric approaches to discourse studies, Shi-xu (2009, p. 41) advocates that Eastern paradigms should (1) formulate locally grounded, globally minded and historically conscious frameworks; (2) bear their own cultural–intellectual identities; (3) be mindful of and reflect upon Eastern past experiences and present conditions; and (4) converse with Western paradigms.

Several of the papers in this Special Issue highlight the need to critique existing approaches to ICC research and propose new frameworks that take the local context into account. Thus, Lando, Muthuri and Odira argue that existing approaches to ICC do not incorporate religion as a salient variable and, therefore, are not useful in terms of analysing the multi-religious reality of many Kenyan workplaces. And Martin and Nakayama criticise existing analytical frameworks in ICC for not considering people's unequal access to power, education and resources in the workplace as part of the analysis of ICC, and they therefore propose a dialectal approach that incorporates both macro- and micro-social issues.

'Culture' in ICC

One issue that has been debated repeatedly in ICC research over the past three decades is how we conceptualise culture, and how much, or how little, importance we should attach to interlocutors' cultural background when we analyse intercultural encounters. In a recent overview of the history of the IALIC, MacDonald and O'Regan (2014) recount how the first IALIC conferences in the mid-1990s were set up to challenge and critique 'the essentialist, nation-based assumptions on which the field of intercultural communication had been founded' (p. 401). The association also criticised the burgeoning intercultural training industry, which, as the authors saw it, 'tended towards the perpetuation of cultural stereotypes rather then their suppression' (pp. 401–402). Out of this critique grew a scholarship, which questioned a conceptualisation of 'culture' as being 'a set of coagulated cognitive and psychological traits', or as 'a causal *a priori*' (p. 402). Rather, it was argued that 'culture' should be seen as a fluid, flexible and multifaceted phenomenon, which is created, negotiated and recreated *in situ* as people engage in talk and other forms of social interaction. This conceptualisation of 'culture' (and other forms of social categorisation) has much in common with the social constructionist approach to discourse (e.g., Parker, 1998), and with discursive approaches to social psychology (e.g., Edwards & Potter, 1992), which were also gaining ground at the time.

In much recent discourse-based research in workplace settings, the social construc-tionist approach is often the preferred paradigm (see, for example, Angouri & Marra, 2011; Holmes, 2006; Mullany, 2007; Schnurr, 2008). Thus, 'culture' is conceptualised as dynamic, flexible and ever-changing, and national culture and ethnic identity are widely discarded as analytical categories with a-priori significance. Some scholars within this tradition of discourse-based workplace research have also argued that the importance of culture is perhaps exaggerated because, they claim, people do not orient to culture when they interact in the workplace. Schnurr and Zaytz (2012) interviewed expatriate leaders in multicultural workplaces in Hong Kong and found that in their meta-discourses about leadership, culture was often brought up by the participants themselves and identified as a salient variable. However, when the authors recorded workplace discourse and studied how these leaders actually communicated with their local Hong Kong Chinese colleagues, they found that 'culture was much less of an issue than claimed in the interviews' (p. 295).

It is a truism that there is often a discrepancy between what people *say* they do (such as orient to 'culture' when 'doing being a leader') and what they *actually* do (such as be focused on 'getting the job done'), but it is equally true that we do not know how much, or how little, culture means for our behaviour. More often than not, we do not orient to culture in our discourse, or talk about 'cultural stuff', but that does not mean, as many of the papers presented at the conference and in this Special Issue will show, that culture is not of paramount importance for what we do, and do not do, in the workplace. One observation appears to be pertinent: when research reports on minority group members, these members themselves will often highlight that culture plays an important role in their lives (cf. the non-local interns in New Zealand workplaces reported in Holmes, or the Chinese students on overseas exchange reported in Jackson; Holmes, 2015; Jackson, 2015). As Edward T. Hall (1976, p. 46) testifies: 'Most cross-cultural exploration begins with the annoyance of being lost', and it is arguably more likely that minority group members will experience the annoyance of being lost. And with this feeling of being lost and misunderstood comes the realisation that this fussy concept of 'culture', which defies easy categorisation and interpretation, has tremendous impact on our lives as we go about doing our business, in the workplace and in all other spheres of life. If we closely scrutinise what the (minority) employees and students in many of the 10 papers that comprise this Special Issue are actually saying, 'culture' is indeed salient.

As MacDonald and O'Regan (2014) recounted: the critical intercultural scholarship, which IALIC and its journal have come to represent, grew out of dissatisfaction with essentialist, nation-based interpretations of ICC, and out of frustration with a 'cultural awareness' industry which appeared to exacerbate cultural differences and stereotypes rather than alleviate them. So, whilst 'culture' in discourse-based research in workplace settings now appears to be widely conceptualised as fluid, multifaceted and constructed *in situ*, it is perhaps time to turn the page and reconsider what we may have lost by rejecting (national) culture and ethnicity as a-priori categories for explaining linguistic and communicative behaviour. Kecskes (2014) proposes a happy marriage between these two opposing conceptualisations of culture as the way forward in intercultural pragmatics. He says:

> Culture has fuzzy boundaries and [should be] considered neither relatively static nor ever-changing, but both. It has both a priori and emergent figures. Culture changes diachronically (slowly through decades) and synchronically (emerges on-the-spot, in the moment speech). (pp. 4–5)

Kecskes goes on to explain why he opposes what he calls the current mainstream approach to culture in ICC, which assumes 'that culture in no way imposes ethnic or cultural characteristics into communicative behavior a priori' (p. 5). This approach, he argues, is just as one-sided as the one that proposes a linear connection between 'culture' and 'communication'. He therefore concludes that we should strive for a compromise between the two approaches: one that acknowledges 'the possibility of ethnic or cultural marking in communicative behavior' (p. 5) but, at the same time, allows for the situational context to be salient and where participants co-construct (inter)cultures *in situ*. Many of the papers in this volume seem to suggest that both approaches to the interpretation of culture in ICC are important.

Overview of themes

A common theme in many of the 10 papers that follow is that they offer, in various ways, a critique of existing paradigms and analytical frameworks in ICC. Common in most critiques is the claim that existing approaches often do not encompass the lives and experiences of people in multilingual, multicultural (global) workplaces, particularly in Asian and African settings. In the first paper, 'Reconsidering intercultural (communication) competence: A dialectal approach', Judith Martin and Thomas Nakayama examine the assumptions about employees' cultural identities that exist in much contemporary ICC research. They critique existing research and training in intercultural competence for its focus on individual characteristics, motivation and skills, often seen through a

Eurocentric lens. As an alternative, they propose a dialectal perspective on ICC in the workplace that emphasises larger societal issues, such as access to power, resources and education. The dialectal approach is similar to social constructionism in that both analyse the role of discourse in constructing and shaping social reality, but they also differ in that the dialectal approach emphasises the larger social contexts that give some people more or less influence in the construction of reality. Thus, employees' (unequal) access to power and resources becomes essential for our understanding of the dynamics of ICC and competence in the workplace.

The next paper, 'Issues of language and competence in intercultural business contexts' by Shanta Nair-Venugopal, deals with the discrepancy between the standard English language norms that exist in multiethnic multilingual Malaysia and employees' actual language use in the workplace. Through an analysis of actual language behaviour in three Malaysian workplaces, Nair-Venugopal shows how interlocutors are able to communicate effectively and appropriately, despite linguistic variability in English within and across countries. Thus, the formulaic approach to business English as evidenced in EFL materials does not reflect employees' actual language performance in Malaysian workplaces. Neither does the dominant organisational rhetoric on in-house language in a commercial bank in Malaysia match that of the trainers' actual language use, which was found to be (a combination of) localised sub-varieties of Malaysian English; standard, colloquial and bazaar Malay; code-switching and code-mixing between English and Malay; workplace jargon; and various ethnolects. The author concludes by critiquing the Anglo-American bias in much ICC research and laments, with Miike (2013), that non-Western cultures often remain peripheral targets of data collection and analysis and, thus, 'fail to become central resources of theoretical insight and humanistic inspiration' (Miike, 2013, p. 116). One remedy, Nair-Venugopal argues, could be more ethnographic participant observation research in non-Western business contexts.

The next paper, 'Examining linguistic proficiency in the multilingual glocal workplace: A Malaysian case study' is written by Sze Seau Lee and Yew Lie Koo, and it explores many of the same issues as the previous paper. Lee and Koo analyse actual language competence and behaviour in a Malaysian airline company, focusing on email communication. The study is motivated by a desire to document employees' actual language proficiency and thus provides a description of the linguistic features that are being used in a multilingual Malaysian workplace. The authors find that while English is still the dominant language, it is far from the standard English language models prescribed by educational policies. Rather, in line with Nair-Venugopal's research, the authors identify a mix of language varieties in play, including functional business English, Malaysian English, and ELF, often mixed with local codes such as Malay and Cantonese. Thus, the authors conclude that a pluralistic view of language proficiency in the glocal workplace is required, and they propose how this view could be reflected in language pedagogy in higher education.

In the fourth paper, Agnes Lando, Linda Muthuri and Paul Odira take us from Asia to Africa. Their paper, entitled 'The importance of interfaith dialogue in the workplace for achieving organizational goals: A Kenyan case study', provides first a critique of existing frameworks in ICC for failing to include religious belief as a potentially salient variable. This, the authors argue, is a problem for multiethnic multi-religious societies like Kenya, where faith is an important dimension of people's lives, including life in the workplace. The authors then outline the details of a study designed to assess the importance of interfaith prayers for achieving organizational goals in two banks in Nairobi, Kenya. The study elicits feedback from Christian, Muslim and Hindu employees who have been involved in interfaith prayers at work. Virtually all attendees agree that interfaith dialogue brings people together across faiths and ethnic groups and breaks down communication barriers and therefore contributes to fulfilling organisational goals. However, the study also includes a caveat: some attendees declared that they had dropped out of the interfaith prayer meetings because they felt pressure to convert to other group members' religion. Thus, interfaith dialogue closely resembles other forms of intergroup dialogue where the ability and willingness to embrace the cultural 'other' in his/her disquieting tension is part of the intercultural experience (cf. Bredella, 2003).

The next two papers discuss and, to some extent, problematise the internationalisation of university education, which is now a prominent feature in tertiary education around the world. In Jane Jackson's paper 'Preparing students for the global workplace: The impact of a semester abroad', the focus is on Chinese university students' experience of 'sojourn', and how it changes their perspective on the world and their place in it. Most of them find that the semester abroad has helped them become more globally oriented citizens, helped them with their communication skills and self-confidence, and also helped them prepare for the global workplace. It was noticeable, for example, that many of the students mentioned their desire to go abroad again to work, and also that the sojourn had made them more open to alternative career paths. However, not all sojourners had developed their global-mindedness during their semester abroad. Some had felt the experience daunting, realising, for example, that 'the Western world' was not at all what they had imagined. For these students, the sojourn meant they ended up determined to have less international exposure in the future.

Jane Vinther and Gordon Slethaug's paper, 'The impact of international students on the university work environment: A comparative study of a Canadian and a Danish university', discusses how the presence of thousands of international students changes the university work environment. They compare a Danish and a Canadian university focusing on internationalisation policies and their effectuation. The authors note first how universities apparently assume that the presence of international students on campus is unproblematic and therefore do not offer any training to lecturers and administrative staff who deal with international students every day. In their study, Vinther and Slethaugh asked university employees to report on their experience with non-local students, and they found that although many felt their presence had enriched and diversified the university work environment and therefore made it a more interesting place to work, there were also numerous problems and frustrations, such as a decline in English proficiency, high enrolment figures, required curriculum changes, and a shift to a more business-oriented approach to education. Overall, there were more similarities than differences between the Danish and the Canadian university.

Building on the notion that there are many ICC challenges due to globalising forces, Prue Holmes explores in her paper, '"The cultural stuff around how to talk to people": Immigrants' intercultural communication during a pre-employment work-placement', the experiences of immigrants entering the New Zealand workforce. Her findings show that immigrants' concerns about ICC are not limited to carrying out workplace responsibilities in a language that may not be their first but extends to the ability to converse in informal situations, such as small talk during tea breaks. Holmes' study also uncovered how differences in expectations, like the belief that one should work independently versus the need to seek affirmation and support from co-workers, constrain immigrants working relations with their supervisors. These findings offer important insights into the benefits and challenges of using work-placement programmes to help immigrants succeed in communication and employment in a new country.

In a similar study, Jane Lockwood's contribution, 'Virtual team management: What's causing communication breakdown?', shares how a large, multinational company designs and implements a needs analysis for business and communication practices concerning the management of geographically displaced work teams. Using interviews, document analysis, surveys and observations, Lockwood shows that while language and cultural misunderstandings are key challenges in managing virtual teams, more significant, institutional struggles exist, like power imbalances, incommensurate expectations about the identity of work teams and general fears regarding company success. Lockwood uses these findings to argue that offshoring and the resulting need to work electronically/ virtually require a greater understanding of ICC in the workplace; however, training programmes that seek to promote the successful management of geographically displaced teams must also not forget larger (and often deeper) institutional challenges and concerns.

'Identities at odds: Embedded and implicit language policing in the internationalized workplace', carried out by Spencer Hazel, demonstrates that careful analyses of actual workplace practices can provide a more nuanced understanding of some of the deeper institutional issues raised by Lockwood. Hazel uses ethnomethodologically informed microanalysis to uncover how employees manage, and at the same time reveal, their normative expectations about language choice and, in doing so, engage in identity work central to carrying out workplace responsibilities.Hazel goes on to argue that multilingual (workplace) settings are important sites of investigation in ICC research, as they reveal how employees align institutional identities and expectations with language choice.

The final contribution in the Special Issue offers a unique, Chinese/Developing World perspective on the discursive and semiotic processes in which Hangzhou, an ancient and renowned tourist city, brands itself for the international community. Shi-xu's paper, 'International city branding as intercultural discourse: Workplace, development and globalization', is revelatory in that it shows how workplace discourse is much more than talk or text at work. Shi-xu argues specifically that urban city branding points to a wider societal mandate, which is achieved and thus represents a complex interplay of communicative acts that operate at various global and local levels. He argues that this nexus of communicative acts requires a much more holistic approach to understanding ICC in the workplace.

Concluding remarks

In many of the approximately 100 papers that were presented at IALIC–2013 in Hong Kong, and in the 10 papers that were selected for publication in this volume, the multifaceted nature of 'culture' has yet again been highlighted. 'Culture' is conceptua- lised not only as an ever-present influence on our communication and social interaction at work but also as an ever-changing fussy concept, which is constantly being (re)created and negotiated as we communicate with cultural 'others'. Some papers have reiterated that for minority group members in the workplace, 'culture' is likely to be perceived as a more salient influence. Not until we are 'lost in translation' do we become acutely aware of 'culture' as constituting reality, as something that inevitably constructs in-groups and out-groups and thus potentially jeopardises communication, despite our attempts engage in dialogue.

Contributors to this Special Issue have also emphasised the need to promote less ethnocentric approaches to ICC research. Despite several notable attempts to introduce non-Western approaches to ICC research, the norms for 'good' research, as well as for 'appropriate' communication, are still widely informed by Eurocentric/Anglocentric practices. It is our hope that with IALIC–2013, and the papers in this volume, we have opened up for a debate about *what* we research in ICC and *how* we research it. Bredella (2003, p. 228) reminds us that 'an indispensable feature of the intercultural experience is that we refrain from imposing *our* categories and values on others but instead learn to reconstruct *their* frame of reference and *see them as they see themselves*' (emphasis added). Therefore, let us remind each other that we as ICC scholars and educators should keep pursuing an agenda that is truly non-ethnocentric, multicultural and anti-racist.

References

Angouri, J., & Marra, M. (Eds.). (2011). *Constructing identities at work*. Basingstoke: Palgrave Macmillan.

Asante, M. K., Miike, Y., & Yin, J. (Eds.). (2013). *The global intercultural communication reader* (2nd ed.). New York, NY: Routledge.

Blasco, M. (2004). Stranger to us than birds in our garden? Reflections on hermeneutics, intercultural understanding and the management of difference. In M. Blasco & J. Gustafsson (Eds.), *Intercultural alternatives: Critical perspectives on intercultural encounters* (pp. 19–48). Copenhagen: Copenhagen Business School Press.

Blommaert, J. (2010). *The sociolinguistics of globalization*. Cambridge: Cambridge University Press.

Bond, M. H., Zegarac, V., & Spencer-Oatey, H. (2000). Culture as an explanatory variable: Problems and possibilities. In H. Spencer-Oatey (Ed.), *Culturally speaking: Managing rapport through talk across cultures* (pp. 47–71). London: Continuum.

Bredella, L. (2003). What does it mean to be intercultural? In G. Alred, M. Byram & M. Fleming (Eds.), *Intercultural experience and education* (pp. 225–239). Clevedon: Multilingual Matters.

Brown, P., & Levinson, S. (1987). *Politeness: Some universals in language usage*. Cambridge: Cambridge University Press.

Chen, G. M., & Miike, Y. (Eds.). (2003). Asian approaches to human communication [Special Issue]. *Intercultural Communication Studies, 12*(4).

Edwards, D., & Potter, J. (1992). *Discursive psychology*. London: Sage.

Geertz, C. (2000). *Available light*. Princeton, NJ: Princeton University Press.

Giddens, A. (2002). *Runaway world: How globalization is reshaping our lives*. London: Profile Books.

Hall, E. T. (1976). *Beyond culture*. New York, NY: Anchor Books.

Hannerz, U. (2001). Thinking about culture in a global ecumene. In J. Lull (Ed.), *Culture in a communication age* (pp. 54–71). London: Routledge.

Herring, S. C. (Ed.). (1996). *Computer-mediated communication*. Amsterdam: John Benjamins.

Herring, S. C. (2004). Slouching towards to ordinary: Current trends in computer-mediated communication. *New Media & Society, 6*(1), 26–36. doi:10.1177/1461444804039906

Hofstede, G. (2001). *Culture's consequences: Comparing values, behaviors, institutions and organizations across nations*. Thousand Oaks, CA: Sage.

Holmes, J. (2006). *Gendered talk at work. Constructing gender identity through workplace discourse*. Oxford: Blackwell.

Holmes, P. (2015). "The cultural stuff around how to talk to people": Immigrants' intercultural communication during a pre-employment work-placement. *Language & Intercultural Communication, 15*(1), 109–124.

Holmes, J., & Stubbe, M. (2003). *Power and politeness in the workplace: A sociolinguistic analysis of talk at work*. London: Pearson Education.

Jackson, J. (2010). *Intercultural journeys: From study to residence abroad*. Basingstoke: Palgrave Macmillan.

Jackson, J. (2015). Preparing students for the global workplace: The impact of a semester abroad. *Language & Intercultural Communication, 15*(1), 76–91.

Kecskes, I. (2014). *Intercultural pragmatics*. New York, NY: Oxford University Press.

Kramsch, C. (2002). In search of the intercultural. *Journal of Sociolinguistics, 6*, 275–285. doi:10.1111/1467-9481.00188

Ladegaard, H. J. (2007). Global culture – myth or reality? Perceptions of 'national cultures' in a global corporation. *Journal of Intercultural Communication Research, 36*(2), 139–163. doi:10.1080/17475750701478729

Ladegaard, H. J. (2012a). The discourse of powerlessness and repression: Identity construction in domestic helper narratives. *Journal of Sociolinguistics, 16*, 450–482. doi:10.1111/j.1467-9841.2012.00541.x

Ladegaard, H. J. (2012b). Rudeness as discursive strategy in leadership discourse: Culture, power and gender in a Hong Kong workplace. *Journal of Pragmatics, 44*, 1661–1679. doi:10.1016/j.pragma.2012.07.003

Ladegaard, H. J. (2015). Personal experience and cultural awareness as resources in teaching intercultural communication: A Hong Kong *case study*. In G. Slethaugh & J. Vinther (Eds.), *International teaching and learning at universities. Achieving equilibrium with local culture and pedagogy* (pp. 111–134). New York, NY: Palgrave Macmillan.

Lockwood, J. (2015). Virtual team management: What's causing communication breakdown? *Language & Intercultural Communication, 15*(1), 125–140.

MacDonald, M., & O'Regan, J. (2014). Editorial. *Language & Intercultural Communication, 14*, 401–405. doi:10.1080/14708477.2014.951158

Matsumoto, Y. (1988). Reexamination of the universality of face: Politeness phenomena in Japanese. *Journal of Pragmatics, 12*, 403–426. doi:10.1016/0378-2166(88)90003-3

Miike, Y. (2009). New frontiers in Asian communication theory: An introduction. *Journal of Multicultural Discourses, 4*(1), 1–5. doi:10.1080/17447140802663145

Miike, Y. (2013). The Asiacentric turn in Asian communication studies: Shifting paradigms and changing perspectives. In M. K. Asante, Y. Miike, & J. Yin (Eds.), *The global intercultural communication reader* (2nd ed.). (pp. 111–133). New York, NY: Routledge.

Mullany, L. (2007). *Gendered discourse in the professional workplace*. Basingstoke: Palgrave Macmillan.

Nakayama, T. K., & Halualani, R. T. (Eds.). (2010). *The handbook of critical intercultural communication*. Oxford: Wiley-Blackwell.

Ohmae, K. (1995). *The end of the nation state*. London: Harper-Collins.

Parker, I. (Ed.). (1998). *Social constructionism, discourse and realism*. London: Sage.

Schnurr, S. (2008). *Leadership discourse at work. Interactions of humour, gender and workplace culture*. Basingstoke: Palgrave Macmillan.

Schnurr, S., & Zaytz, O. (2012). 'You have to be adaptable, obviously'. Constructing professional identities in multicultural workplaces in Hong Kong. *Pragmatics, 22*, 279–299.

Scollon, R., Scollon, S. W., & Jones, R. (2011). *Intercultural communication: A discourse approach* (3rd ed.). Oxford: Wiley-Blackwell.

Shi-xu (2009). Reconstructing Eastern paradigms of discourse studies. *Journal of Multicultural Discourses, 4*(1), 29–48. doi:10.1080/17447140802651637

Shi-xu (2013). Constructing new forms of intercultural communication. In Shi-xu, *Discourse and culture. From discourse analysis to cultural discourse studies* (pp. 377–393). Shanghai: Shanghai Foreign Language Education Press.

Smith, A. D. (1990). Towards a global culture? In M. Featherstone (Ed.), *Global culture: Nationalism, globalization and modernity* (pp. 171–191). London: Sage.

11

Thurlow, C., & Jaworski, A. (2010). *Tourism and discourse: The language of global mobility.* Basingstoke: Palgrave Macmillan.

Vinther, J., & Slethaugh, G. (2015). The impact of international students on the university work environment: A comparative study of a Canadian and a Danish university. *Language & Intercultural Communication, 15*(1), 92–108.

Waldvogel, J. (2007). Greetings and closings in workplace email. *Journal of Computer-Mediated Communication, 12*, 456–477. doi:10.1111/j.1083-6101.2007.00333.x

Reconsidering intercultural (communication) competence in the workplace: a dialectical approach

Judith N. Martin[a] and Thomas K. Nakayama[b]

[a]School of Human Communication, Arizona State University, Tempe, AZ, USA; [b]Department of Communication Studies, Northeastern University, Boston, MA, USA

Scholars and practitioners from a variety of disciplinary backgrounds (sociolinguistics, language education, communication, business, etc.) have investigated and promoted the notion of competence in intercultural interaction for many years. They have addressed complex issues and proposed culture general and culture specific models and applied these models in various contexts including workplace interaction. In this paper, we examine the assumptions about the cultural identities of workers in contemporary research and training in intercultural competence. These assumptions seem to reinscribe the colonialist traveler/cosmopolitan – focusing on individual characteristics, motivation, and skill sets, often through a Eurocentric lens. A dialectical perspective foregrounds individual characteristics of competence with larger societal attitudes and laws that impact the treatment of women, gays, and others. A dialectical perspective can help us better understand the opportunities and constraints facing different people in workplaces around the world. By complicating our understanding of competence and taking a dialectical perspective, we hope to advance theory and practice in this important topic area.

Chercheurs et praticiens de divers milieux disciplinaires (sociolinguistique, l'enseigne-ment des langues, la communication, les entreprises, etc.) ont étudié et promu la notion de compétence en interaction interculturelle depuis de nombreuses années. Ils ont abordé des questions complexes et proposé des modèles de culture-générale et culture-spécifique et appliqués ces modèles dans divers contextes, y compris l'interaction dans les lieux de travail. Dans cet article, nous examinons les hypothèses sur les identités des travailleurs dans la recherche contemporaine et de la formation en compétences interculturelles. Ces hypothèses semblent réinscrire le voyageur colo-nialiste/cosmopolite mettant l'accent sur les caractéristiques individuelles, la motiva-tion et les compétences, souvent par l'intermédiaire d'une lentille eurocentrique. Une perspective dialectique peut nous aider à mieux comprendre les possibilités et les contraintes auxquelles sont confrontées des personnes différentes dans des lieux de travail à travers le monde. En compliquant notre compréhension de la compétence et de prendre un point de vue dialectique, nous espérons faire avancer la théorie et la pratique dans ce sujet important.

Introduction

The concept of intercultural competence has been one of the traditional areas of intercultural scholarship. Scholars and practitioners from a variety of disciplinary backgrounds, including psychology (Thomas, 2003), language education (Aguilar, 2009; Byram, Gribkova, & Starkey 2002; Byram & Zarate, 1997; Byram, 2012; Dasli, 2012a; Fantini, 2012; Kramsch, 2009; Méndez García, 2012; Rathje, 2007), communication (Arasaratnam, 2007; Arasaratnam, Banerjee, & Dembek, 2010; Bennett, 2009; Chen, 2014; Chen & Starosta, 1996; Ting-Toomey, 2009; Wiseman & Koester, 1993; Yep, 2000), business (Bartel-Radic, 2009; Johnson, Lenartowicz, & Apud, 2006; Matveev, 2004; Morley & Cerdin, 2010), education (Deardorff, 2009; Holmes, 2006), have investigated and promoted the notion of competence in intercultural interaction for many years.

One of the most important contexts for intercultural interaction in the twenty-first century is the global workplace. In fact, one might argue that the workplace is the setting where individuals are most likely to encounter persons of different cultural backgrounds – as globalization, world immigration patterns, and technological advances shrink the cultural distances between some workers (Washington, Okoro, & Thomas, 2012). In fact, many business leaders identify intercultural communication competence (ICC) as a requisite skill set for workers entering the current job market (Milhauser & Rahschulte, 2010).

However, it must be noted that the majority of ICC models have been based on Eurocentric, ethnocentric, and egocentric perspectives (Bruneau, 2002; Yep, 2000), and therefore may be limited in their applicability to multiple cross-cultural encounters or contexts (Greenholtz, 2005; Martin, 1993; Spitzberg & Changnon, 2009): 'Generalizations and assumptions derived from models with such a skewed perspective have a tendency to be unfairly normative, ineffective, and inconsiderate' (Kupka, Everett, & Wildermuth, 2007, p. 21). Specifically, these individual-centered models tend to focus on national culture, conceptualize culture as bounded and static, and ignore issues of power and the larger structures that constrain and impact individual attitudes and actions. However, more recent scholarship has challenged these notions, emphasizing the dynamic, fluid nature of culture, cultural identity and intercultural encounters (Feng, 2009; Holliday, 2009, 2010a; Jack, 2009; Jenks, Bhatia, & Lou, 2013; Verschueren, 2008; Young & Sercombe, 2010), recognizing the important role of political and other macrostructures in investigations of intercultural competence (Block, 2013; Hoskins & Sallah, 2011; Phipps, 2014). In this paper, we propose a dialectical approach to ICC scholarship, in an attempt to contribute to this more complex and nuanced understanding of competence and advance theory and practice in this important topic area.

We first describe the characteristics and challenges of the twenty-first century global workplace and then outline and critique traditional approaches to ICC. Specifically we note how the positivistic individual-centered approaches that call for 'mutual accommodation' and 'shared meaning' may not adequately reflect the realities of dynamic, structural (societal and organizational) hierarchies of the global workplace. Finally we present a critical dialectical perspective that offers a dynamic, relational approach to competence and foregrounds individual characteristics of competence with *larger societal attitudes and laws* that impact an individual's competence skills (Martin & Nakayama, 2010).

The twenty-first century global workplace

Business experts and scholars agree that the twenty-first century workplace, regardless of location, is somewhat different from the work contexts of even 25 years ago as a result of (1) economic globalization (Akram, Fahim, Bin Dost, & Abdullah, 2011), (2) shifting demographic patterns (Karoly & Panis, 2004), and (3) the rapid pace of technological change. Economic globalization affects industries worldwide and segments of the workforce insulated from trade-related competition in the past. The shift in workplace demographics arise from local and global migration patterns. People have always encountered cultural others, migrating because of war, famine, or search for a better life and work, and current migration is no exception. The post WWII labor migration from Turkey, Spain, and Italy to Germany, for instance, brought huge complexity to a fragile peace and a country rebuilding from the ground up. Rural Pakistani and Bangladeshi moving to communities in northwest mill towns in England in the early 1900s, or the great migration of African-Americans from southern to northern USA in the same era also saw increasing intercultural contact, not without conflict. Current statistics reveal women migrating and entering the workforce in greater numbers than ever before; people in many countries are working later in life – leading to a shift in workplace demographics and a more balanced distribution by age, sex, and race/ethnicity and greater participation in the workforce by those with low labor force experience (Karoly & Panis, 2004; *World Migration in Figures*, 2013).

A final factor that impacts the current global workplace is technological change, especially communication technologies (Karoly & Panis, 2004, p. xiv), resulting in the increase in virtual work and global virtual teamwork of often culturally diverse team members (Lloyd & Härtel, 2010; Phadnis & Caplice, 2013), raising the question of how online encounters impact intercultural competences (Maroccia, 2012). Technological advances have also led to the proliferation of job outsourcing to emerging economy locales. All these factors are 'catapulting people, practices, and beliefs from different cultures into shared and contested physical and virtual spaces in workplaces ... in unprecedented ways' (Sorrells, 2012, p. 372), leading to complex and challenging power and relational dynamics (Holliday, 2012; Kramsch & Uryu, 2012; Sorrells, 2013).

Power issues and hierarchies have always been a taken-for-granted element of the workplace (Coleman, Kugler, Mitchinson, & Foster, 2013) and cultural variation in the expectations and practices regarding these hierarchies (e.g. Hofstede's [2001] power distance variable) have been well documented (Bochner & Hesketh, 1994; Matusitz & Musambira, 2013; Varela, Salgado, & Lasio, 2010). However, a more challenging (and also endemic) hierarchy is the structural inequality among various identity groups (nationality, language, gender, race, ethnicity, sexual orientation, etc.) that come together in the contemporary workplace (Gates & Mitchell, 2013; Warren, 2012).

These complex structural inequalities often stem from historical social power relations and some economists suggest that these inequities may be heightened as a result of globalization, due to increased power of global capital over labor (Śliwa, 2007; Walby, 2003). For just one example, there are a number of recent studies highlighting the effect of globalization on gender inequities in the Chinese workplace. Several studies explore the far-reaching effect of China's economic restructuring and globalization, identifying factors (age, less education) that contribute to women's increasing disadvantageous position in the work unit and their increased vulnerability in the changing labor market. That is, women are more likely to be offered lower wages and less likely to work in high paying foreign firms – globalization changes the nature of job queues and men and women are matched into jobs accordingly (Liu, 2007; Sheldon, Kim, Li, & Warner, 2011; Shu, Zhu, & Zhang, 2007).

There are other examples of women and children being transported across borders (both legally and illegally) to serve as servants and concubines; sweatshops in cities around the world employ undocumented immigrants with few legal rights. For example, Ladegaard (2013) documents, through narratives of foreign domestic helpers in Hong

Kong, the exploitation and abuse often suffered by these women and he calls for more attention by language/communication scholars to the larger sociocultural contexts and discursive ideologies that allow for and even promote negative stereotyping and prejudice, and discrimination. There are additional studies, reviewed later in the paper, that explore workplace inequities of other identity groups. The question here is how to understand/investigate ICC in these workplace encounters?

The implications for twenty-first century global worker competences in this current environment with complex structural/historical inequities are enormous and a review of literature on ICC in this context of increasing diversity (and concomitant power relations) reveals two views: (1) increased diversity/inequities require enhanced training in how to manage the increased cultural diversity in national and international contexts (Arakelian, 2009; Dooley, 2003; Guilherme, Glaser, & Méndez García, 2009; Johnson et al., 2006; Mughan, 2009; Tomalin, 2009) with special attention to legal requirements (Collins, 2012); and an opposing view is (2) that traditional diversity training may be intensely inadequate, as diversity management is impacted by both macro (societal) and micro (individual) issues (Keating, Guilherme, & Hoppe, 2010; Syed & Pio, 2010; Warren, 2012) and that a simple ahistorical 'diversity' framework approach to competence, without attention to macro issues, may actually reinforce Eurocentric and often colonial power relations (Sorrells, 2012). Jack (2009) notes that in his management and marketing courses, he asks students to critically 'confront and consider social, political and ethical issues associated with a broader conception of the intercultural. ... a more politicized understanding of intercultural competence' (p. 96). We tend to agree with Jack (2009) and favor this second, more challenging view.

Current research in intercultural (communication) competence

While there has been active investigation of the concepts of communication competence, intercultural competence, and ICC for the past 50 years in a variety of disciplines, there remain many conceptual and practical challenges. The first challenge is the plethora of terms used across disciplines by authors who seldom cite each other's work. In an attempt to remedy this, let us clarify. The term used in our discipline (communication) is *intercultural communication competence*. The related terms, *intercultural communicative competence*, or more recently, *the intercultural speaker,* are often used by language education scholars – in the tradition of the Council of Europe Common European Framework led by Michael Byram et al. (2002; Byram & Zarate, 1997; MacDonald & O'Regan, 2012, etc.). Generally speaking these two terms/approaches have much in common; a difference seems to be the latter's privileging of language and language-centered scholarship,[1] although some acknowledge that intercultural competences are not always calibrated with language skills (Dervin, 2010; Zarate, 2003).

A second challenge is to reconcile the interplay between individual competence and societal forces. As described in an earlier paper (Nakayama & Martin, 2014), the majority of competence scholarship in the communication discipline has been conducted from a postpositive variable-analytic approach and attempts to identify and model the various dimensions of ICC on the individual level (Chen, 1989, 1990, 1992, 1995, 2014; Chen & Starosta, 1996; Hammer, 1989; Martin, 1989; 1993; Wiseman, 2002; Wiseman & Koester, 1993). Intercultural *communicative* competence scholarship seems to have followed the same trajectory (MacDonald & O'Regan, 2012). The recent theoretical integration, resulting in useful conceptual frameworks, reveals that most models/theories, whether conceptualizing intercultural competence, ICC, or intercultural *communicative* competence, reflect the 'ABC' (Affect, Behaviors, and Cognition/Knowledge) triumvirate (see Spitzberg & Changnon [2009] and Chen [2014] for excellent summaries and presentation of the various lists of corresponding elements, briefly outlined here):

(1) Affective – e.g., respect, open-mindedness, nonjudgmentalness, empathy, curiosity, and attitudes.

(2) Cognitive – e.g., self-knowledge and cultural knowledge, language proficiency, mindfulness, and ability to create new categories.

(3) Behavioral – both macro (e.g., adaptability, flexibility, social skills, and decoding skills) as well as micro (e.g., eye gaze, head nods, self-disclosure, and message skills).

Subsequent empirical research following this ABC 'list' approach added additional dimensions to the mix, including *motivation* (Wiseman, 2002), *outcomes* (e.g. communication and relational satisfaction, effectiveness, goal attainment, task accomplishment, etc.), *contexts* (see Johnson et al., 2006; Spitzberg & Changnon, 2009; Warren, 2012), and stressed the importance of the relational dimension – that competence cannot be conceptualized as residing *in an individual* – but rather is a process of negotiation in an ongoing relationship (Byram, 2003; Cupach & Imahori, 1993).

The overall *process* of intercultural (communication) competence from this perspective can be described thusly:

> two (or more) interactants come to an encounter, characterized by their cultural differences, and through accommodation and mutual display of the ABC's, they achieve shared meaning, mutual understanding, and arrive at a mutually satisfying relationship. (Kupka et al., 2007)

And indeed, Spitzberg and Changnon, after reviewing the extensive previous research conclude: 'the more a model incorporates specific conceptualization of interactants' motivation, knowledge, skills, context, and outcomes, in the context of an ongoing relationship over time, the more advanced the model' (p. 44).[2]

As noted earlier, much of the global business literature surveyed seems to take this same approach – emphasizing that in order to be interculturally competent, business personnel (especially managers/leaders) need to understand the variety of cultural differences/backgrounds that employees bring to the workplace context (Bird, Mendenhall, Stevens, & Oddou, 2010; Dooley, 2003; Kim Keum, 2012; Moran, Youngdahl, & Moran, 2009; Morley & Cerdin, 2010; Washington et al., 2012), including language issues (Cheng, 2009; Deprez-Sims & Morris, 2010; Harzing & Pudelko, 2013; Mughan, 2009; Yunxia, 2008), and then adapt and accommodate to these differences.

Yep (2000) noted 15 years ago that this approach is limited in several ways:

(1) Competence is viewed through an individual-centered 'lens' and often from a privileged center (Xiao & Chen, 2009). While some scholars have noted the importance of environment and contextual factors that facilitate/impede intercultural competence, it is not enough to simply add 'context' or 'environment' as a separate dimension, because of the dynamic, fluid nature of the intercultural interaction (Dervin, 2011) and the impacts of societal forces and power hierarchies on individual behaviors.

(2) The focus on national culture groups that are presumed to be homogenous, and stable ignores intersections with other fundamental social positions such as gender, social class, sexuality, and race (Block & Corona, 2014; Yep, 2000) and while many scholars acknowledge that these conceptualizations are outdated and acknowledge the

fluid, dynamic, contested nature of intercultural interactions, in their/our investigations and models, they/we fall back on easy categorizations of people into national, ethnic, religious groups, termed by Dervin (2010) as 'Janusian interculturality' – referring to the two-faced god.

We would argue that, in reality, intercultural workplace encounters are complicated and dynamic and involve multiple identities simultaneously and that historical transnational/ cultural/organizational structural hierarchies often mitigate against arriving at shared meaning and mutual relational satisfaction. The limitations of some previous conceptualizations seem to call for a more complicated, dynamic, historically and contextually situated approach to intercultural competence. Several scholars have begun to identify the need for such a shift in Language and Intercultural Communication (LAIC) in recent years, calling for a critical approach to language and culture, one that recognizes the interplay of individual agency and societal forces (Block, 2013), that focuses on emancipation and social justice (Dasli, 2012b; Phipps, 2014), that allows for 'dissonance, contradiction and conflict as well as consensus, concurrence, and transformation' (Guilherme, 2002, p. 219). We do not suggest that one model would fit all contexts, but our own contribution adds to this discussion with a dialectic approach.

A dialectical approach to ICC

Incorporating a dialectic view into research investigating dimensions of ICC may offer a way to extend the rather static, individual-centered focus of previous research on competence and also lead to a less western, ethnocentric bias. Based on Bakhtin's (1982) work, the dialectic approach emphasizes the processual, relational, and the contradictory nature of human interaction and relationships. According to the dialectic view, intercultural relating is a dynamic, fluid, and ongoing process. In the field of Communication, Baxter (2004) and colleagues have established a solid dialectic approach in interpersonal relationship dynamics and in previous work, we have identified six intercultural dialectics and other scholars have built on our foundational work (Martin & Nakayama, 1999, 2010): Individual-cultural, differences-similarities, past/present-future, personal-contextual, privilege-disadvantage, static-dynamic. These dialectics presupposes that the business of relating is *simultaneously* as much about individual characteristic as cultural (societal) constraints, cultural differences as similarities, and disadvantage as privileges, etc. To paraphrase Baxter (2004, p. 115), relating is a complex knot of contradictory interplays, and these bipolar forces (individual/societal, differences/similarities, privilege/disadvantage, etc.) do not exist in parallel to one another but interweave in ongoing dialectical interplay.

Much of the current discussion on culture is framed around 'macro'versus 'constructivist' approaches (Angouri, 2010). The macro approaches tend to focus on the nation-state as the site of culture, e.g., French culture equals France. This tends to create a static and stereotypical view of cultures. Individual agents have no role in the construction of French (or any other) culture. There is little sense of the dynamic character of culture, as well as the myriad of competing interests in how it is defined and hierarchies created.

Recent scholarship which some term 'critical' and 'constructivist' seem to stress a language/culture learner that is critically engaged (Byram, 2003; Dasli, 2012b; Holliday, 2012) with the learning and with other interactants, where competence is seen as negotiated (between people) as a process. The social constructivist view focuses 'on the co-construction of culture as a process enacted in discourse' (Angouri, 2010, p. 209).

Thus, the 'social constructivist approach to social reality which puts individual agency at the forefront' (Block, 2013, p. 128), is different from the dialectical approach that places inequities resulting from larger social contexts at the forefront. In the social constructivist approach, there is little emphasis on the notion that different actors speak from different power positions and therefore not all are equal in the construction of social reality.

The dialectical approach is distinctive from the constructivist approach in that it foregrounds the forces that constrain communicative choices. Individuals are not equal in their power relations in that some social realities are created in the interests of some, over other social realities that might benefit others. Rather than the emphasis on the individual that runs through much of the constructivist work, the dialectical approach connects individual agency with larger, structural constraints into dialectical relationships (see Block, 2013). These dialectics reveal the complexities of culture, as well as the various interests at work in driving cultural hierarchies.

By taking a look at how ICC plays out in various global workplaces, we can see the strengths and limitations of focusing on the traditional individual characteristics of competence. These examinations also highlight the ways that a dialectical perspective can complement traditional ways of thinking about competence in a global workplace. The three studies discussed below also show the dynamic complexity of intercultural interaction – that various identities (not just nationality) are involved and interrelated and competence cannot be viewed as comprising only national (or ethnic or racial) identity.

In his study of a workplace in Singapore, Park (2013) shows how diversity management (ICC scholarship in action) and the neoliberal discourse of 'diversity management' works to rationalize and justify workplace inequities. We see neoliberalism as 'an ideological hegemonic project' (Springer, 2012, p. 136), a belief in the market system that masks and justifies unequal power relations through a discourse that lauds the free market system. Through a close analysis of several interactions of employees (Chinese Singaporean, Indian, Korean), within the regional headquarters of a large multinational enterprise in Singapore, he discusses why Korean employees are consistently denied promotion, in spite of effective functioning within the organization. He suggests that this is not a case of simple discrimination against Korean employees, but a more complex process. So, when an employee was not granted a promotion, the employee internalizes the rejection as an individual characteristic, e.g., it 'takes the form of employees adopting a particular model of behavior and disposition that is evaluated in terms of morality and responsibility' (p. 574). In dialectical terms, this disadvantage can also be viewed as an advantage in a different cultural frame: 'in the context of transnational South Korea, for example, they are in fact privileged transnational elites, who have moved beyond the bounds of Korean society using the linguistic and cultural capital they accumulated through their work at global MNCs' (p. 574).

In another example of global workplace interactions, Leonard (2010) describes the complex (and dialectical) negotiations of white male and female workers in postcolonial Hong Kong and the interplay between global and local discourses and the formation of white, gendered subjectivities and shows how workplace competencies can ONLY be understood in dialectics: individual-societal, privilege-disadvantage, past-present/future. That is, in her study, she found that the traditional privileged identity position of white Britishness in Hong Kong is in dialectical tension with the present day situation in which 'the cages of white Britishness are being rattled' (p. 356). The privilege of the past is undergoing changes with the emerging new Hong Kong identities and past privilege is in dialectical tension with the present and future increasing disadvantage. Within the shifting global workplace, then, the individual's competence can only function within a range of effectiveness in a larger changing social context. The previous privileged position of white Britishness is being displaced by Chinese Hong Kongese who can speak not only English, but also Cantonese and Putonghua, and possibly other Chinese dialects. The image of white Britishness is receding to become the image of the past, not the future. In the contemporary context, Hong Kongers appear to be much more focused on their identity in relationship to Mainland Chinese (Tse, 2014). This shift is largely due to the governmental shift from the UK to China in 1997 and its attendant consequences throughout Hong Kong. Thus, the main 'other' identity in dialectical tension with Hong Kongers is the Mainland Chinese identity that many Hong Kongers view negatively (Kit, 2014; Ladegaard, 2012). An important dialectical tension opens up in the contemporary context: Hong Kongers feel a unified Chinese identity while also feeling different as Hong Kongers from Mainland Chinese. A dialectical perspective helps us better track the shifting dialectics from the British to Mainland Chinese and how that influences competence in communicating across these various identities.

In a third example, Kim (2004) describes the hierarchical and dialectic relations between less assimilated Korean (foreign) managers who supervise more assimilated Korean-Americans in a Korean company located in the USA and examines how ethnicity/ nationality/generation is salient and interrelated in this global workplace. This study 'displays the impact of globalization at the workplace, since Koreans and Korean-Americans have been brought together to work side by side as a result of the movement of businesses across countries' (p. 72). Kim's analysis reveals the dialectics of individual-cultural, privilege-disadvantage, past-present/future. There is also a dialectical tension that runs throughout the work relationships between 'Americanness' and 'Koreanness.' These cultural identities shape the expectations and work assignments of the Korean-Americans who come from different immigrant generations. In this case, the workers and managers' individual competence skills needs to be set against the backdrop of the cultural expectations in a Korean company, located in the USA. The relative privilege of the Korean managers is in dialectical tension with the relative disadvantage they experience with limited English language skills. The relative disadvantage of the Korean-American workers in relation to the managers is in dialectical tension with their ability to understand traditional Korean values and negotiate tasks in English. Whatever individual competencies the Korean-American workers have, they are stereotyped by the Korean managers for their Americanization, and lack of a Korean 'work ethic:' 'the ethnic interpretation of work behaviours not only essentializes certain qualities as generational characteristics but also justifies the limited opportunities for the younger Korean-Americans' (p. 89).

Here we can see how equating nations with cultures is problematic, as Korean-Americans are seen as both and neither Koreans and US-Americans. Thus, in this Korean transnational corporation, the assimilation into US-American culture is both valued and devalued, underscoring the dialectical tension between the Korean managers and Korean-Americans: on the one hand, foreign Korean managers value the 'Korean' Korean-Americans who share their own Korean work ethic and comply with their work expectations, by talking positively about the 'Koreanization' of these Korean-Americans. But on the other hand, they are critical of them, viewing those who seek employment in Korean transnational corporations (TNCs) as not competent enough to assimilate completely to the US-American ways of living.

The individual competencies of Korean-American workers to navigate both Korean-ness and US-Americanness are set against the backdrop of these other tensions that must be taken into consideration when we think about competence. We can gain a much better understanding of competence by situating it within the larger social and cultural contexts where competence functions. The same skills, motivations, and knowledge may not function as effectively for all depending upon the specific contexts in which their communication takes place. People read a range of communicative behaviors differently, in this workplace, depending upon who is doing the communicative behaviors.

In all of these examples, the dynamics of other intersecting identities also play a key role in the construction of how intercultural competencies play out. For example, gender, class, race, and age carry important values in all of these cultural contexts and impact what is seen as competent and how that competence is performed. In his work on class difference in language teaching, Block (2012) underscores the importance of class in language and identity. A dialectical perspective would infuse these case studies with complexities of lived everydayness by helping us better understand the dialectical tensions that frame all of these interactions. A dialectical perspective helps us break any notion of a monolithic cultural identity, but instead focus on the various dialectical tensions that rivet throughout all intercultural interactions.

So what does this mean about how we should consider intercultural competence in the workplace?

(1) The global workplace is a dynamic environment that is being constructed by the unequal participation by various actors, in all encounters. For example, the recent rise of South Korea as a player in creating TNCs has created different work relationships, e.g., with Korean-Americans that did not emerge earlier. The dynamic nature of the workplace underscores the processual nature of a dialectical approach. The individual characteristics of competence can be helpful at a macro-level, but the specific aspects of cultural competence in particular work environments, at particular moments, remain ever elusive. Just as Korean immigrants vary in generational differences, so too will Korean managers, as traditional Korean practices change from transnationalism in Korea as well. Intercultural competence is a process as much as all intercultural communication and the dialectical perspective underscores this processual nature.

(2) The global workplace heightens our awareness of the larger cultural, economic, political, and historical tensions that are a part of the work environment. In this context, the traditional building blocks of competence (motivation, knowledge, and skills) cannot be understood uniquely as individual characteristics. A dialectical approach places these individual competence traits in tension with the motivations, knowledge, and skills of the organization, the other workers, and the larger cultural contexts.

(3) A dialectical approach emphasizes the ongoing, processual nature of the continual configuring and reconfiguring of the context. Context in a dialectical approach is not simply another variable to be added on to the existing framework of intercultural competence. A dialectical approach is a radical rethinking of 'context' in which context is a fluid and dynamic space that is shaped by both local and global forces that constantly reconfigure it. Understanding the dialectical tensions that drive these changes is key to beginning to grasp the relationships between context and competence. The global workplace is very connected to the shifting nature of globalization with different workers, skill sets, economies, and histories. The dialectical approach is similar to the social constructionist approach as both emphasize the central role of communication and discourse in the construction of

social reality; however, they differ in that the dialectical approach foregrounds the larger contexts that allow some voices more or less influence in the construction of social reality. These power relations are key to the dialectical approach.

In practice, the dialectical approach is a useful way of thinking about intercultural competence. For example, in intercultural training, the dialectical approach responds to calls by several LAIC scholars and practitioners, in that it offers an alternative to giving out lists of cultural traits that tend to stereotype various cultural groups (Fleming, 2009; Holliday, 2010b; Jack, 2009; Keating et al., 2010; Phipps, 2010). The dialectical approach gives people an alternative way to think about intercultural competence and how it might be conceptualized and enacted while avoiding reliance on stereotypes and fixed notions of cultures.

We also see the dialectical perspective as consonant with MacDonald and O'Regan's (2013) favoring the 'multiple over the singular, the variable over the stable and the mess over the arranged' (p. 1016). The dialectical approach also pushes people to think about the larger global, economic, political, and social contexts in which their intercultural interaction is taking place. This self-reflexive move is always part of the dialectical approach, as individuals must swing between the self and larger contexts. We are already situated and positioned in many ways before we engage in intercultural interaction. Understanding that notion can be helpful in intercultural training, as it asks us all to be reflective on where we enter and what intercultural competence could mean in this specific situation.

This means that the dialectical approach foregrounds the inevitable inequities in power relations that are characteristic of all intercultural interactions. While these inequities can be created by economic differences, they are also fueled by cultural attitudes about race, gender, class, age, ethnicity, religion, and more. Helping intercultural actors understand the inevitable inequities that are a part of any intercultural interaction empowers them to better negotiate and understand why and how intercultural interactions succeed or fail. In practical terms, the dialectical approach offers a framework for intercultural competence.

Notes

1. Kramsch (2012) notes that European educators, proponents of the intercultural competence approach, have recently moved to incorporate a discourse dimension in their study of intercultural competence. This would appear to bring the two strands of scholarship – intercultural communicative competence and intercultural competence – closer together.
2. We are aware of additional 'components' proposed by Language Education scholars (e.g. Byram's five *Savoirs*, the notion of interculturality) as well as Deardorff's (2009) comprehensive intercultural competence (2006) model, the Rainbow Model of Intercultural Communication Competence (Kupka et al., 2007), and others, but our critiques of the ABC model mostly hold for these other models as well.

Disclosure statement

No potential conflict of interest was reported by the authors.

References

Aguilar, M. J. C. (2009). Intercultural communicative competence in the context of the European higher education area. *Language & Intercultural Communication, 9*, 242–255. doi:10.1080/14708470902785642

Akram, M. A. C., Faheem, M. A., Bin Dost, M. K., & Abdullah, I. (2011). Globalization and its impacts on the world economic development. *International Journal of Business and Social Science, 2*, 291–297.

Angouri, J. (2010). 'If we know about culture it will be easier to work with one another': Developing skills for handling corporate meetings with multinational participation. *Language & Intercultural Communication, 10*, 206–224. doi:10.1080/14708470903348549

Arakelian, C. (2009). Professional training: Creating intercultural space in multi-ethnic workplaces. In A. Feng, M. Byram, & M. Fleming (Eds.), *Becoming interculturally competent through education and training* (pp. 174–192). Bristol: Multilingual Matters.

Arasaratnam, L. A. (2007). Research in intercultural communication competence: Past perspectives and future directions. *Journal of International Communication, 13*(2), 66–73. doi:10.1080/13216597.2007.9674715

Arasaratnam, L., Banerjee, S., & Dembek, K. (2010). The integrated model of intercultural communication competence (IMICC): Model test. *Australian Journal of Communication, 37*(3), 103–116.

Bakhtin, M. (1982). *The dialogic imagination* (M. Holquist, Ed.; C. Emerson & M. Holquist, Trans.). Austin, TX: University of Texas Press.

Bartel-Radic, A. (2009). La compétence interculturelle: État de l'art et perspectives [Intercultural competence: State of the art and perspectives]. *Management International, 13*(4), 11–26.

Baxter, L. A. (2004). Dialogues of relating. In R. Anderson, L. A. Baxter, & K. N. Cissna (Eds.), *Dialogue: Theorizing difference in communication studies* (pp. 107–124). Thousand Oaks, CA: Sage.

Bennett, J. (2009). Cultivating intercultural competence. In D. K. Deardorff (Ed.), *The Sage handbook of intercultural competence* (pp. 121–140). Thousand Oaks, CA: Sage.

Bird, A., Mendenhall, M., Stevens, M. J., & Oddou, G. (2010). Defining the content domain of intercultural competence for global leaders. *Journal of Managerial Psychology, 25*, 810–828. doi:10.1108/02683941011089107

Block, D. (2012). Class and SLA: Making connections. *Language Teaching Research, 16*, 188–205. doi:10.1177/1362168811428418

Block, D. (2013). The structure and agency dilemma in identity and intercultural communication research. *Language & Intercultural Communication, 13*(2), 126–147. doi:10.1080/14708477.2013.770863

Block, D., & Corona, V. (2014). Exploring class-based intersectionality. *Language, Culture and Curriculum, 27*(1), 27–42. doi:10.1080/07908318.2014.894053

Bochner, S., & Hesketh, B. (1994). Power distance, individualism/collectivism and job-related attitudes in a culturally diverse work group. *Journal of Cross-Cultural Psychology, 25*, 233–257. doi:10.1177/0022022194252005

Bruneau, T. (2002). Intercultural communication competence: A critique. *Human Communication: A Journal of the Pacific and Asian Communication Association. 5*(1), 1–14.

Byram, M. (Ed.). (2003). *Intercultural competence*. Strasbourg: Council of Europe.

Byram, M. (2012). Conceptualizing intercultural (communicative) competence and intercultural citizenship. In J. Jackson (Ed.), *The Routledge handbook of language and intercultural communication* (pp. 85–98). New York, NY: Routledge.

Byram, M., Gribkova, B., & Starkey, H. (2002). *Developing the intercultural dimension in language teaching: A practical introduction for teachers.* Strasbourg: Council of Europe.

Byram, M., & Zarate, C. (1997). Definitions, objectives, and assessment of sociocultural competence. In M. Byram, G. Zarate, & G. Neuner (Eds.), *Sociocultural competence of language learning and teaching* (pp. 7–43). Strasbourg: Council of Europe.

Chen, G. M. (1989). Relationships of the dimensions of intercultural communication competence. *Communication Quarterly, 37*(2), 118–133. doi:10.1080/01463378909385533

Chen, G. M. (1990). Intercultural communication competence: Some perspectives of research. *Howard Journal of Communications, 2*, 243–261. doi:10.1080/10646179009359718

Chen, G. M. (1992). A test of intercultural communication competence. *Intercultural Communication Studies, 2*, 63–82.

Chen, G. M. (1995). A model of intercultural communication competence. *Mass Communication Research, 50*, 81–95.

Chen, G. M. (2014). Intercultural communication competence: Summary of 30-year research and directions for future study. In X.-D. Dai & G. M. Chen (Eds.), *Intercultural communication competence: Conceptualization and its development in cultural contexts and interactions* (pp. 14–40). Newcastle: Cambridge Scholars.

Chen, G. M., & Starosta, W. J. (1996). Intercultural communication competence. In B. Burleson (Ed.), *The communication yearbook, 19* (pp. 353–383). Thousand Oaks, CA: Sage.

Cheng, W. (2009). Professional communication competence: 4 key industries in Hong Kong. In W. Cheng & K. C. C. Kong (Eds.), *Professional communication: Collaboration between academics and practitioners* (pp. 31–50). Hong Kong: Hong Kong University Press.

Coleman, P. T., Kugler, K. G., Mitchinson, A. & Foster, C. (2013). Navigating conflict and power at work. *Journal of Applied Social Psychology, 43*, 1963–1983. doi:10.1111/jasp.12150

Collins, E. C. (2012). Global diversity initiatives. *The International Lawyer, 46*, 987–1006.

Cupach, W. R., & Imahori, T. T. (1993). Identity management theory: Communication competence in intercultural episodes and relationships. In R. L. Wiseman & J. Koester (Eds.), *Intercultural communication competence* (pp. 112–131). Newbury Park, CA: Sage.

Dasli, M. (2012a). Are we there yet? Intercultural encounters with British studies. *Language & Intercultural Communication, 12*, 179–195. doi:10.1080/14708477.2012.691098

Dasli, M. (2012b). Theorizations of intercultural communication. In G. S. Levine & A. Phipps (Eds.), *Critical and intercultural theory and language pedagogy* (pp. 95–11). Boston: Cengage Heinle.

Deardorff, D. K. (Ed.). (2009). *The Sage handbook of intercultural competence.* Thousand Oaks, CA: Sage.

Deprez-Sims, A.-S., & Morris, S. B. (2010). Accents in the workplace: Their effects during a job interview. *International Journal of Psychology, 45*, 417–426.

Dervin, F. (2010). Assessing intercultural competence in language learning and teaching: A critical review of current efforts. In F. Dervin & E. Suomela-Salmi (Eds.), *New approaches to assessing language and (inter-)cultural competences in higher education* (pp. 157–174). New York, NY: Peter Lang.

Dervin, F. (2011). A plea for change in researching intercultural discourse: A 'liquid' approach to the study of acculturation of Chinese students. *Journal of Multicultural Discourses, 6*(1), 37–52. doi:10.1080/17447143.2010.532218

Dooley, R. (2003). Four cultures, one company: Achieving corporate excellence through working cultural complexity (part 1). *Organization Development Journal, 21*(1), 56.

Fantini, A. (2012). Language: An essential component of intercultural communicative competence. In J. Jackson (Ed.), *The Routledge handbook of language and intercultural communication* (pp. 263–278). New York, NY: Routledge.

Feng, A. (2009). Becoming interculturally competent in a third space. In A. Feng, M. Byram, & M. Fleming (Eds.), *Becoming interculturally competent through education and training* (pp. 71–91). Bristol: Multilingual Matters.

Fleming, M. (2009). Introduction; education and training: Becoming interculturally competent. In A. Feng, M. Byram, & M. Fleming (Eds.), *Becoming intercultural competent through education and training* (pp. 1–12). Bristol: Multilingual Matters.

Gates, T. G., & Mitchell, C. G. (2013). Workplace stigma-related experiences among lesbian, gay, and bisexual workers: Implications for social policy and practice. *Journal of Workplace Behavioral Health*, *28*(3), 159–171.

Greenholtz, J. F. (2005). Does intercultural sensitivity cross cultures? Validity issues in porting instruments across languages and cultures. *International Journal of Intercultural Relations*, *29*(1), 73–89.

Guilherme, M. (2002). *Critical citizens for an intercultural world*. Clevedon: Multilingual Matters.

Guilherme, M., Glaser, E., & Méndez García, M. C. (2009). The pragmatics of intercultural competence in education and training: A cross-national experience on 'diversity management'. In A. Feng, M. Byram, & M. Fleming (Eds.), *Becoming interculturally competent through education and training* (pp. 193–210). Bristol: Multilingual Matters.

Hammer, M. R. (1989). Intercultural communication competence. In M. K. Asante & W. B. Gudykunst (Eds.), *Handbook of international and intercultural communication* (pp. 247–260). Newbury Park, CA: Sage.

Harzing, A.-W., & Pudelko, M. (2013). Language competencies, policies and practices in multinational corporations: A comprehensive review and comparison of Anglophone, Asian, Continental European and Nordic MNCs. *Journal of World Business*, *48*(1), 87–97. doi:10.1016/j.jwb.2012.06.011

Hofstede, G. (2001). *Culture's consequences: Comparing values, behaviors, institutions, and organizations* (2nd ed.). Thousand Oaks, CA: Sage.

Holliday, A. (2009). The role of culture in English language education: Key challenges. *Language & Intercultural Communication*, *9*, 144–155. doi:10.1080/14708470902748814

Holliday, A. (2010a). Complexity in cultural identity. *Language & Intercultural Communication*, *10*, 165–177.

Holliday, A. (2010b). Cultural descriptions as political cultural acts: An exploration. *Language & Intercultural Communication*, *10*, 259–272. doi:10.1080/14708470903348572

Holliday, A. (2012). Culture, communication, context and power. In J. Jackson (Ed.), *The Routledge handbook of language and intercultural communication* (pp. 37–51). New York, NY: Routledge.

Holmes, P. (2006). Problematising intercultural communication competence in the pluricultural classroom: Chinese students in a New Zealand university. *Language & Intercultural Communication*, *6*(1), 18–34. doi:10.1080/14708470608668906

Hoskins, B., & Sallah, M. (2011). Developing intercultural competence in Europe: The challenges. *Language & Intercultural Communication*, *11*(2), 113–125. doi:10.1080/14708477.2011.556739

Jack, G. (2009). A critical perspective on teaching intercultural competence in a management department. In A. Feng, M. Byram, & M. Fleming (Eds.), *Becoming interculturally competent through education and training* (pp. 95–14). Bristol: Multilingual Matters.

Jenks, C., Bhatia, A., & Lou, J. (2013). The discourse of culture and identity in national and transnational contexts. *Language & Intercultural Communication*, *13*(2), 121–125. doi:10.1080/14708477.2013.770862

Johnson, J. P., Lenartowicz, T., & Apud, S. (2006). Cross-cultural competence in international business: Toward a definition and a model. *Journal of International Business Studies, 37*, 525–543.

Karoly, L. A., & Panis, C. W. A. (2004). *The 21st century at work*. Santa Monica, CA: The RAND Corporation. Retrieved from http://www.rand.org/content/dam/rand/pubs/monographs/2004/RAND_MG164.pdf

Keating, C., Guilherme, M., & Hoppe, D. (2010). Diversity management: Negotiating representations in multicultural contexts. In M. Guilherme, E. Glaser, & M. C. Méndez García (Eds.), *The intercultural dynamics of multicultural working* (pp. 168–185). Bristol: Multilingual Matters.

Kim, J. H. (2004). 'They are more like us': The salience of ethnicity in the global workplace of Korean transnational corporations. *Ethnic and Racial Studies*, *27*(1), 69–94.

Kim Keum, H. (2012). Cultural divergence between Korean and Malay industrial workers as reflected in their 'definition of the situation'. *Korea Journal, 52*(2), 188–220.

Kit, C. C. (2014). China as 'other': Resistance to and ambivalence toward national identity in Hong Kong. *China Perspectives, 1*, 25–34.

Kramsch, C. (2009). Discourse: The symbolic dimension of intercultural competence. In A. Hu & M. Byram (Eds.), *Intercultural competence and foreign language learning* (pp. 107–122). Tübingen: Gunter Narr Verlag.

Kramsch, C. (2012). Theorizing translingual/transcultural competence. In G. S. Levine & A. Phipps (Eds.), *Critical and intercultural theory and language pedagogy* (pp. 15–31). Boston, MA: Cengage Heinle.

Kramsch, C., & Uryu, M. (2012). Intercultural contact, hybridity, and third space. In J. Jackson (Ed.), *The Routledge handbook of language and intercultural communication* (pp. 211–225). New York, NY: Routledge.

Kupka, B., Everett, A., & Wildermuth, S. (2007). The rainbow model of intercultural communication competence: A review and extension of existing research. *Intercultural Communication Studies, 16*, 18–35.

Ladegaard, H. J. (2012). Discourses of identity: Out group stereotypes and strategies of discursive boundary-making in Chinese students' online discussions about 'the other'. *Journal of Multicultural Discourses, 7*(1), 59–79.

Ladegaard, H. J. (2013). Beyond the reach of ethics and equity? Depersonalisation and dehumanisation in foreign domestic helper narratives. *Language & Intercultural Communication, 13*(1), 44–59. doi:10.1080/14708477.2012.748789

Leonard, P. (2010). Organizing whiteness: Gender, nationality and subjectivity in postcolonial Hong Kong. *Gender, Work and Organization, 17*, 340–358.

Liu, J. (2007). Gender dynamics and redundancy in urban China. *Feminist Economics, 13*, 125–158. doi:10.1080/13545700701445322

Lloyd, S., & Härtel, C. (2010). Intercultural competencies for culturally diverse work teams. *Journal of Managerial Psychology, 25*, 845–875. doi:10.1108/02683941011089125

MacDonald, M. N., & O'Regan, J. P. (2012). Editorial. *Language & Intercultural Communication, 12*, 173–178. doi:10.1080/14708477.2012.694260

MacDonald, M., & O'Regan (2013). The ethics of intercultural communication. *Educational Philosophy & Theory, 45*, 1005–1017.

Maroccia, M. (2012). The internet, intercultural communication and cultural variation. *Language & Intercultural Communication, 12*, 353–368.

Martin, J. N. (Ed.). (1989). Intercultural communication competence. *Special Issue: International Journal of Intercultural Relations, 13*, 227–428. doi:10.1016/0147-1767(89)90010-2

Martin, J. N. (1993). Intercultural competence: A review. In R. L. Wiseman & J. Koester (Eds.), *Intercultural communication competence* (pp. 16–29). Newbury Park, CA: Sage.

Martin, J. N., & Nakayama, T. K. (1999). Thinking dialectically about culture and communication. *Communication Theory, 9*, 1–25.

Martin, J. N., & Nakayama, T. K. (2010). Intercultural communication and dialectics revisited. In R. T. Halualani & T. K. Nakayama (Eds.), *Handbook of critical intercultural communication* (pp. 51–83). Malden, MA: Blackwell.

Matusitz, J., & Musambira, G. (2013). Power distance, uncertainty avoidance, and technology: Analyzing Hofstede's dimensions and human development indicators. *Journal of Technology in Human Services, 31*(1), 42–60.

Matveev, A. V. (2004). Describing intercultural communication competence: In-depth interviews with American and Russian managers. *Qualitative Research Reports in Communication, 5*, 55–62.

Méndez García, M. C. (2012). The potential of CLIL for intercultural development: A case study of Andalusian bilingual schools. *Language & Intercultural Communication, 12*, 196–213.

Milhauser, K. L., & Rahschulte, T. (2010). Meeting the needs of global companies through improved international business curriculum. *Journal of Teaching in International Business, 21*(2), 78–100. doi:10.1080/08975930.2010.483912

Moran, R. T., Youngdahl, W. E., & Moran, S. V. (2009). Intercultural competence in business: Leading global projects. In D. K. Deardorff (Ed.), *The Sage handbook of intercultural competence* (pp. 100–120), Thousand Oaks, CA: Sage.

Morley, M. J., & Cerdin, J.-L. (2010). Intercultural competence in the international business arena. *Journal of Managerial Psychology, 25*, 805–809. doi:10.1108/02683941011089099

Mughan, T. (2009). Exporting the multiple market experience and the SME intercultural paradigm. In A. Feng, M. Byram, & M. Fleming (Eds.), *Becoming interculturally competent through education and training* (pp. 32–52). Bristol: Multilingual Matters.

Nakayama, T., & Martin, J. (2014). Ethical issues in intercultural communication competence: A dialectical approach. In X.-D. Dai & G. M. Chen (Eds.), *Intercultural communication competence: Conceptualization and its development in cultural contexts and interactions* (pp. 97–117). Newcastle: Cambridge Scholars.

Park, J. S. Y. (2013). Metadiscursive regimes of diversity in a multinational corporation. *Language in Society, 42*, 557–577.

Phadnis, S., & Caplice, C. (2013). Global virtual teams: How are they performing? *Supply Chain Management Review, 17*(4), 8–9.

Phipps, A. (2010). Training and intercultural education: The danger in good citizenship. In M. Guilherme, E. Glaser, & M. C. Méndez García (Eds.), *The intercultural dynamics of multicultural working* (pp. 59–75). Bristol: Multilingual Matters.

Phipps, A. (2014). 'They are bombing now': 'Intercultural dialogue' in times of conflict. *Language & Intercultural Communication, 14*(1), 108–124.

Rathje, S. (2007). Intercultural competence: The status and future of a controversial concept. *Language & Intercultural Communication, 7*, 254–266. doi:10.2167/laic285.0

Sheldon, P., Kim, S., Li, Y., & Warner, M. (Eds.). (2011). *China's changing workplace: Dynamism, diversity and disparity.* New York, NY: Routledge.

Shu, X., Zhu, Y., & Zhang, Z. (2007). Global economy and gender inequalities: The case of the urban Chinese labor market. *Social Science Quarterly, 88*, 1307–1332.

Śliwa, M. (2007). Globalization, inequalities and the 'polanyi problem'. *Critical Perspectives on International Business, 3*(2), 111–135.

Sorrells, K. (2012). Intercultural training in the global context. In J. Jackson (Ed.), *The Routledge handbook of language and intercultural communication* (pp. 372–389). New York, NY: Routledge.

Sorrells, K. (2013). *Intercultural communication: Globalization and social justice.* Thousand Oaks, CA: Sage.

Spitzberg, B. H., & Changnon, G. (2009). Conceptualizing intercultural competence. In D. K. Deardorff (Ed.), *The Sage handbook of intercultural competence* (pp. 2–64). Thousand Oaks, CA: Sage.

Springer, S. (2012). Neoliberalism as discourse: Between Foucauldian political economy and Marxian poststructuralism. *Critical Discourse Studies, 9*(2), 133–147.

Syed, J., & Pio, E. (2010). Veiled diversity? Workplace experiences of Muslim women in Australia. *Asia Pacific Journal of Management, 27*(1), 115–137.

Thomas, A. (2003). Interkulturelle kompetenz: Grundlagen, probleme und konzepte [Intercultural competence: Principles, problems and concepts]. *Erwägen, Wissen, Ethik, 14*(1), 137–221.

Ting-Toomey, S. (2009). Intercultural conflict competence as a facet of intercultural competence development: Multiple conceptual approaches. In D. K. Deardorff (Ed.), *The Sage handbook of intercultural competence* (pp. 100–120). Thousand Oaks, CA: Sage.

Tomalin, B. (2009). Applying the principles: Instrument for intercultural business training. In A. Feng, M. Byram, & M. Fleming (Eds.), *Becoming interculturally competent through education and training* (pp. 115–130). Bristol: Multilingual Matters.

Tse, T. (2014). Constructing Chinese identity in post-colonial Hong Kong: A discursive analysis of the official nation-building project. *Studies in Ethnicity & Nationalism, 14*, 188–206. doi:10.1111/sena.12073

Varela, O. E., Salgado, E. I., & Lasio, M. V. (2010). The meaning of job performance in collectivistic and high power distance cultures. *Cross Cultural Management, 17*, 407–426.

Verschueren, J. (2008). Intercultural communication and the challenges of migration. *Language & Intercultural Communication, 8*(1), 21–35.

Walby, S. (2003). Policy developments for workplace gender equity in a global era: The importance of the EU in the UK. *Review of Policy Research, 20*(1), 45–65.

Warren, M. (2012). Professional and workplace settings. In J. Jackson (Ed.), *The Routledge handbook of language and intercultural communication* (pp. 481–494). New York, NY: Routledge.

Washington, M. C., Okoro, E. A., & Thomas, O. (2012). Intercultural communication in global business: An analysis of benefits and challenges. *The International Business & Economics Research Journal, 11*(2), 217.

Wiseman, R. L. (2002). Intercultural communication competence. In W. B. Gudykunst & B. Mody (Eds.), *Handbook of intercultural and international communication* (pp. 207–224). Thousand Oaks, CA: Sage.

Wiseman, R. L., & Koester, J. (Eds.). (1993). *Intercultural communication competence*. Newbury Park, CA: Sage.

World Migration in Figures. (2013, October). New York, NY: United Nations Department of Economic and Social Affairs, Population Division.

Xiao, X., & Chen, G.-M. (2009). Communication competence and moral competence: A Confucian perspective. *Journal of Multicultural Discourses*, *4*(1), 61–74.

Yep, G. A. (2000). Encounters with the other: Personal notes for a reconceptualization of intercultural communication competence. *The CATESOL Journal*, *12*(1), 117–144.

Young, T., & Sercombe, P. (2010). Communication, discourses and interculturality. *Language & Intercultural Communication*, *10*, 181–188.

Yunxia, Z. (2008). New Zealand and Chinese managers' reflections on language use in business settings: Implications for intercultural communication. *Language & Intercultural Communication, 8*(1), 50–68.

Zarate, G. (2003). Identities and plurilingualism: Preconditions for the recognition of intercultural competences. In M. Byram (Ed.) *Intercultural competence* (pp. 84–118). Strasbourg: Council of Europe.

Issues of language and competence in intercultural business contexts

Shanta Nair-Venugopal

Institute of Malaysian and International Studies, University Kebangsaan Malaysia, Selangor, Malaysia

This paper explores some of the tension between language ability as a type of workplace competence and standardized language use in Malaysian business contexts, which are set against the backdrop of the globalized workplace. Standardized English language use is prioritized as a value-added skill, over contextualized or localized language use as authentic language ability, in these contexts which are natural sites of intercultural communication in multilingual, multiethnic Malaysia. It is contended that standardized English may not be able to compete with the authenticity of contextualized or localized language use for it is the latter that ensures that the work of the localized workplace gets done first before it can lay claim to the globalized economy. The tension between such authentic language use as innate ability and prescribed language use as skills can impinge on intercultural communication competence (ICC). Three studies that demonstrate such tension in the localized Malaysian and globalized business contexts are discussed following an examination of ICC in Anglo-American contexts.

Artikel ini menyelidiki ketegangan kebolehan berbahasa sebagai kecekapan di tempat bekerja, dan penggunaan bahasa *standard* dalam konteks perniagaan di Malaysia yang dibandingkan dengan tempat bekerja global. Penggunaan bahasa Inggeris *standard* yang dilihat sebagai kecekapan yang lebih bernilai, diutamakan berbanding penggunaan bahasa berkonteks dan tempatan sebagai kemampuan berbahasa yang sahih, di dalam konteks komunikasi antarbudaya di Malaysia yang terdiri dari pelbagai bahasa dan bangsa. Artikel ini dicadangkan bahawa bahasa Inggeris *standard* mungkin tidak dapat bersaing dengan penggunaan bahasa Inggeris berkonteks atau tempatan yang sahih. Ini adalah kerana penunaan bahasa berkonteks dan tempatan dapat memastikan bahawa segala urusan kerja di tempat bekerja tempatan akan diselesaikan terlebih dahulu sebelum kerja di tempat bekerja global akan dilakukan dan disiapkan. Ketegangan antara penggunaan bahasa yang sahih sebagai kebolehan semulajadi dan penggunaan bahasa yang disarankan akan memberi kesan terhadap kecekapan berkomunikasi antarbudaya. Tiga kajian yang menunjukkan ketegangan sedemikian dalam konteks perniagaan di Malaysia dan global akan dibincangkan setelah meneliti kecekapan berkomunikasi antarbudaya dalam konteks Anglo-Amerika.

Introduction

In this paper I discuss some of the tension between language ability, as a type of workplace competence, and standardized language use in Malaysian business contexts, against the backdrop of the globalized workplace, in the prioritization of standardized English language use as a value-added skill over contextualized or localized language use as authentic language ability. The Malaysian business context is seen as a site of intercultural communication (IC) given Malaysia's multilingual and multiethnic diversity. I contend that standardized English may not be able to compete with the authenticity of contextualized or localized language use for it is the latter that ensures that the work of the localized workplace gets done first before it can lay claim to the globalized economy. Since language 'directly mediates every transaction' (Fantini, 2010, p. 270) it is the link in intercultural development that affects intercultural communication competence (ICC). Thus the tension between authentic language use as innate ability and prescribed language use as skills can impinge on ICC. I draw on three studies to illustrate this tension in localized Malaysian and globalized business contexts. First, I examine the notion of culture and how it operates in the intercultural nexus. Then I discuss how language contributes to ICC in intercultural business contexts in which ICC has to be understood in relation to what constitutes culture in the workplace. I then examine the claims made for models of ICC in Anglo-American contexts in relation to whether or not the impetus to be interculturally competent is a hegemonical preserve since research in these contexts leads the field. Their findings, which define and dominate knowledge production in the field, usually reflect Western cultural values. When these findings are extended to other intercultural contexts and situations, they come embedded with the same cultural values. Shi-Xu (2009) points out that the dominance of Western knowledge production and dissemination is the act of exercising the power of global communication.

Culture in the intercultural nexus

Although hugely problematic to define and reach consensus on, culture is an inextricable link in the intercultural nexus. While the intercultural is defined by differences rather than similarities, the locus of IC is not only the mediation between behaviours and world views among peoples of different languages and cultures, but it is also the dialogue between minority and dominant cultures along cleavages that may be present in any society (Kramsch, 1998, 2001) including that with a national language and culture. We not only need to problematise culture, but we also need to look at it less defensively as structure (Block, 2013) while affirming the self-agency of individuals to act for themselves and not merely as members of societies (Nair-Venugopal, 2003a, p. 18). Individuals may resist ascribed norms or prescribed meanings, patterns of behaviour, practices and attitudes of the societies they 'belong' to.

Nevertheless, whichever way we look culture continues to be predicted by provenance. The meanings of symbols and artefacts, ideas, beliefs, values and norms, as well as patterns of behaviour, practices and attitudes are shared and understood as objective reality (Kroeber & Kluckhohn, 1952; Spencer-Oatey, 2000). These are conventionally learned as part of primary socialization or enculturation or as 'a process of making and remaking collective sense of changing social facts' (Baumann, 1996, p. 189). Most of us carry much of this cultural knowledge in an emotional backpack as a fallback guide or interpretative framework for most of our lives. In the largely taken for granted view, culture shapes attitudes and priorities and deems what is acceptable or relevant to the community as 'ways of doing things' in a community as human activities (following Goodenough, 1994). To summarize, 'culture is a verb' (Street, 1993). It is that 'which needs to be known in order to operate reasonably effectively in a specific human environment' (Street, 1993, p. 38). Since language is integral to communication, 'ways of speaking' (Hymes, 1974a, 1974b) also become 'ways of doing things' in the community. Hall once declared, 'culture is communication and communication is culture' (1959, p. 186).

Intercultural communication

Considering language in an intercultural context merits some discussion of the defining parameters of IC, because IC is communication that mediates 'cultures' and impacts on language use whichever way we understand 'cultures'. IC is frequently used interchangeably with cross-cultural communication to mean cross-country communication on the assumption that one can distinguish between the cultures of different societies. The USA led in the early work on IC because of its attempts to explain difference in its long history of assimilating diverse groups of immigrants as citizens, understanding its own natives and protecting its global strategic and military interests. These efforts were supported by its Foreign Service Institute, in which Edward Hall, who is credited with using the term 'IC', worked for about five years.

IC is not only bounded by political, geographical and social borders and boundaries, but it is also restrained by contextually dependent and relational situations. It therefore includes the discourse of the minorities within them, whether defined by localities or by 'other' cultures, or sub-fields within the margins of territories, communities and disciplines, respectively. And while the broadly defining metaphor of IC is that of staying within borders, rather than that of crossing them, it is also the discourse of the glocal, the cosmopolitan and the a-cultural, and of universal rather than of distinctive or particular applicability. It includes state and non-state players in a world of both porous and dissolving borders and boundaries. Thus in embracing these dichotomies, IC includes not only the interactive space between what is generally understood as distinct cultures, but also that within the interstices, i.e. the 'space' within smaller specific cultures, and across the larger distinct ones. Membership in the larger distinct cultures within or without the same society is not diminished relative to that in the smaller specific cultures. For example, academics, as members of specific professional cultures, will relate more to their counterparts from other cultures than they will to factory workers in their own, although they may share ethno-cultural values and traditions with the latter. This contrasts with the otherization and cultural reductionism of individuals when viewed only as members of 'national' cultures.

It is also in that 'space' within and across 'cultures' that social identities are negotiated and communicated (see Jenks, Bhatia, & Lou, 2013). Identity behaviour is implicated as ways of doing things that are typical or are influenced by some considerations of provenance, such as for example, race/ethnicity, religious affiliation and sexuality. They may be manifested as inequities too, as with regard to gender (Holmes, 2006; Ladegaard, 2011) or age/generation, sexuality and ability. In the workplace, these identities may have implications for IC if they are marked and affect job-related decisions. Thus it is important to understand what constitutes culture in the workplace in order to understand IC in the workplace, even if it is becoming rather difficult to identify 'cultural' identity, particularly in the globalized workplace.

Culture and IC in the workplace

The workplace quite apart from being a fundamental site of language contact and socialization, also operates as a microcosm of wider society and manifests culture both in the fairly conventional sense, and as social categories, or as the 'small' cultures of 'any cohesive social grouping' (Holliday, 1999, p. 237). Culture in the workplace appears to operate on at least two levels. One is at the level of interpersonal and intercultural relations between individuals who belong to the 'large' and distinctive cultures of provenance, or to sub- and/or co-cultures as 'small' cultures. Sub-cultures may be seen as either the variable patterns of thought and behaviour of similar groups of people, or as onion skin like variations that 'deviate from the normative ideals of adult communities', or 'elements in ideological tension with ... dominant large cultures' (Holliday, 1999, p. 239, citing Thornton, 1997; Gelder, 1997, respectively). In co-cultures, individuals share values and norms, beliefs and interests that distinguish them from those of the larger cultures but with whom they share common beliefs as groups within them. Women, or the aged, for example, may be viewed in all human societies as members of smaller cultures that cut across the large or 'meta' ones (Dahl, 2003).

Secondly, culture operates in the workplace at the level of interaction between individuals as members of the same organization. They subscribe to particular values and ways of doing things, as organizational culture that they share and simultaneously define through their collective behaviour. Although, as Holliday suggests, multinational organization cultures are small cultures (1999, p. 239), these organizational cultures become emblematic of regularization, standardization and normativity affecting a range of decisions including language choice and use. It is in these corporations that the commonalities of 'how to' cultural training are prevalent.

It is also in the multinational corporations and transnational conglomerates that expatriate staff and guest workers reconfigure the locational aspects of the workplace with the fluidity of working within the space and borderlessness of globalization. In challenging geographical borders and national boundaries and spaces, globalization allows for the emergence of a type of worker who subsists within the local spaces of borders and boundaries, yet works for globalized interests that also satisfy self-interests. These globalized interests naturally value competencies that mediate cultural differences. And intercultural communicative competence is valued from among the plethora of desirable workplace competencies that can range from new literacies to professional and communication competencies. But, as Dervin and Kuoppala (in press) note, intercultural competences are often polysemic and rely heavily on problematic concepts such as culture and identity, and not everyone agrees on what intercultural competences mean either.

IC has been very much associated with the mantras of national cultures and globalization. Hofstede (1980/2001; 1991/2005) was already a byword on the dimensions of national cultures from the 1990s onwards. Trompenaars and Hampden-Turner were also 'Riding (their) Waves of Culture in Understanding (in what was posited to be) Cultural Diversity in Business' (1997). Cultural sensitivity emerged as 'the ability to discriminate and experience relevant cultural differences' (Hammer, Bennett, & Wiseman, 2003, p. 422), as a predictor of intercultural competence. It has since been claimed (Plum, Achen, Dræby, & Jensen, 2008) that it is cultural intelligence, a combination of emotional drivers, cultural knowledge and practical methods, that can bridge differences in the (inter)cultural encounter as it can handle and prevent cultural conflict by synergizing differences.

National cultures (Hofstede 1980/2001, 1991/2005), the 'default' cultures that are synonymous with nation states, were based on conventional understandings of what constituted a nation's culture in the heydays of Anglo-American multinational proliferation. Such readings of culture might have served as early warning signals for reading the 'cultural other' and might have helped novices to globalized workplaces make some sense of some of the unfamiliar and uncertain in their new environments. However, as homogenized representations of locality, they get in the way of understanding contextually dependent and relational situations in transnational workplaces that have since become increasingly globalized and cosmopolitan due to considerable demographic changes in the workforce.

Moreover, the face of the multinational/transnational corporation has changed somewhat from being almost wholly Anglo-American to increasingly Asian (China, Korea and Japan), Other-European (Scandinavian) and mixed. Predicting national cultures is not useful or reliable given rapid globalization. They have become 'imaginaries' (Dervin, Paatela-Nieminen, Kuoppala, & Riitaoja, 2012; Holliday, 1999). Similarities have become more important within the homogenizing impulse of globalization, while its obverse, glocalization, encapsulates the tension between the local and the global (Robertson, 1995). And in being both localized and globalized, i.e. glocalized, the transnational workplace may be seen as cosmopolitan space in its 'incorporation' of the global outsider within the insiderness of locality.

Workplace competence

Understanding workplace competence has to precede an understanding of ICC. Spitzberg and Changnon (2009) argue that the term *competence* is a contested conceptualization that has, for some time, been too loosely bandied about and variously equated with understanding, relationship development, satisfaction, effectiveness, appropriateness and adaptation, with each of these criteria defended or criticized elsewhere. It is also 'sometimes conceptually equated with a set of abilities or skills which is by far the most common approach and fits with the more normative semantic sense of the term' and 'at other times, a subjective evaluative impression' (p. 6). While competencies may be generally understood as a set of abilities or skills, workplace 'competencies' commonly refer to a set of desirable skills that are specific to particular jobs. Workplace competence is defined (Spencer & Spencer, 1993) as an underlying characteristic of an individual that is causally related to criterion-referenced effective, or superior performance, or both in a job or situation. The argument is that individuals can get and keep desired jobs, and find new ones if they possess the desired competencies of knowledge and skills, and personal attributes or dispositions (Hillage & Pollard, 1998). Thus, while the ability to use word processing software and other technologies as hands-on knowledge at work is considered basic workplace competence today, the ability to speak another language as ICC may be an additional skill. Many organizations establish the relationship between core competencies and employability skills, and integrate critical skills into work-based projects aligned to core competencies. Developed from the early 1980s, work-based competency is a methodology for describing desired performance commonly used in large companies and government agencies worldwide. It has been argued, however, that established methodologies have inherent strengths that can challenge the competence philosophy (Stewart & Hamlin, 1992).

Intercultural communication competence

Compounded by mondialization, increasing mobility and migration, ICC appears to have become an aspirational aspect of workplace competence. ICC is defined as:

> impression management that allows members of different cultural systems to be aware of their cultural identity and cultural differences, and to interact effectively and appropriately

with each other in diverse contexts by agreeing on the meaning of diverse symbol systems, with the result of mutually satisfying relationships. (Kupka, 2008, p. 16)

Unarguably, the interaction will be deemed appropriate only if it does not significantly violate valued rules, norms and expectations, and considered effective if valued goals or rewards are attained.

Despite its applicability to the globalized workplace, a definition of ICC that can be applied across intercultural contexts globally appears unavailable. Kupka (2008), for instance, points out the limitations to his study (despite the promise it holds). What any one definition or model would do is, like many other so-called 'universal' standards, homogenize from a particular vantage point of dominance. In the workplace, it is likely to perpetuate Western/Anglo-American human resources (HR) managerial hegemony and ignore the potential capacity for transformational change in specific context dependent situations. As an example of dominant discourse, gross domestic product (GDP) is considered to be one of the 'traditional' markers of human progress despite concerns for some time about the adequacy of its figures to measure societal well-being. Its relevance as an indicator of economic performance and social progress of a nation is only now being reconsidered albeit by the leading economists, Stiglitz, Sen and Fitoussi (Newcombe, 2012) after being imposed for so long as a measure of economic, environmental and social sustainability.

Another example of dominance is how in the UK, the Western biomedical model exerts hegemony by subjugating traditional systems of medicine, such as Ayurveda, to Western biomedical practices. This robs Ayurveda of its status as a form of traditional medicine with its potential for autonomous transformation (Nair-Venugopal, 2012). So as a powerful legitimizing tool, Western scientific validation can either affirm or replace the authority of other traditions.

There are thus lessons to be learnt here for ICC too in the hope that 'experts' can 'decide what the components of the definition are' for ICC (Lapointe, 1994, p. 275). Although critical approaches have weakened such hopes, 'top intercultural scholars and academic administrators' were consulted to 'document consensus … on what constitutes intercultural competence and the best ways to measure this complex construct' (Deardorff, 2006, p. 242) in a claim that it is the first study to do so. However, although 'the ability to communicate effectively and appropriately in intercultural situations based on one's intercultural knowledge, skills, and attitudes' (Deardorff, 2006, p. 247) may not be controversial, the list of components identified may be. It raises the usual contestable issues of culture and social categorization, and identity and power, despite the affirmation that it represents the first crucial step towards such measurement.

Some of the challenges of reaching consensus were made explicit in the Centre for Information for Language Teachers commissioned work undertaken by O'Regan and MacDonald (2007) on national occupational standards in intercultural working in the UK. Reaching consensus on most component skills, even from a defined multicultural perspective within the UK, was not straightforward (see MacDonald, O'Regan, & Witana, 2009) despite the articulation by the European Institute for Comparative Cultural Research of a concept of 'intercultural dialogue' within the European context of cultural diversity (*ERICarts*, 2008). Considering such difficulties in conceptualizing ICC, the challenge is to be able to apply any one definition or model of ICC reliably to every intercultural encounter. Even within a single area, region or country, each intercultural encounter is dependent on context and relations. The other challenge is 'whether multiple models of competence should be developed in particular contexts with high levels of specificity' (Macdonald & O'Regan, 2012, p. 558).

Arasaratnam's (2009) avers that her model of ICC is one of the few that has been constructed entirely based on data from participants who represented multiple cultural perspectives, and which performs well in culturally diverse participant groups. The logic behind it is that a person who is competent in one intercultural exchange is intrinsically able to be competent in a different exchange. It is based on the findings of a previous study (Arasaratnam & Doerfel, 2005) in which participants from 15 different countries were asked to describe a competent intercultural communicator (among other tasks). The variables identified were empathy, intercultural experience/training, motivation, global attitude and good listening ability. The study claims that there arc identifiable variables in a competent intercultural communicator that transcend cultural context and cultural identity of the perceiver. Culture and context remain intractable entities in the ICC nexus that exacerbate the problems of model application.

Language and ICC in intercultural business contexts

Language is more identifiable than culture and knowing additional languages is advantageous within the ethno-cultural diversity of the globalized workplace today. Before culture became the focus of contestation in IC, Clyne (1994) produced an account of the Australian workplace within an interactionist view of the relation between language and culture. That culture 'determines the areal networks promoting similarities in discourse patterns and expectations' (p. 204), may seem simplistic and even essentialist today. But, if 'linguistic competence plays a key role' (Byram, 1997, p. 34) in ICC, then the new and diverse cultural and linguistic contexts of the contemporary workplace must also value 'communicative competence' (Bachman, 1990; Canale & Swain, 1980; Hymes, 1968; Savignon, 1983) in a foreign language, alongside knowledge of information and communication technologies.

Ultimately, global economic competiveness depends on the effective use of information and communication technologies (ICTs) matched by high levels of literacy developed and maintained through the use of the Internet and other ICTs. However, even if certain kinds of knowledge that underlie the performance of particular tasks do not require linguistic ability, language remains a valuable resource in the new globalized economy (see Heller, 2003, 2005, 2010). Language may be only one of many competencies required to thrive in the workplace, but it is integral to ICC in the workplace, as the language–culture relationship is communicated through 'language at work', which entails a considerable amount of contextualized language use.

The Malaysian context

In Malaysia, linguistic diversity is complemented by multiethnic diversity. Although it is generally described as being multicultural, Malaysia is still very much a composite, plural society (see Milner, 2003; Ratnam, 1965) of communities living largely separate social lives, and for the most part peacefully, despite politically generated dissonance, misplaced nationalism and jingoism. Malaysian society is composed of a largely Malay Muslim native (*Bumiputra*) majority, Chinese (mainly) and Indian minorities and various smaller indigenous groups (*Pribumi*) speaking a polyglot of languages. Despite the linguistic diversity, global economic competitiveness is believed to rest on the pervasive ideology of the value-addedness of the English language as *the* language of employability in

Malaysian business (see Nair-Venugopal, 2013). Yet, the English language situation in Malaysia is largely that of a quasi-second language since Malay, as Bahasa Malaysia, the national language, is the main medium of instruction in national schools for countless Malaysians alongside Mandarin and Tamil in vernacular schools. However, its pluricultural diversity makes the Malaysian workplace an intercultural space in which, like any other workplace anywhere else, the social identities of individuals categorized as members of the sub- or co-cultures of age/generation, gender, ethnicity/race, religious affiliation, sexual orientation, etc. are negotiated and communicated in interactions that involve localized or contextualized language use.

Generally speaking, opportunities to enter workplace sites to research relevant subjects are, more often than not, difficult in Malaysia. Although there are research collaborations and consultancy work with universities, frequently when entry is gained into organizations, researchers tend to interact less with employees than with their employers. Access is usually only gained through negotiations with middle management. Approval is obtained from top management, so protocol is hardly breeched. Management tends to allow access to research proposals that suit institutional purposes and frequently research outcomes fit management expectations. Unsurprisingly then, Malaysian workplace literature abounds with the perceptions and expectations of stakeholders, gatekeepers and invariably senior management (Kaur & Chuah 2012; Kaur & Clarke, 2009; Moslehifar & Ibrahim, 2012; Muthiah, 2002, 2003; Ong, Leong, & Kaur, 2011; Sarudin, Mohd Noor, Zubairi, Tunku Ahmad, & Nordin, 2013; Wahi, O'Neill, & Chapman, 2011). The locus of much workplace research is on how to prepare graduates adequately in English for the workplace with employability skills that are invariably associated with communication skills. Very little, however, is available on how the daily grind of work is managed, given the less than desirable levels of English language skills frequently lamented by management, or even how, in many large business organizations, Malay is competing with English. When the attention of gatekeepers is drawn to this antinomy, it is argued that language is not as important as work-based/job-related knowledge. Nevertheless, there is no letting up on the desirability of English language skills, which are frequently and disadvantageously conflated with communicative skills for employability (Nair-Venugopal, 2013) as part of a national logic on economic global competitiveness.

This state of affairs perpetuates a cycle of disconnect between what is posited as relevant or appropriate language skills for the workplace rather than what actually matters for work-based competence. The mismatch between actual workplace language competence and taught language skills appears to be an iterative global phenomenon too that is not surprisingly reified by lucrative publishing in English Language Teaching/English as a Second Language/English for Specific Purposes (ELT/ESL/ESP). A lucrative global industry continues to capture world markets with publications on how to teach business English as *the* language of business, how to communicate interculturally or how to become interculturally competent in the classroom or training room, very much like making rats perform under laboratory conditions. These perspectives come mainly from the canonical centres of ELT/ESL/English as a Foreign Language (EFL)/ESP with a heavy reliance on feedback obtained from foreign students privileged to study abroad, rather than from an experiential understanding of the sociolinguistic movement on the ground. The periphery that is encroached is not always understood. Such practices are evident in the work on ICC too.

Evidence of language 'tension' in localized and globalized business contexts

I now discuss three previous studies (Nair-Venugopal, 2003b, 2006, 2009) that demonstrate this language 'tension'. Understanding language tension requires an understanding of the role of language as natural resource, i.e. as a way of talking or a type of organizational discourse (see Bargiela, 2005; Holmes & Stubbe, 2003) to get things done, as a rule of thumb criterion, rather than as a set of commodified skills that are prescribed. This is regardless of the size of the ethno-cultural space occupied *in situ* by interlocutors. A study (Crosling & Ward, 2002) in English speaking Australia found, for instance, that since workplace communication was mostly informal in nature, practice in making formal presentations alone was not sufficient preparation for business graduates.

The three studies identified for discussion on language 'tension' focus on the following aspects:

1. Interactions among Malaysians in a localized business context and between two businessmen in the globalized context of international trade as speakers of English as another language/lingua franca (Nair-Venugopal, 2003b);
2. Comparisons between Business English materials and contextualized language use (Nair-Venugopal, 2006); and
3. Organizational imperatives for training vis-à-vis trainer language choice (Nair-Venugopal, 2009).

The first study (Nair-Venugopal, 2003b) illustrates the phenomenon of intelligibility in English in localized and globalized intercultural business contexts. Two out of the three data examples discussed are taken from Malaysian business contexts while the third is an oft-quoted extract taken from Firth (1990) on negotiations in international commodity trading conducted via telephone. Both types of interactions demonstrate the different routes that communication can take in different contexts for different purposes and attest to how intelligibility, as comprehensibility, has to go beyond the 'good enough' English of pronunciation and accent in intercultural contexts of communication in English.

The first two examples (Nair-Venugopal, 2003b, pp. 42–43) showed that intelligibility is facilitated by the interlocutors' membership within the same speech community, that is, of Malaysian speakers of English. Drawn from Malaysian business contexts, they showed how trainer comprehensibility of trainees is facilitated by familiar social context, shared cultural background or schematic knowledge, insider awareness of linguistic norms and interactive engagement, with regard to the relevance of intelligibility in ICC. It is clearly the modalities of the localized variation of English, inclusive of the alternation of codes as individual sociolinguistic repertoires that interface ICC in these contexts.

The third example (Nair-Venugopal, 2003b, p. 44) is drawn from Firth (1990, p. 275). Here the interactions are between two businessmen, a Syrian and a Dane, as speakers of English as another language or lingua franca. Comprehensibility was neither facilitated nor impeded as members of the wider global community of speakers of English. It hinged more crucially on both as non-native speakers of English interacting with each other to somehow achieve a communicative breakthrough to successfully relay, receive and understand a message. Firth's well-known strategies of 'let it pass' and 'make it normal' appear to underpin successful interactions that are not only 'real, authentic, effective, expedient' (Firth, 1996). They are also contextually relevant and appropriate in what are quintessentially intercultural encounters, inclusive of the limitations in English language ability. Today the telephone can be replaced by the use of Skype and a webcam. They will reveal some paralinguistic features, such as facial expressions and some gestures.

These can alter the dynamics of the interactions into face-to-face communication, despite being mediated still by technology.

The language tension in the three data examples lay in the expectations regarding each interlocutor's English language ability to communicate in the intercultural encounter, and the use of available language resources for appropriate and effective communication. The study proved that, despite linguistic variability in English within and across countries, 'cultures' and contexts, individuals can interact effectively and appropriately with each other in diverse ethno-linguistic contexts to achieve mutually satisfying relationships. This has been defined as the characteristic outcome of ICC (Kupka, 2008, p. 16).

In the second study (Nair-Venugopal, 2006), the English in Business English materials produced by international publishing houses, mainly centred in the UK, was compared to that of the English in an interactional model of English that had already been identified for business contexts (Nair-Venugopal, 2000, 2001) in Malaysia in a previous large-scale study. A sampling of more than 30 of published materials in Business English revealed that most set out to teach grammar, vocabulary, pronunciation and communication skills that were posited as appropriate for business purposes. Speaking was ranked as the most important skill to develop with some practice provided in listening skills. The study showed that the prescribed language forms and patterns of speech and communication in the commercially produced texts and multimedia materials surveyed were clearly pretentious and stilted in the context of speaking English in Malaysian business contexts. The dissonance was particularly apparent because the interactional model of English identified for business contexts (Nair-Venugopal, 2000, 2001) operates as a functional model of interaction too. Such evidence counters the marketing mythologies of purportedly universal forms of language use in business contexts worldwide. The language of Business English is frequently that of register or specific content (as applicable to a particular job type or specialization), mixed with general-purpose language use in context.

This dissonance points to the dichotomy that exists between prescribed patterns of English usage (such as those available in the plethora of commercially produced materials), and those of contextualized language use in real-time Malaysian workplace interactions. To ignore it is to deny the pragmatic relevance of speaking English as one of the localized languages of business in Malaysian contexts. The following examples of 'signalling devices' used in presentations, taken from the sampling of publications studied, illustrate the discordance: 'Let me start by'; 'I'd like to begin by'; 'Let me turn now to'; 'Let's look at this in more detail'; 'I will deal with this later'; 'if I may, but for now'; 'I'd like to sum up now'. Instead of these it was 'okay' and 'right' that were used as signalling devices. They were also two of the most common discourse markers in the interactional model (see Nair-Venugopal, 2006). The interactional model, in fact, reflects the linguistic diversity of Malaysia in its sub-varieties of Malaysian English (ME), standard, colloquial and bazaar Malay, code-switches into Malay and English, code-mixes of English and Malay, formal and informal referents mixed with workplace register and ethnically distinctive ways of speaking as 'ethnolects' (Nair-Venugopal, 2000, 2001). Not least of all, it provides support for an indigenous response to a pervasive global ideology at work by exposing the gap between contextualized language use and prescribed usage in commercially produced texts. In representing language change and choice in Malaysian business contexts, it may be taken to be evidence of functional language use in the Malaysian workplace and provides an appropriate model for the development of authentic language materials as an alternative response.

It appears that the writers of the materials on Business English relied on a formulaic approach to ESL/EFL materials production based on the assumption that native speakers were the arbiters of the norms perpetuating some of the *World Englishes (WE)* debates on language hegemony. The business transactions contexts were almost exclusively within Anglophone speaker domains of control, even when the interlocutors were non-native speakers. Hardly any of the interactions were set in Singapore, for instance, which is viewed as one of the most globalized nations today. As for the assignments set in Jakarta, Indonesia, the key and top management figures were all white Caucasians and mainly male. This was true for the Japanese scenarios too. Ironically, if the texts were meant to simulate or reflect 'realistic' business contexts in Asia, they did succeed by reflecting Anglo-American monopoly of multinational and transnational businesses worldwide based on a 'new world order' of free market enterprise.

Furthermore in one of the texts that claims to be 'certified' as realistic business materials, one of the main protagonists in an 'assignment' is a Kuwaiti businessman. Yet, there is no mention of the prerequisite dietary label *halal* (permissible in Islam) in the 'assignment', which involves the import of poultry into Kuwaiti which is a Muslim country. This displays a clear lack of cultural knowledge of Kuwait. It constitutes a reality gap with regard to assumptions regarding local values and taboos, such as for instance, the prohibition against the consumption of non-*halal* meat (i.e. not slaughtered according to Islamic injunctions) in Muslim countries.

It does also appear that, while the producers of these materials had aspired for 'large' cultural changes for their users, they did not display in their pedagogical objectives, either relevant cultural knowledge or sensitivity, or the willingness, to modify their own cultural biases and communicative behaviour to suit those of the target users. Relevant knowledge or willingness would have demonstrated some 'cultural' awareness' at least as a dimension of the ICC they could have projected as the writers. Additionally, the claim that a certain type of language usage is 'the kind of standard business practice that *most* students of Business English are likely to encounter in their working environment' (Jones & Alexander, 1996, p. 6), does not demonstrate any tolerance for the high probability of ambiguity (or redundancy) in language use that some students will encounter and learn to cope with in such environments. More recent publications such as *The Business* by Macmillan (2009), and *Market Leader* by Pearson/Longman (2008) have introduced topics such as corporate image, risk management, managing conflict and investment, and drawn on authentic and authoritative content from *the Financial Times* and other media sources, respectively. Yet, cultural awareness, sensitivity or intelligence still appear to be in short supply.

Lastly, in the third study (Nair-Venugopal, 2009), actual language use of in-house trainers in a commercial bank was observed and the trainers subsequently interviewed. The aim was to find out if, in fact, the dominant organizational rhetoric on in-house language use matched that of the trainers' actual language use, and whether the institutional directives impinged on language ability (or 'ways of speaking') as a type of workplace competence vis-à-vis standardized English language use prescribed by management as de rigueur. The disconnect between institutional preaching and practice was clearly evident in the training sessions observed, despite the institutional directives on the use of standardized English. There was much evidence of contextualized language use in the form of the localized sub-varieties of ME, standard, colloquial and bazaar Malay, code-switches into Malay and English, code-mixes of English and Malay, formal and informal referents, workplace jargon and inevitably the ethnically distinctive ways of speaking as 'ethnolects' (Nair-Venugopal, 2000, 2001). The findings of this study have since been compared to those of the large-scale one conducted in the 1990s for a longitudinal perspective on language choice in Malaysian business contexts, and they confirm those of the earlier study (see Nair-Venugopal, 2013).

Considering the global dispersion of English, it is still moot in ELT work to ask questions of ownership with regard to who decides for whom in matters of language teaching and learning as many writers within the *WE* paradigm have (see Canagarajah, 1999; Kumaravadivelu, 2003). Who or what has the authority to sanction and affirm particular traditions, and thereby their absorption into the fabric of societies, is a serious issue. Without pushing the envelope too much I think we should ask the same questions of ICC? Who decides for whom? This question has far greater salience for ICC than asking the same of ELT. ELT could at least lay claim to a cannon and a centre until the empire struck back. But ICC is premised on language and culture both of which imbue all of us as human beings, even if culture is less identifiable than language. Can lists of component skills and categories, and measurements of quotients and scales, lay claim to the knowledge of particular ramifications of cultural behaviour in specific context dependent situations? Whose values and norms will decide which perspective is more important in determining competence? Do some have greater claims to making these decisions than others? Is the impetus to be communicatively competent interculturally a hegemonical preserve? Not least of all, what would justify such dominance?

Conclusion

Much of the early literature, emanating as it did from Anglo-American sites, shows a clear cultural bias in attending to IC as a problem of understanding for Anglo-Americans as receivers. Although much of it (too long a list to cite here) is very impressive as formative work, it has been built on this perspective. Alternative views have since been developed (see Asante, Miike, & Yin, 2014). Miike argues that 'Non-Western cultures, more often than not, remain as peripheral targets of data analysis and rhetorical criticism and fail to become central resources of theoretical insight and humanistic inspiration' (2014, p. 116). In an era of global consciousness, such issues have become acute with cosmopolitanism as global political consciousness igniting the debates of global citizenship. Furthermore, in a mondialized world of much mobility and migration propelled by innovations in telecommunications, rapid transport systems and cheap travel, it may become difficult to identify an intercultural exchange based on what may be nebulous cultural identities. Indeed the notion of the 'cultural other' may become indefensible in a world that is being homogenized by popular forms of global consumption, through cultural diffusion, and the continuing localization and hybridization of language forms, such as the emergence of *Globish*, a variant subset of English, that claims to be a global means of simplified communication (see McCrum, 2010).

Generally speaking, one can be adjudged to be communicatively competent if one achieves the communication goal of successfully accomplishing a communicative task effectively and appropriately for such an accomplishment can be self-reported and evaluated. ICC, however, may depend on achieving much more. Following Fantini (2010, p. 271), it is perhaps the accomplishment of a task of mutual interest and benefit to two parties without much loss of understanding between them, while maintaining good relations, that points to successful ICC. Arasaratnam and Doerfel opine that 'regardless of one's internal capacity, being perceived as competent by a culturally different other in an intercultural interaction contributes significantly to favorable outcomes' for both participants (2005, p. 141). While this may ring true it would be useful to know who decides what is perceived as 'competent' communication and who the 'cultural other' is. It may not be easy to identify one in a rapidly changing world of direct human contact and communication. The diffusion of small cultures across borders and boundaries, and the global consciousness of cosmopolitanism, will only serve to further fudge the large cultures of nation and race, and reinforce interculturality.

Arasaratnam suggests (2007, p. 71) that it would be helpful 'to start thinking of intercultural communication in terms of cultural distance and its effects on message construction/interpretation instead of thinking in terms of national/ethnic boundaries or ... cultural taxonomies', and that it is necessary 'to incorporate a culture-general approach to instrument development and study design in intercultural research'. Although there is a general rejection of national cultures (see McSweeney, 2002; Paramasivam & Nair-Venugopal, 2012) as a model of cultural differences, a culture-general approach to instrument development may not be completely without issue either. Nevertheless, it is useful to consider 'how the advent of new technologies has influenced intercultural communication in a generation to which communicating with someone across the globe is mostly routine' (Arasaratnam, 2007, p. 72). We should also look at how language communicates in all its forms and variations (inclusive of technological mediation) across 'cultures', in addition to other means of communication.

Lastly, I would like to posit that any attempt at ICC should be recognized for what it is, as a worthy attempt, and commended for the effort it involves, in spite of the language differences and inadequacies at intercultural relations that will accompany 'cultural' differences. With specific reference to intercultural contexts in both localized and globalized workplaces, ICC does not necessarily translate into the use of a supra-global language like English for effective or appropriate IC to take place, nor does it have to be standardized for perceived communicative competence to be considered work-based competence.

Finally, without trivializing any of the impressive work and serious debates on ICC, I would like to suggest that it is in the interstices of much of the normative language use of institutional imperatives and contextualized language use that IC resonates with ICC, if it is defined as the ability to communicate effectively and appropriately. Long-standing ethnographic participant observation in the intercultural business contexts of the Malaysian workplace has only affirmed this for me.

Acknowledgements

I would like to thank the organizers of *IALIC-2013* for the honour of presenting the original version of this paper as a keynote speaker at the 13th International Conference of the International Association for Languages and Intercultural Communication, from 29 November to 1 December, at Hong Kong Baptist University.

Disclosure statement

No potential conflict of interest was reported by the author.

References

Arasaratnam, L. A. (2007). Research in intercultural communication competence: Past perspectives and future directions. *Journal of International Communication, 13*(2), 66–73. doi:10.1080/13216597.2007.9674715

Arasaratnam, L. A. (2009). The development of a new instrument of intercultural communication competence. *Journal of Intercultural Communication, 20.* Retrieved from http://www.immi.se/intercultural/

Arasaratnam, L. A., & Doerfel, M. L. (2005). Intercultural communication competence: Identifying key components from multicultural perspectives. *International Journal of Intercultural Relations, 29,* 137–163. doi:10.1016/j.ijintrel.2004.04.001

Asante, M. K., Miike, Y., & Yin, J. (2014). *The global intercultural communication reader.* New York: Routledge.

Bachman, L. (1990). *Fundamental considerations in language testing.* Oxford: Oxford University Press.

Bargiela, F. (2005). Language at work: The first ten years. *ESP Across Cultures, 1,* 22–34.

Baumann, G. (1996). *Contesting culture.* Cambridge: Cambridge University Press.

Block, D. (2013). The structure and agency dilemma in identity and intercultural communication research. *Language and Intercultural Communication, 13*(2), 126–147. doi:10.1080/14708477.2013.770863

Byram, M. (1997). *Teaching and assessing intercultural communicative competence.* Clevedon: Multilingual Matters.

Canagarajah, S. (1999). *Resisting linguistic imperialism in English teaching.* Oxford: Oxford University Press.

Canale, M., & Swain, M. (1980). *Theoretical bases of communicative approaches to second language teaching and testing.* Cambridge: Cambridge University Press.

Clyne, M. G. (1994). *Intercultural communication at work: Cultural values in discourse.* Cambridge: Cambridge University Press.

Crosling, G., & Ward, I. (2002). Oral communication: The workplace needs and uses of business graduate employees. *English for Specific Purposes, 21*(1), 41–57. doi:10.1016/S0889-4906(00)00031-4

Dahl, S. (2003). *An overview of intercultural research, society for intercultural training and research UK 1/10 (2/2003).* Retrieved from www.unice.fr/.../_dahal%20-%20overview-of-intercultural-research.pdf

Deardorff, D. K. (2006). Identification and assessment of intercultural competence as a student outcome of internationalization. *Journal of Studies in International Education, 10,* 241–266. doi:10.1177/1028315306287002

Dervin, F., & Kuoppala K. (in press). Developing a portfolio of intercultural competences in teacher education: The case of a Finnish international programme. *Scandinavian Journal of Educational Research.*

Dervin, F., Paatela-Nieminen, M., Kuoppala, K., & Riitaoja, A.-L. (2012). Multicultural education in Finland – Renewed intercultural competences to the rescue? *International Journal of Multicultural Education, 14*(3), 1–13.

European Institute for Comparative Cultural Research (ERICarts). (2008). *What is intercultural dialogue?* Retrieved from http://www.interculturaldialogue.eu/web/intercultural-dialogue.php

Fantini, A. E. (2010). Language: An essential component of intercultural communicative competence. In J. Jackson (Ed.), *The Routledge handbook of intercultural communication* (pp. 263–278). Oxon: Routledge.

Firth, A. (1990) 'Lingua franca' negotiations: Towards an interactional approach. *World Englishes, 9*(3), 269–280.

Firth, A. (1996). The discursive accomplishment of normality: On Conversation Analysis and 'Lingua Franca' English. *Journal of Pragmatics, 26,* 237–259.

Goodenough, W. H. (1994). Toward a working theory of culture. In R. Borofsky (Ed.), *Assessing cultural anthropology* (pp. 262–275). New York, NY: McGraw Hill.

Hall, E.T. (1959). *The silent language.* New York, NY: Doubleday.

Hammer, M. R., Bennett, M. J., & Wiseman, R. (2003). Measuring intercultural sensitivity: The intercultural development inventory. *International Journal of Intercultural Relations*, *27*, 421–443. doi:10.1016/S0147-1767(03)00032-4

Heller, M. (2003). Globalization, the new economy and the commodification of language and identity. *Journal of Sociolinguistics*, *7*, 473–492. doi:10.1111/j.1467-9841.2003.00238.x

Heller, M. (2005, July). *Paradoxes of language in the globalised new economy*. Paper presented at the International Conference on Global Communication Cardiff, Wales.

Heller. (2010). Language as resource in the globalized new economy. In N. Coupland (Ed.), *Handbook of language and globalisation* (pp. 349–365). Oxford: Wiley-Blackwell.

Hillage, J., & Pollard, E. (1998). *Employability: Developing a framework for policy analysis* (Research Report No. 85). Nottingham: Department for Education and Employment (DfEE).

Hofstede, G. (1980/2001). *Culture's consequences: International differences in work related values/ comparing values, behaviours, institutions, and organisations across nations*. Beverly Hills, CA: Sage.

Hofstede, G. (1991/2005). *Cultures and organizations: Software of the mind/intercultural cooperation and its importance for survival*. London: McGraw-Hill.

Holliday, A. (1999). Small cultures. *Applied Linguistics*, *20*(2), 237–264.

Holmes, J. (2006). *Gendered talk at work: Constructing gender identity through workplace discourse*. New York and Oxford: Blackwell.

Holmes, J., and Stubbe, M. (2003). *Power and politeness in the workplace: A sociolinguistic analysis of talk at work*. London: Pearson.

Hymes, D. (1968). The ethnography of speaking. In J. A. Fishman (Ed.), *Readings in the sociology of language* (pp. 99–133). The Hague: Mouton.

Hymes, D. (1974a). On communicative competence. In J.B. Pride & J. Holmes (Eds.), *Sociolinguistics* (pp. 269–293). Harmondsworth: Penguin.

Hymes, D. (1974b). Ways of speaking. In R. Baumann and J. Sherzer (Eds.), *Explorations in the ethnography of speaking* (pp. 433–451). Cambridge: Cambridge University Press.

Jenks, C., Bhatia, A., & Lou, J. (2013). Special issue: The discourse of culture and identity in national and transnational contexts. *Language and Intercultural Communication*, *13*(2), 121–125. doi:10.1080/14708477.2013.770862

Jones, L., & Alexander, R. (1996). *New international business English*. Cambridge: Cambridge University Press.

Kaur, S., & Clarke, C. (2009). Analysing the English language needs of human resource staff in multinational companies. *English for Specific Purposes*, *8*(3). Retrieved from http://www.esp-world.info.

Kaur, M., & Chuah S. C. (2012). Manufacturing industry employers' perception of graduates' English language skills proficiency. *International Journal of Applied Linguistics & English Literature*, *1*(4), 114–124.

Kramsch, C. (1998). *Language and culture*. Oxford: Oxford University Press.

Kramsch, C. (2001). Intercultural communication. In R. Carter & D. Nunan (Eds.), *The Cambridge guide to teaching English to speakers of other languages* (pp. 201–206). Cambridge: Cambridge University Press.

Kroeber, A. L., & Kluckhohn, C. (1952). *Culture: A critical review of concepts and definitions*. Papers. Peabody Museum of Archaeology & Ethnology, Harvard University. Cambridge, MA: Mass. Vol *47*(1). Retrieved from http://www.archive.org/details/papersofpeabodymvol47no 1peab

Kumaravadivelu, B. (2003). *Beyond methods: Macrostrategies for language teaching*. New Haven and London: Yale University Press.

Kupka, B. (2008). *Creation of an instrument to assess intercultural communication competence for strategic international human resource management* (Unpublished doctoral dissertation). University of Otago, Otago.

Ladegaard, H. J. (2011). 'Doing power' at work: Responding to male and female management styles in a global business corporation. *Journal of Pragmatics*, *43*(1), 4–19. doi:10.1016/j. pragma.2010.09.006

Lapointe, A. E. (1994). Measuring global competence. In R. D. Lambert (Ed.), *Educational exchange and global competence* (pp. 275–276). New York, NY: Council on International Educational Exchange.

MacDonald, M. N., & O'Regan, J. P. (2012). A global agenda for intercultural communication research and practice. In J. Jackson (Ed.), *The Routledge handbook of intercultural communication* (pp. 553–567). Oxon: Routledge.

MacDonald, M. N., O'Regan, J. P., & Witana, J. (2009). The development of national occupational standards for intercultural working in the UK. *Journal of Vocational Education & Training, 61*, 375–398. doi:10.1080/13636820903363600

McCrum, R. (2010). *Globish: How English became the world's language*. New York, NY: W.W. Norton & Co.

McSweeney, B. (2002). Hofstede's model of national cultural differences and their consequences: A triumph of faith – A failure of analysis. *Human Relations, 55*(1), 89–117

Miike, Y. (2014). The Asiacentric turn in Asian communication studies: Shifting paradigms and changing perspectives. In M. K. Asante, Y. Miike, & J. Yin (Eds.), *The global intercultural communication reader* (pp. 111–133). New York: Routledge.

Milner, A. (2003). Who created Malaysia's plural society? *Journal of the Malaysian Branch of the Royal Asiatic Society, LXXVI*(2), 1–24.

Moslehifar, M. A., & Ibrahim, N. A. (2012). English language oral communication needs at the workplace: Feedback from human resource development (HRD) trainees. *Procedia – Social and Behavioral Sciences, 66*, 529–536.

Muthiah, P. (2002). *'Welcome to the real world': A comparative study of the orientation to the evaluation of business correspondence by ESL instructors and business practitioners and its implications for teaching and assessment* (Unpublished PhD thesis). The University of Melbourne, Melbourne.

Muthiah, P. (2003). English language proficiency at the workplace: Expectations of bank officers in Malaysia. *Asian Englishes, 6*(2), 64–81.

Nair-Venugopal, S. (2000). *Language choice and communication in Malaysian business*. Bangi: Penerbit UKM/UKM Press.

Nair-Venugopal, S. (2001). The sociolinguistics of choice in Malaysian business settings. *International Journal of the Sociology of Language, 152*, 121–153.

Nair-Venugopal, S. (2003a). Approximations of social reality as interpretations of culture: Extending a framework of analysis in intercultural communication. *Journal of International Communication, 9*(2), 13–28.

Nair-Venugopal, S. (2003b). Intelligibility in English: Of what relevance to intercultural communication? *Language and Intercultural Communication, 3*(1), 36–47. doi:10.1080/14708470308668088

Nair-Venugopal, S. (2006). An interactional model of Malaysian English. A contextualised response to commodification. *Journal of Asian Pacific Communication, 16*(1), 51–75.

Nair-Venugopal, S. (2009). Localised perspectives Malaysia. In F. Bargiela (Ed.), *Handbook of business discourse* (pp. 387–399). Edinburgh: Edinburgh University Press.

Nair-Venugopal, S. (2012). *The gaze of the west and framings of the east*. Basingstoke: Palgrave Macmillan.

Nair-Venugopal, S. (2013). Linguistic ideology and practice: Language, literacy and communication in a localized workplace context in relation to the globalized. *Linguistics and Education, 24*, 454–465. doi:10.1016/j.linged.2013.05.001

Newcombe, S. (2012). Global hybrids? 'Eastern traditions' of health and wellness in the West. In S. Nair-Venugopal (Ed.), *The gaze of the West and framings of the East* (pp. 202–217). Basingstoke: Palgrave Macmillan.

O'Regan, J. P., & MacDonald, M. N. (2007). *Consultation report on the development of national occupational standards in intercultural working: Phase I* (Unpublished report). CILT Project to Develop Standards for Intercultural Working, London.

Ong, T. L., Leong C. K., & Kaur, P. (2011). Employer expectations of language at the workplace. *Malaysian Journal of ELT Research, 7*(2), 82–103. Retrieved from www.melta.org.my

Paramasivam, S., & Nair-Venugopal, S. (2012). Indian collectivism revisited: Unpacking the western gaze. In S. Nair-Venugopal (Ed.), *The gaze of the west and framings of the east* (pp. 156–169). Basingstoke: Palgrave Macmillan.

Plum, E., Achen, B., Dræby, I., & Jensen, I. (2008). *Cultural intelligence: The art of leading cultural complexity (management, policy + education)*. Middlesex: Middlesex University Press.

Ratnam, K. J. (1965). *Communalism and the political process in Malaya*. Singapore: University of Malaya Press.

Robertson, R. (1995). 'Glocalization'. In S. Lash, M. Featherstone, & R. Robertson (Eds.), *Global modernities* (pp 25–44). London: Sage.

Sarudin, I., Mohd Noor, Z., Zubairi, A. M., Tunku Ahmad, T. B., & Nordin, M. S. (2013). Needs assessment of workplace English and Malaysian graduates' English language competency. *World Applied Sciences Journal, 21*, 88–94. doi:10.5829/idosi.wasj.2013.21.sltl.2141

Savignon, S. (1983). *Communicative competence: Theory and classroom practice*. Reading, MA: Addison-Wesley.

Shi-Xu. (2009). Asian discourse studies: Foundations and directions. *Asian Journal of Communication, 19*(4), 384–397.

Spencer, L. M., & Spencer, S. M. (1993). *Competence at work*. New York, NY: Wiley.

Spencer-Oatey, H. (2000). *Culturally speaking: Managing rapport through talk across cultures*. London: Continuum.

Spitzberg, B. H., & Changnon, G. (2009). Conceptualizing intercultural competence. In D. K. Deardorff (Ed.), *The SAGE handbook of intercultural competence* (pp. 2–51). Thousand Oaks, CA: Sage.

Stewart, J., & Hamlin, R. G. (1992). Competence-based qualifications: The case for established Methodology. *Journal of European Industrial Training, 16*(10): 9–16. Retrieved from http://search.proquest.com/docview/215396850?accountid=28110

Street, B. (1993). Culture is a verb. In D. Graddol, L. Thompson, & M. Byram (Ed.), *Culture and language* (pp. 23–43). Clevedon: Multilingual Matters / British Association of Applied Linguistics.

Trompenaars, F., & Hampden-Turner, C. (1997). *Riding the waves of culture: Understanding cultural diversity in business* (2nd ed.). London: Nicholas Brealey.

Wahi, W., O'Neill, M., & Chapman, A. (2011). Investigating English language academic literacy for employability of undergraduate students: A case in a Malaysian public university. In S. A. M. Pandian, M. Ismail, & C. H. Toh (Eds.), *Teaching and learning in diverse contexts: Issues and approaches* (pp. 90–101). Penang: School of Languages, Literacies and Translation, Universiti Sains Malaysia.

Examining linguistic proficiency in the multilingual glocal workplace: a Malaysian case study

Sze Seau Lee[a] and Yew Lie Koo[b,c]

[a]Faculty of Social Sciences and Humanities, Universiti Kebangsaan Malaysia, Malaysia; [b]School of Education, Charles Darwin University, Casuarina, NT, Australia; [c]Faculty of Languages and Cultures, SOAS, University of London, London, UK

The study was conceived from the concern that the twenty-first-century workplace in Malaysia lacks locally sited and empirically based research that provide evidence for a grounded view of language proficiency and use beyond the dominant idealized notion of Standard English language models for education policy. A qualitative case study of a Malaysian airline company was conducted to provide an analytic description of the features of linguistic proficiency and their use in the multilingual glocal workplace. Using emails, interviews and field observations, the findings point to a pluralistic view of linguistic proficiency that embraces functional business English, Malaysian English, English as a lingua franca and the use of other language codes. While the English language is shown to be dominant in the workplace, the data demonstrate the importance of a pluralistic view of linguistic proficiency in diverse glocal contexts. The study also provides insights into how language pedagogy in higher education can support diversity in the workplace.

Kajian ini bertitik tolak daripada kekurangan kajian empirikal tempatan yang berfokus kepada tempat kerja dalam abad ke-21 di Malaysia yang memberi sokongan berasaskan bukti kepada usulan yang mendorong pendapat terhadap kecekapan linguistik untuk menjauhi ideologi dominan yang mementingkan Bahasa Inggeris Standard. Oleh sedemikian, sebuah kajian kes kualitatif yang bertempat di sebuah syarikat penerbangan di Malaysia telah dijalankan untuk memberi keterangan analitikal terhadap penguasaan bahasa yang diperlukan di tempat kerja. Sumber data kajian ini merangkumi e-mel, temu bual dan pemerhatian lapangan. Hasil kajian yang berpandukan persepsi majmuk terhadap kecekapan linguistik merangkumi sumber kepelbagaian bahasa dari segi Bahasa Inggeris Tempat Kerja fungsional, Bahasa Inggeris Malaysia, Bahasa Inggeris sebagai bahasa perantaraan, penggunaan kod-kod bahasa lain, dan juga menekankan bahawa repertoar linguistik sebegini merupakan sumber penting dalam konteks glokal pelbagai bahasa. Kajian ini diharapkan dapat memberikan pengertian terhadap bagaimana pendidikan bahasa di institusi pengajian tinggi dapat menyediakan pendidikan bahasa yang dapat menyokong kepelbagaian di tempat kerja.

Introduction

While there are extensive theories on how work in the twenty-first century has changed (for example, Cope & Kalantzis, 2009; Gee, 2000), few studies have empirically explored how linguistic proficiency is engaged in the multilingual workplace. This is particularly true for the region investigated in this study, where most research on workplace literacies in Malaysia are solely based on employers' perceptions (Koo, Pang, & Mansur, 2008; Pandian, Azman, & Haroon, 2010; Shah, 2008; Wye & Lim, 2009) and the dominant ideology of the role of an idealized form of Standard English as the basis of economic success in the Malaysian workplace (Nair-Venugopal, 2013) is rarely questioned.

This gap in the literature has motivated the researchers to address the following question. What does linguistic proficiency mean in a multilingual glocal worksite in Malaysia, *glocal* referring to the site where the requirements of a global economy meet situational realities? In other words, what are the features of linguistic proficiency which are in use in the glocal workplace? With the actual analytical description of the aspects of linguistic proficiency in a multilingual glocal worksite in Malaysia, it is hoped that the prevailing ideology which emphasizes the importance of an idealized form of Standard English (Nair-Venugopal, 2013) could be contested. Such a dominant view which currently informs language education policy is viewed as unhelpful in addressing the actual needs of students and employees. Addressing the research question would help provide insights into how policies on curriculum and pedagogy can be reconceptualized to empower learners in line with global requirements and local realities in language and communication.

The examination of linguistic proficiency is underpinned by the idea that workplace literacies are socially situated and culturally pluralistic. Understood in this manner, 'literacies are part of social practices' and 'are patterned by social institutions and power relationships' (Barton & Hamilton, 2012, p. xvii). Workplace literacies reflect the need to negotiate (sometimes simultaneously) diverse cultures, including national, ethnic, religious, generational, ideological and organizational ones. Based on this notion of workplace literacies, the present study examines Malaysian English, English as a lingua franca and multilingualism as understood in terms of the Multiliteracies Framework (Cope & Kalantzis, 2000, 2009; The New London Group, 1996, 2000).

The site of study is *SuperFly* (pseudonym), a Malaysian airline company recognized as a global player in the industry. Hence, the site can be classified as a glocalized workplace. The multiple sources of data for the study include selected emails, semi-structured interviews and a single-day field observation.

Theoretical descriptions of the new workplace in the twenty-first century

There are a few defining characteristics of the new workplace in the twenty-first century. The new workplace has been extensively affected by globalization (International Monetary Fund, 2008; Kakabadse, Bank, & Vinnicombe, 2004) and new technology (Friedrich, Peterson, Koster, & Blum, 2010; Kakabadse et al., 2004). Technological advances have changed patterns of employment by increasing the demand for highly educated and skilled knowledge workers (Organization for Economic Cooperation and Development [OECD], 2001). The view that information and knowledge are at the centre of economic growth is so dominant that the concepts of *knowledge economy* and *knowledge worker* have been created (OECD, 2001). Knowledge workers are 'those in jobs requiring the production and use of knowledge', so they 'require high levels of competencies and skills' (OECD, 2001, p. 112).

Language use has also been radically transformed by new communications media (Cope & Kalantzis, 2000; Lankshear & Knobel, 2004) in the sense that communication is less dominated now by the written word and is enhanced by multimodal forms. The researchers posit that the glocal workplace is a communicative space which is a complex intersection of institutional and everyday languages and discourses.

In terms of social relations, the new workplace is served more by collaborative than hierarchical relations. Gee (2000) suggests that the workers bond through a 'common endeavour' organized around 'multiple but integrated functions' and supported by 'affective ties' (p. 53). Their 'extensive knowledge' could be acquired through 'networks of relationship' (Gee, 2000, pp. 53–54). The workers also need 'flexibly rearrangeable portfolio of the skills, experiences and achievements' that are gained through their participation and interaction with other workers in the workplace (Gee, 2000, p. 61). In response to these theoretical descriptions of the new workplace, we seek to discuss the ways in which linguistic proficiency, that is the features that are strategically used by the knowledge worker (OECD, 2001) in a Malaysian workplace, is sited at the intersection of new knowledge economy requirements and local situational realities. Indeed, we seek to show that an idealized notion of Standard English in use is challenged by the empirical data where features of a worker's linguistic proficiency are resourcefully engaged through the use of various strategies. Such strategies involve the strategic use of linguistic features of Malaysian English, English as a lingua franca and, in some cases, the use of other languages.

Examining linguistic proficiency: Malaysian English, English as a lingua franca and the Multiliteracies Framework

Linguistic proficiency is one of the most researched categories of workplace literacies in Malaysia. The selected definition for linguistic proficiency is the 'abilities and use of particular languages' as appropriate to diverse cultural contexts (Koo et al., 2008, p. 4). Because the prescriptive approach to language has been criticized for failing to document actual language use (Yuen, 2007), the intention of this study is to be descriptive, not prescriptive. The prescriptive approach is generally used 'to "prescribe" how a language should be instead of describing how it is used' (Yuen, 2007, p. 116). For example, linguistic forms that do not conform to idealized native English norms are unquestionably classified as 'mistakes' (Kachru, 1983, p. 45). The view held here is that descriptive documentation of how language proficiency is used in context is crucial for reflecting on the current understanding of linguistic proficiency in the workplace.

Considering the global and local trajectories that are influencing the Malaysian workplace, we have decided to study linguistic proficiency through the lenses of three established paradigms: Malaysian English (ME henceforth), English as a lingua franca (ELF henceforth) and the Multiliteracies Framework (Cope & Kalantzis, 2000, 2009; The New London Group, 1996, 2000).

Malaysian English

The complexities of how the English language has been localized in Malaysia require some discussion. We would like to point out that '[b]esides Malay, the indigenous languages of the East Malaysian states of Sabah and Sarawak, and the non-native Chinese and Indian languages, English is pervasive as a localized variety at many levels of interaction and within particular domains' (Nair-Venugopal, 2013, p. 455).

Moreover, Koo (2009) has argued that ME actually comprises different varieties within itself, and she classifies ME in terms of the acrolect–mesolect–basilect cline. According to Gill (2002, p. 52), the acrolect, or the standard ME, could be more suitable for international communication. The mesolect is the colloquial variety that is used for intranational communication between Malaysians of diverse ethnicities. The basilect, because of its marked differences from the standard, is almost unintelligible outside of the speech community in which it is developed. In addition, the three sub-varieties have been proposed to be belonging to a continuum (Baskaran, 1994; Pillai, 2006).

Considerations of ME for the workplace implicate a point of tension. On the one hand, a strong trend in Malaysian research, which suggests the English language incompetency of Malaysians as a factor for their unemployability (such as Pandian et al., 2010; Talif & Noor, 2009), shows no considerations for the viability of ME. A dominant view of an idealized prescriptive is that Standard English informs such studies. In addition, the official language policy in Malaysia is based on the so-called 'standard' native speaker models, as evidenced more recently by the Ministry of Education's 'Native Speaker Programme' that has been implemented since 2011. This programme aims to enhance the English language proficiency of ME language teachers by employing language mentors who are perceived as native speakers (Jusoh, 2014). Therefore, it has been pointed out that '[n]otwithstanding its prevalence, ME has no legitimacy in the public domain and does not derive any mainstream pedagogical support as an appropriate language model' (Nair-Venugopal, 2013, p. 455). On the other hand, there is a movement in local research that proposes ME as a possible model of interaction for the Malaysian business context (such as Gill, 2002; Yuen, 2007).

To the best of our knowledge, previous studies that argue for the feasibility of ME in the workplace (such as Gill, 2002; Yuen, 2007) are based on research with Malaysian participants exclusively. The present study would explore the use of ME as part of the linguistic repertoire of global workers who are engaged in a multicultural and multinational workplace that has both Malaysians and non-Malaysians among its employees.

English as a lingua franca

Following a research tradition, which focuses on English in international business contexts among non-native speakers of English (Louhiala-Salminen, 2002; Louhiala-salminen, Charles, & Kankaanranta, 2005; Nickerson, 2005), the present study examines the use of ELF as an aspect of linguistic proficiency required in the workplace. ELF is viewed as the English variety that serves as a 'means of communication among speakers of different first languages' (Jenkins, 2012, p. 486). ELF is not a language variety in the traditional sense since it is 'additionally acquired' for all the speakers involved, including native English speakers (Jenkins, 2012, p. 486). There are some 'typical ELF forms' which are commonly shared among ELF speakers with different lingua-cultural backgrounds such as zero-markings of third-person singular and merging of 'who' and 'which' (Jenkins, 2012, p. 489).

The questions of intelligibility and communication efficiency have been of huge interest to ELF researchers. Seidlhofer (2004, p. 222) argues:

> Proficiency in the language code accounts for part of the success or failure of communication; at least as important is a more general communicative capability, such as sensitivity to the limits of shared systemic and schematic knowledge, as well as accommodation skills.

Research on ELF in international business contexts has shown increasing focus on strategies that contribute to effective communication (Nickerson, 2005), with a pragmatic and flexible approach to language use instead of a preoccupation with linguistic correctness being suggested to be more supportive of communication efficiency (Louhiala-Salminen et al., 2005). Kirkpatrick's (2008) research on English as the official working language in the ASEAN region, for example has highlighted some effective strategies used by ELF speakers, such as non-use of local idioms, let-it-pass and paraphrasing. The use of accommodation strategies and code switching are also crucial characteristics of ELF (Cogo, 2008; Jenkins, 2012). We have drawn on ELF studies in our notion of linguistic proficiency in the workplace where both features of language as well as its use are integral.

The Multiliteracies Framework

According to the Multiliteracies Framework (Cope & Kalantzis, 2000, 2009; The New London Group, 1996, 2000), multiple linguistic and cultural diversities in the globalized world permeate all aspects of our lives – in work and in both the public and private domains. In the new globalized world, differences have to be negotiated in 'increasingly globally interconnected working and community lives' (Cope & Kalantzis, 2000, p. 6).

As a result of this diversity, the English language is now 'a common language of global commerce, media and politics' while, at the same time, 'breaking into multiple and increasingly differentiated Englishes, marked by accent, national origin, subcultural style and professional or technical communities' (Cope & Kalantzis, 2000, p. 6). In addition, the various multilingual backgrounds that each individual comes from have to be negotiated even more in day-to-day interactions (Cope & Kalantzis, 2009).

It needs to be pointed out that in the context of this study, even if English is viewed as the current dominant language of international political negotiation, information, economy and in academia, the spread of English has always been uneven in the workplace. In fact, to alternate and integrate elements from various languages is 'normal linguistic behaviour' for most Malaysians (Nair-Venugopal, 2013), and multilingualism has been suggested to be a powerful resource in the workplace (Chan & Abdullah, 2013). This study examines how the multilingual backgrounds (Cope & Kalantzis, 2009) of workers are negotiated in the glocal workplace, as well as their multiple and increasingly differentiated Englishes (Cope & Kalantzis, 2000).

Methodology

The present study aims to describe the aspects of linguistic proficiency that are engaged in a locally situated workplace, which has been affected by globalization and new technology. The airline company that we focus on in the study, referred to with the pseudonym *SuperFly*, sits at a conjuncture of global–local influences. The main office is situated in Malaysia but the company possesses characteristics of globalized companies, such as offering international services, having culturally diverse employees and collaborations with companies beyond national borders.

The research participants are employers, employees and partners of the airline company. Being representatives of the company's various internal departments and collaborating industries, such as media companies, business process outsourcing and information technology, they mainly fall within the category of *knowledge workers* whose jobs require 'the production and use of knowledge', so they 'require high levels of competencies and skills' (OECD, 2001, p. 112). The participants have to negotiate their multilingual backgrounds with each other daily (Cope & Kalantzis, 2009).

The selection of the main participant, Jenny, was both expedient and purposeful. Besides being available and interested in this study, she is arguably a *knowledge worker* (OECD, 2001). Born and raised in Malaysia, Jenny is a Chinese Malaysian woman in her early 40s who graduated from Universiti Kebangsaan Malaysia (the National University of Malaysia) in communication studies. She is the head of Commercial Services and her responsibilities include devising and providing overall commercial strategy and direction for Marketing, Distribution and Revenue Management. Commercial advice and support on new route development, airport negotiations, liaison with tourism ministries and other related government bodies also fall under her portfolio. Jenny's proficiency in several languages and dialects reflects her multilingual identity. She ranks her overall language proficiency in English and Bahasa Malaysia (Malay language, the national language of Malaysia), and her spoken proficiency in Mandarin, Cantonese and Hokkien as good.

The study adopts a multiple data collection technique to provide in-depth understanding and representation of the issues in question (Denzin & Lincoln, 2003). The primary data include selected email communication between Jenny and her colleagues or clients. The secondary data consist of two semi-structured interviews with Jenny and on-site observations of her work routines in a single day, including the meetings that she attends.

Jenny's email communication during a typical day at work was selected as the main data for analysis. In work contexts, email may replace more traditional means of communication such as the phone and even face-to-face communication (Ahdoot, 2007; DeKay, 2010). For Jenny, it is not unusual to produce 2000 emails in one working day. Jenny screened the emails collected on 1 June 2010 for confidentiality and sensitive issues; finally, 132 emails were selected for analysis. One subject title may include multiple strands of sent, received and forwarded emails from the involved participants. Therefore, although there were 132 emails, there were only 41 subject titles. The emails as categorized under the subject titles are listed in Table 1. The original wordings of the subject titles have been kept as close to the raw data as possible but when necessary, the names of involved individuals and organizations have been given pseudonyms to protect anonymity. For example, the Malay word for 'invoice' in E34 is retained, but organization names such as *Top Money* (E2), *TravelMag* (E6) and *Insync PR* (E22) are pseudonyms. As far as possible, the pseudonyms given to the participants reflect the actual ethnicity of the participants.

The two semi-structured interviews with Jenny were conducted using online chats because Jenny prefers mobile text-based communication and we think that online chats provide immediate and exact documentation of the interviews. Jenny's work routines, which include mainly meetings, were observed for one day on 1 June 2010. Louhiala-Salminen (2002) has shown how detailed analysis of a single day of observation could produce salient findings. Field notes were made and meetings were recorded whenever convenient and were later applied to the analysis of data.

All the sources of data are coded and these codes are narrowed into a few significant themes (Creswell, 2008). Thematic analysis is driven by the research aim, which is to analytically describe the aspects of linguistic proficiency in the multilingual glocal workplace. Findings from previous studies based in Malaysia, such as those suggesting the viability of ME in the Malaysian workplace (such as Gill, 2002; Nair-Venugopal, 2003), are used as a guide for the process, but the study is open to significant themes that have not previously been identified. Triangulation is attempted through comparisons with different sources of data as well as input from Jenny who was able to provide valuable information on each of the participants.

Table 1.   Selected email titles.

Email reference	Subject title
E1	Google analytics in-house Training
E2	Editorial support for Top Money
E3	Invitation to Register for Complimentary Subscription to ABC Asia
E4	*SuperFly* Megastore's Special Showcase @ Bluefort –Today & Tomorrow!
E5	URGENT: Query regarding overseas billing for Indonesia
E6	*SuperFly* Insure snips and write-ups in TravelMag
E7	Kuching Hub
E8	Sponsorship Mileage –XY Entertainment
E9	Midweek All Seats All Flights
E10	Request for documents
E11	Blue Skies Project Status
E12	Airport Fees
E13	Content for *SuperFly* Inflight Magazine
E14	Revised Timing: *SuperFly* Call Centre-Biz Plan Presentation
E15	Commence Date for Mei Ling
E16	Press conference –8th June @ 11 am
E17	Basah the Musical Season 2
E18	Levy of UDF at ABC Airport
E19	*SuperFly* GSA for Bangladesh
E20	IVR based CC processing (India –Call Centre Support)
E21	*SuperFly* adds 2nd DailyFlight to Phnom Penh
E22	Meeting agenda –3rd June @ 230 pm with Insync PR
E23	Media Owner Contracts
E24	Summary of Briefing for Next Week Campaign
E25	*SuperFly*– Project Update
E26	*SuperFly*
E27	Baggage analysis YTD April'10
E28	*SuperFly*–Amex Alliance
E29	Asia Spa & Wellness Festival
E30	Google Alert –*SuperFly*
E31	Google Alert –*SuperFly*
E32	[No subject]
E33	When are we meeting or dining?
E34	invois meter application –URGENT
E35	ABC Bank 20% savings –Promo
E36	RE: Meeting in KL
E37	WAKE UP Guys…!
E38	Brik informal sharing session on *SuperFly*
E39	Standee for baggage (urgent)
E40	Recap of OOH brief and discussion –Regional OOH
E41	Recap of OOH brief and discussion –Malaysia OOH

Findings and discussion
Functional business English as a prominent code

A major finding of this study is identifying a prominent code of English being used in the workplace that we would like to term as *functional business English*. This code of English possesses a hybrid mix of standard and non-standard characteristics, written and spoken features. The balance of standard and non-standard characteristics is determined by the nature of the interaction. In more formal situations, the sentence structures are mostly complete. Truncated forms, ellipsis and occasional slips are acceptable in situations such as when the message, speed of communication and collaborative work relations are deemed more important than linguistic correctness based on the prescriptive view. As mentioned earlier, linguistic prescriptivism generally aims 'to "prescribe" how a language should be instead of describing how it is used' (Yuen, 2007, p. 116). The aims served by functional business English include discussing marketing ideas, reporting meetings, negotiating business partnerships, describing problems and proposing solutions. These aims contrast with another local study (Ng, 2003) and a few non-local studies (Gains, 1999; Waldvogel, 2005) that suggest commercial emails mainly disseminate information and make requests.

In the following excerpt, Ng Fun Fun, a Malaysian Chinese who is a magazine editor-in-chief, tries to negotiate the decisions regarding magazine publications for *SuperFly* in an email to Jenny:

No worries – I'm sure I'll be seeing more of you in the coming months and you have my number and know where I sit so you can pop by for a visit anytime.

Firstly, I think we need to distinguish between advertorial and editorial support – the former is (usually paid-for) promotional material while the latter isn't. (E6)

We can see from this excerpt that the sentence structures are by and large complete, even complex. However, expressions such as 'pop by' and 'No worries' echo spoken language. As the discussion moves towards a more serious turn, more written language features surface, such as the adverb, firstly, which is usually used to signal content development in written discourse.

The next example is an excerpt from a lengthy email (E25) written by Shobana Arasu, an Indian national who is a business development manager from a company that provides business process and technology services to *SuperFly*. The aim is to inform Jenny about the progress of a new project launch:

Quality:

- Shah Inderjit will be the quality lead from our SQMS team. QA candidates are being screened.
- QA monitoring form to be finalized. We request you to share the current QA process followed and we will be glad to share our proposal for call monitoring.

The sentences in this excerpt resemble listing. Specialized abbreviations such as 'SQMS' shared by and known only to the participants actively involved in the project mentioned are utilized. Hence, her understanding of the email is not based solely on her linguistic proficiency, but her knowledge is also acquired through the 'networks of relationship' (Gee, 2000, pp. 53–54) in her workplace. Other specialized registers found in the data are instances of IT terms such as 'riverbed', 'firewall' and 'router'; common abbreviations typical of the airline industry such as 'BKK' for Bangkok and 'KUL' for Kuala Lumpur; and common email abbreviations such as 'FYI' and 'pls'.

The ease with which emails can be sent and received could result in information overload (Ahdoot, 2007). We would like to suggest that certain rhetorical practices such as the use of bullets and subheadings could possibly minimize the effect of information overload. Another popular rhetorical practice which assists in information processing is highlighting the main purpose of the email in the subject title. For example, subject titles such as 'Revised Timing: *SuperFly* Call Centre-Biz Plan Presentation' (E14), 'Press conference – 8th June @ 11 am' (E16), 'Meeting agenda – 3rd June @ 230 pm with Insync PR' (E22), and 'Brik informal sharing session on *SuperFly*' (E38) accurately reflect the main purposes of the emails. Jenny also commented that she does pay more attention to emails marked '*Urgent*', and she tends to overlook emails that have no subject titles, such as E32. Moreover, some participants use different coloured fonts for emphasis. This rhetorical practice appears to be helpful when the discussion is long and involves multiple participants. For instance, Dave highlights the date in bold red to emphasize the exact time the passengers would be charged a newly implemented fee: 'The collection of UDF (user development fee) is w.e.f. 15Jun'10' (E18). There are 13 strands of emails in E18 and the discussions aim to clarify the confusion over how airfares to a particular destination would be affected by a newly implemented local tax.

Apart from the specialized registers mentioned earlier, there are also traces of very informal registers used even by individuals holding important portfolios. An executive director from Singapore, for example apologizes very informally to a sales manager who is hierarchically below him in the workplace with a single line email: 'Thanks Sig, sorry about the wrong cc [to] Jenny.:) fingers faster than brain in the morning' (E38). In fact, when matters are urgent, the polite openings and closings taught in business writing textbooks are not used at all. For instance, in this email sent by a marketing manager, there is only a one-sentence expression of how he feels about meeting for a discussion: 'Hi, Ok. Let's do it. Thanks'. The tone of informality suggests that the workplace is more collaborative than hierarchical (Gee, 2000). The informal tone is also more apparent when emails are sent from portable digital devices.

In summary, based on the analysis of 132 emails, functional business English could be distinguished through these characteristics: (1) usually straightforward; (2) hybrid features that would not be approved by linguistic prescriptivism; (3) includes specialized industry-related registers; (4) supports collaborative relations in the workplace; (5) affected by digital technology. The specialized registers could be manifestations of the English language 'breaking into multiple and increasingly differentiated English' (Cope & Kalantzis, 2000, p. 6), in this case marked by professional and technical communities. When collaborative relations and pragmatism are valued above prescribed linguistic correctness based on Standard English models, the language features violate the guidelines given by publications on business writing (such as Taylor, 2012). As emphasized by Jenny in the interview:

> Gone are the days where corporate workers buy an 'Official Business Writing' book as a reference to ensure accurate language use. Digital communication [has] greatly diminished 'good' letter writing skills, or command of language in general. Speed and efficiency [are] valued above language proficiency.

Lastly, while information technology could result in information overload (Ahdoot, 2007), the analysis has demonstrated how certain rhetorical practices made possible by information technology such as the use of colours and bullets could minimize this undesirable effect.

Malaysian English and the use of other languages in the workplace

We ascertain that ME ranging from the acrolectal to the mesolectal (Gill, 2002; Koo, 2009) is utilized in communication as a language of solidarity, both in written emails and face-to-face communication, when the participants are all Malaysians. One of the most appropriate emails to demonstrate the purposeful uses of ME is E39. The discussion in 'RE: Standee for baggage (urgent)' (E39) considers the need to reinforce the baggage standee for the passengers' convenience. Anand from the Ancillary Income Department code switches to ME when he tries to appeal to his co-workers that urgent action needs to be taken. These are the opening sentences in an email to his co-workers:

> I think we would need to reinforce the standee for the baggage la bro. its very flimsy and seems like it could break very easily. We have already taken 7 with us. We would not move with the rest until the supplier reinforces it please.

This excerpt shows that Anand, a Malaysian Indian, is capable of expressing himself in acrolectal ME but uses language tags such as '-la', which is a meaning enhancer in ME mesolect and basilect clines (Koo, 2008). This language tag could have originated from Hokkien, one of the Chinese dialects spoken in Malaysia (Koo, 2008), but we also find the same language tag in Cantonese. Besides reinforcing a point, this language tag also represents the Malaysian way of expressing informality, solidarity and friendliness (Koo, 2008; Platt & Weber, 1980). It is also typical of male speakers of ME who share a close relationship to address each other as 'bro' as an expression of fraternity.

Our conclusions about the use of functional business English and ME in emails are in contrast to a study on commercial email writing in the UK. According to Gains (1999), the participants in his study, who are employees of a large UK insurance company, follow 'the standard conventions for written business English, that is fully-formed and correctly punctuated sentences which a normal speaker of British English would regard as "grammatical" in their written form' (p. 86). The discrepancies between the two studies confirm the idea that literacies are socially situated (Barton & Hamilton, 2012). For example, the present study is socially situated in a global work site involving multilingual Malaysians as well as participants from the Asia Pacific. Their education, sociolinguistic and cultural realities are far removed from Gains' (1999) British context. Indeed, our experience has been that British English use may alienate others as it is linked to a history of colonialism and privilege (Seidlhofer, 2005; Holliday, 2009). English language communication is increasingly viewed as a working language which is appropriate in context. Because the participants from our study come from diverse multilingual and English language learning backgrounds, they will attempt to find common grounds for interaction by focusing on the functionality of the message and tending to accept some differences in ways of saying and writing. The focus in ELF is on adequate comprehension which is negotiated according to a particular speech community's norms. *SuperFly* is a global airline targeted mostly at the Asia Pacific mass market. Its staff come from diverse linguistic and cultural backgrounds and hence the staff have attempted to resourcefully engage with each other to achieve sufficient mutual understanding despite variations in ways of communicating. Furthermore, the perceived variation may reflect the idea that meaning-making has been changed and is being changed by new communications media (Cope & Kalantzis, 2000; Lankshear & Knobel, 2004) since writing technologies most probably have metamorphosized written discourse, at least after Gains' (1999) study.

While the use of functional business English is shown to be dominant in the primary data of emails, secondary data such as on-site observation reaffirms that multilingual

Malaysian speakers engage various language codes when involved in oral communication in the workplace (Chan & Abdullah, 2013). During the on-site observation, interactions in small groups, even in work meetings, have been observed to include the languages that affectively bond the speakers. Jenny, for example, code mixes English and Cantonese when interacting with a speaker who shares her background and proficiency in Cantonese. In a meeting negotiating possible partnerships for outdoor advertisements with Alec Koh (an account director from an advertising company), both speakers speak mainly in English but code switch to Cantonese frequently:

Jenny: We basically want more advertisements inside, outside and around airports. Some ideas please?

Alec: I think advertisements in the Maldives can be put on beach umbrellas. Lei dim tai ah? [Cantonese for 'What do you think?']

Jenny: OK, any other ideas?

Alec: More advertisements on light boxes in Singapore.

Jenny: OK. Zhong yau leh? [Cantonese for 'What else?']

This is an interesting finding considering that emails written by Jenny and Alec Koh (E40 and E41) show no traces of other languages than English.

In another meeting involving five other Malaysian participants who are working with Jenny to develop a more attractive corporate package, the main language of communication is English but there is a significant degree of code switching to Malay, although there are only two participants who speak Malay as their mother tongue. Although all the participants are fluent English speakers, they code switch to interact in Malay, the national language, the language that most possibly affectively brings them together. This is a short excerpt from their meeting:

Jenny: We need more refreshing ideas for the corporate package. The pen is pretty lame. Ada tak idea baru sikit? [Malay for 'Is there any new idea?']

Farah: I was thinking of adding more designs to the caps. They seem to be very popular.

Jenny: Boleh juga. [Malay for 'That is an acceptable idea'.] What about recycled bags? Can we have some interesting designs?

Hafiz: I think I can look into that. Nanti I check dengan supplier. [Malay for 'I can check with the supplier later'.]

Therefore, while English remains the dominant language of oral communication in this global workplace, we still get a sense that the 'affective ties' that support the 'common endeavour[s]' in the workplace (Gee, 2000, p. 53) influence aspects of linguistic proficiency.

Linguistic proficiency and accommodation skills in ELF

Assuming ELF as a 'means of communication among speakers of different first languages' (Jenkins, 2012, p. 486), non-Malaysian bilinguals and multilinguals who wield extensive corporate power in *SuperFly* have been observed to use ELF. The emails written by an executive in a regional office in Bangladesh (E19) and a marketing director from Indonesia (E37), for instance, embody linguistic features of ELF contradicting prescriptive notions of language proficiency and use. Budi, a marketing director from Indonesia, motivates his marketing and sales team to be more aggressive than *SuperFly*'s competitors by adjusting their strategies: 'But base on our experience, they have offer many attractive deals but our price can be push a little bit' (E37). In another example, an executive from Bangladesh wrote to Jenny to complain about the standard procedure of remittance that *SuperFly* appears to be violating and requested a meeting:

> Our company been one of the oldest and reputed organization would not want to be involved in any illegal business and at the same time I strongly believe that [SuperFly] been a global brand would not want their name and reputation been tarnish because of this shoddy arrangement. The present arrangement of remittance that been practice might one day cause big problem to [SuperFly] if any of its competitors were to highlight to the relevant authorities. (E19)

The use of the verb 'to be' and the non-marking of the past participle in the excerpts from E19 (for example, 'Our company been') and E37 (for example, 'base on our experience') clearly do not conform to Standard English norms. These are examples of ELF linguistic features in use that require a flexible approach as a response instead of preoccupation with linguistic correctness (Louhiala-Salminen et al., 2005) and accommodation skills to ensure communication efficiency with ELF users (Seidlhofer, 2004).

The flexible approach and let-it-pass strategy typical in ELF interactions are demonstrated in Jenny's emails to the ELF users. For example, in response to the email cited above (E19), Jenny used the let-it-pass strategy (Kirkpatrick, 2008) and accommodated to the writer by demonstrating goodwill and a proactive attitude:

> Your email caught me by surprise and I will need to investigate this. I would prefer to have this meeting with Kate Toh as she is my boss and she is in the know of all matters related to Bangladesh from day one. I appreciate your detailed explanation and will definitely sort this out within the month.

Jenny focuses on the essentials of the message and lets the ELF linguistic features pass, features which may not conform to Standard English norms. By offering to investigate the issue further and consulting her superior about the issue, she is proactively attending to the issue raised. She uses the adverb 'definitely' to emphasize her proactive response. Such flexibility typifies ELF use indicating that the higher concerns are on the functional understanding of an adequate message and less on the accuracies and/or niceties of linguistic expression.

Linguistic proficiency and other skills

The *knowledge workers* (OECD, 2001) in this study come from a myriad of workplaces such as Singapore, Indonesia, India and Bangladesh apart from *SuperFly*'s main office in Malaysia. In fact, work sites which are physically outside of Malaysia are involved in 39% of the total email subject titles. The heterogeneity of workplaces have resulted in wide-ranging types of misunderstandings, problems and tensions, such as on remittance procedures (E19), confusions over sales strategies of different regions (E35), contrasting practices in different region's call centres (E20) and conflicting understandings of the operations of the media industry (E22). For example, Sharifah, a public relations executive, emphasizes to Jenny that the operations of the media industry in India are different from Malaysia (E22):

> We would also like to suggest the way and means to go about the media here in India. I think it would be important to note the distinctions and difference in the mindsets here. We should discuss in a meeting for an induction of the team in Malaysia so that they get a better appreciation and understanding of things in India.

Jenny responded by agreeing with Sharifah that a meeting should be arranged to resolve the misunderstandings.

In the interview, Jenny emphasizes the importance of the willingness to form intercultural understanding and learn more when resolving problems in the glocal workplace through language use:

> We need to always respect the locals and listen. That is the best way of doing business anywhere and globally. Knowing the culture and history of each country/province before dealing with them would be best. So we read up a lot prior to any interaction. We also communicate with the locals to understand more. For example, I will ask my Indian advertising agency to share a consumer study just to understand the consumer insights. Understanding people is the first step to good communication/business.

Thus, we would like to emphasize that our expanded notion of linguistic proficiency needs to be viewed in relation to other vital skills such as the willingness to cultivate intercultural understanding in the glocal workplace.

Implications for higher education

In terms of linguistic proficiency that is engaged at the glocal workplace, we recommend policy-makers, researchers and practitioners to consider a pluralistic view instead of a prescriptive approach that propagates Standard English norms which do not connect with the sociolinguistic realities on the ground. While English is identified as the dominant corporate language in the multilingual glocal workplace, the aspects of linguistic proficiency described in this study demonstrate plurality and include contextually intelligible features and the resourceful use of various codes such as functional business English, ME and ELF in written communication, and the use of other languages in glocal interactions. Therefore, subjecting students to diverse linguistic task requirements that include the use of repertoires of linguistic codes, including standard and so-called non-standard English, the English language and other languages, would empower learners for work in global sites where diverse cultures and languages are negotiated daily.

Moreover, the accommodation skills required to collaborate with global ELF users should be developed. The question of incorporating ELF's variability into teaching is a consistent challenge as there is minimal description of an ELF-oriented pedagogy (Jenkins, Cogo, & Dewey, 2011). We recommend exposing learners to ELF type interactions based on the extensive corpuses that have been developed by ELF researchers such as the Asian Corpus of English (2009–2014). This may help students to foresee how pragmatic strategies can be engaged to support communication efficiency.

Because the email data show that information overload in emails (Ahdoot, 2007) is managed by certain rhetorical practices, such as the use of bullets and subheadings, workplace writing courses should expose students to these rhetorical practices. Although the norms in the real workplace are fluid because they are negotiated by the workers involved, students can still be taught the possible rhetorical effects of certain practices. While rhetorical practices may be obvious to teachers and *knowledge workers* (OECD, 2001), it is not common knowledge for new undergraduates in the developing countries who do not use emails daily. Thus, we agree with DeKay (2010) that document design for email writing should not be overlooked in language education.

The present study also suggests that aspects of intercultural awareness and understanding should be considered in designing industrial training for undergraduates. Undergraduates in education and training should be exposed to collaborations with diverse cultures which are now an integral part of the twenty-first-century workplace. As far as possible, students should be alerted to the idea that linguistic proficiency alone would not solve their problems in the workplace. They need to develop a willingness to listen to and learn about people of diverse languages and cultures which are vital attributes of glocal citizens.

Conclusion

We hope that we have illustrated the complexities of linguistic proficiency and the dynamics of language use in a multilingual glocal workplace influenced by globalization, new technology and local sociolinguistic realities. The study recommends that stakeholders and actors in higher education adopt an expanded concept of linguistic proficiency which exposes students to multilingualism, ELF interactions, purposeful rhetorical practices and intercultural openness instead of adopting a one-size-fits-all prescriptive model of Standard English use.

Future studies utilizing longitudinal ethnography and mixed-methods studies may enrich perspectives on the role of language education in preparing graduates for the workplace and their citizenship in the wider world. It would be relevant to examine the changes in forms and uses of languages in the global–local nexus of the twenty-first century to help global communicators from diverse language and cultural backgrounds to establish common ground as such globalized communication is expected to intensify further.

Disclosure statement

No potential conflict of interest was reported by the authors.

References

Ahdoot, J. (2007). *Email overload: Information overload and other negative effects of email communication* (Unpublished master's thesis). California State University.

Asian Corpus of English (ACE). (2009–2014). The Asian Corpus of English. Kirkpatrick, A. (Director), & Lixun, W., Patkin, J., Subhan, S. (Researchers). Retrieved from http://corpus.ied.edu.hk/ace/About.html

Barton, D., & Hamilton, D. (2012). *Local literacies: Reading and writing in one community.* London: Routledge.

Baskaran, L. (1994). The Malaysian English Mosaic. *English Today, 10*(1), 27–32. doi:10.1017/S0266078400000857

Chan, S. H., & Abdullah, A. N. (2013). Norms of language choice and use in relation to listening and speaking: The realities of the practice in the Malaysian banking sector. *Pertanika Journal of Social Sciences & Humanities, 21*(S), 117–130.

Cogo, A. (2008). English as a lingua franca: Form follows function. *English Today, 24*(3), 58–61. doi:10.1017/S0266078408000308

Cope, B., & Kalantzis, M. (2000). Introduction: Multiliteracies – the beginnings of an idea. In B. Cope & M. Kalantzis (Eds.), *Multiliteracies: Literacy learning and the design of social futures* (pp. 3–8). London: Routledge.

Cope, B., & Kalantzis, M. (2009). "Multiliteracies": New literacies, new learning. *Pedagogies: An International Journal, 4*, 164–195. doi:10.1080/15544800903076044

Creswell, J. W. (2008). *Educational research – Planning, conducting, and evaluating quantitative and qualitative research* (3rd ed.). Upper Saddle River, NJ: Pearson International Edition.

DeKay, S. H. (2010). Designing email messages for corporate readers: A case study of effective and ineffective rhetorical strategies at a Fortune 100 company. *Business Communication Quarterly, 73*(1), 109–119. doi:10.1177/1080569909358103

Denzin, N. K., & Lincoln, Y. S. (2003). Introduction: The discipline and practice of qualitative research. In N. K. Denzin, & Y. S. Lincoln (Eds.), *The landscape of qualitative research: Theories and issues* (2nd ed., pp. 1–45). Thousand Oaks. CA: Sage.

Friedrich, R., Peterson, M., Koster, A., & Blum, S. (2010). The rise of generation C: Implications for the world of 2020. Retrieved from http://www.booz.com/media/uploads/Rise_Of_Generation_C.pdf

Gains, J. (1999). Electronic mail – A new style of communication or just a new medium? An investigation into the text features of e-mail. *English for Specific Purposes, 18*(1), 81–101. doi:10.1016/S0889-4906(97)00051-3

Gee, J. P. (2000). New people in new worlds: Networks, the new capitalism and schools. In B. Cope & M. Kalantzis (Eds.), *Multiliteracies: Literacy learning and the design of social future* (pp. 43–68). London: Routledge.

Gill, S. K. (2002). *International communication: English language challenges for Malaysia.* Serdang, Selangor: Universiti Putra Malaysia Press.

Holliday, A. (2009). English as a lingua franca, 'Non-native Speakers' and cosmopolitan realities. In S. Farzad (Ed.), *English as an international language: Perspectives and pedagogical issues* (pp. 21–33). Clevedon: Multilingual Matters.

International Monetary Fund. (2008). *Globalization: A brief overview. IMF Issues Brief 2.* Washington, DC: International Monetary Fund. Retrieved from http://www.imf.org/external/np/exr/ib/2008/053008.htm

Jenkins, J. (2012). English as a lingua franca from the classroom to the classroom. *ELT Journal, 66*, 486–494. doi:10.1093/elt/ccs040

Jenkins, J. Cogo, A., & Dewey, M. (2011). Review of developments in research into English as a lingua franca. *Language Teaching, 44*, 281–315. doi:10.1017/S0261444811000115

Jusoh, I. (2014). Opening keynote address at the 18th Malaysian Education Summit 2014. Retrieved from http://www.asli.com.my

Kachru, B. B. (Ed.). (1983). *The Indianisation of English: The Indian language in India.* Delhi: Oxford University Press.

Kakabadse, A., Bank, J. & Vinnicombe, S. (2004). *Working in organisations* (2nd ed.). Aldershot: Gower Publishing Limited.

Kirkpatrick, A. (2008). English as the official working language of the Association of Southeast Asian Nations (ASEAN): Features and strategies. *English Today, 24*(2), 27–34. doi:10.1017/S0266078408000175

Koo, Y. L. (2008). Malaysian Chinese pluricultural meaning-makers: Malaysian English texts and contexts. *Journal of the Malaysian Modern Languages Association, 5*, 669–684.

Koo, Y. L. (2009). Englishisation through World English as a cultural commodity: The literacy practices of multilingual students in Global Malaysian Higher Education. In K. K. Tam (Ed.).

Englishization in Asia: Language and cultural issues (pp. 88–118). Hong Kong: Open University of Hong Kong Press.

Koo, Y. L., Pang, V., & Mansur, F. (2008). Employer perceptions on graduate literacies in higher education in relation to the workplace. *English for Specific Purposes World, 4*(20), 1–16. Retrieved from www.esp-world.info/Articles_20/DOC/Koo_vp_employer_Journal18Oct09.pdf

Lankshear, C., & Knobel, M. (2004, December). 'New' literacies: Research and social practice. Paper presented at the Annual Meeting of the National Reading Conference, San Antonio, TX.

Louhiala-Salminen, L. (2002). The fly's perspective: Discourse in the daily routine of a business manager. *English for Specific Purposes, 21*, 211–231. doi:10.1016/S0889-4906(00)00036-3

Louhiala-Salminen, L., Charles, M., & Kankaanranta, A. (2005). English as a lingua franca in Nordic corporate mergers: Two case companies. *English for Specific Purposes, 24*, 401–421. doi:10.1016/j.esp.2005.02.003

Nair-Venugopal, S. (2003). Malaysian English, normativity and workplace interactions. *World Englishes, 22*(1), 15–29. doi:10.1111/1467-971X.00269

Nair-Venugopal, S. (2013). Linguistic ideology and practice: Language, literacy and communication in a localized workplace context in relation to the globalized. *Linguistics and Education, 24*, 454–465. doi:10.1016/j.linged.2013.05.001

The New London Group. (1996). A pedagogy of multiliteracies: Designing social futures. *Harvard Educational Review, 66*, 60–92.

The New London Group. (2000). A pedagogy of multiliteracies: Designing social futures. In B. Cope & M. Kalantzis (Eds.), *Multiliteracies: Literacy learning and the design of social futures* (pp. 9–37). London: Routledge.

Ng, Y. K. (2003). A discourse analysis of e-mail messages in a Malaysian business community. *GEMA Online Journal of Language Studies, 3*(1), 37–46.

Nickerson, C. (2005). English as a lingua franca in international business contexts. *English for Specific Purposes, 24*, 367–380. doi:10.1016/j.esp.2005.02.001

Organization for Economic Cooperation and Development. (2001). Competencies for the knowledge economy. In *Education policy analysis 2001* (pp. 99–118). OECD. Retrieved from http://www.oecd.org/dataoecd/42/25/1842070.pdf

Pandian, A., Azman, H., & Haroon, H. A. (2010). Summary. In M. Sirat & A. Pandian (Eds.), *University curriculum and employability needs* (pp. 59–68). Penang: National Higher Education Research Institute.

Pillai, S. (2006). Malaysian English as a first language. In M. K. David (Ed.), *Language choices and discourse of Malaysian Families: Case studies of families in Kuala Lumpur* (pp. 61–75). Malaysia: SIRD.

Platt, P., & Weber, H. (1980). *English in Singapore and Malaysia*. Kuala Lumpur: Oxford University Press.

Seidlhofer, B. (2004). Research perspectives on teaching English as a lingua franca. *Annual Review of Applied Linguistics, 24*, 209–309. doi:10.1017/S0267190504000145

Seidlhofer, B. (2005). Key concepts in ELT: English as a lingua franca. *ELT Journal, 59*, 339–341. doi:10.1093/elt/cci064

Shah, N. Z. (2008). Are graduates to be blamed? Unemployment of computer science graduates in Malaysia. *Electronic Journal of the American Association of Behavioral and Social Sciences, 11*(6). Retrieved from http://aabss.org/Perspectives2008/AABSS2008Article6NORSHIMAZ-SHAH.pdf

Talif, R., & Noor, R. (2009). Connecting language needs in the workplace to the learning of English at tertiary level. *Pertanika Journal of Social Science & Humanities, 17*(2), 65–77.

Taylor, S. (2012). *Model business letters, emails and other business documents* (7th ed.). Harlow: Pearson Education Limited.

Waldvogel, J. (2005). *The role, status and style of workplace email: A study of two New Zealand workplaces* (Unpublished doctoral dissertation). Victoria University of Wellington, Wellington.

Wye, C. K., & Lim, Y. M. (2009). Perception differential between employers and undergraduates on the importance of employability skills. *International Education Studies, 2*(1), 95–105. doi:10.5539/ies.v2n1p95

Yuen, C. K. (2007). The realities of indigenised forms of language: The case for Malaysian English. In H. Azman, K. S. Lee, & N. M. Noor (Eds.), *Transforming learning realities in the ELT world* (pp. 114–123). Malaysia: Pearson Longman.

The importance of interfaith dialog in the workplace for achieving organizational goals: a Kenyan case study

Agnes Lucy Lando, Linda Muthuri and Paul R. Odira

Communication Department, Daystar University, Nairobi, Kenya

Workplaces present divergent cultural conventions for engaging in work- and nonwork-related activities. However, when cultures in workplaces are mentioned, most people tend to think of cultures in the narrow sense of behavioral interaction, yet culture also includes variables of faith or religions. Therefore, just as people of different cultures may have the potential to clash when they come in contact, so would people of different faiths. Just like culture, diverse faiths have the potential of either enhancing or jeopardizing organizational cohesiveness and achievement of organizational goals. Interfaith dialog as practiced in some banking institutions in Kenya is a case in point. Diamond Trust Bank and Co-operative Bank of Kenya's workforce constitute Christians, Muslims, and Hindus, and as a practice, this workforce meets once a week to pray. This study assesses the effects of interfaith dialog in the workplace in achieving organizational goals. This research presents alternative frameworks for analyzing intercultural communication in the workplace based on the principles of faith. By providing a critique of existing models of language and intercultural communication in the workplace from an interfaith perspective, the aforementioned case could lead to presenting a scenario for the formulation/shaping of a theory of interfaith relations in intercultural workplaces.

Les lieux de travail présentent des conventions culturelles divergentes pour l'engagement dans des activités, soit au travail, soit en dehors. Souvent, les cultures au travail tendent à être réduites au sens étroit d'interactions comportementales. Or la culture inclut également des éléments variables de foi ou de religion. De même que des personnes de différentes cultures peuvent s'affronter, de la même façon le conflit peut surgir entre personnes différentes par la foi. Comme pour la culture, la diversité de foi peut favoriser ou mettre en danger la cohésion de l'organisation et la réalisation de ses objectifs. Le dialogue entre religions, pratiqué dans quelques institutions bancaires du Kenya, en est un exemple typique. Le personnel employé par la Banque Diamond Trust et par la Banque Coopérative du Kenya comprend chrétiens, musulmans et Hindous qui prient ensemble une fois par semaine. La présente étude évalue les effets du dialogue entre les religions dans la réalisation des objectifs de l'organisation. Cette recherche présente un cadre alternatif qui permet d'analyser la communication interculturelle au travail en se basant sur les principes de la foi. Le cas mentionné ci-dessus pourrait permettre d'élaborer une théorie des relations interreligieuses dans des lieux de travail interculturels.

Introduction and research background

McLuhan (1964) foresaw a time where cultures would be united through technology in what he called the global village. This would be the new form of social organization that would inevitably unite the entire world into one great social, political, and cultural system (Baran & Davis, 2009). It is argued in much of the literature on the intercultural workplace that with an increasingly globalized community comes an increasingly globalized and diverse workforce. As Blommaert (2010) correctly puts it, the world has increasingly become interconnected and is marked by more and more mobility of both people and commodities, including language *and faith* (italics added). Thus, one's faith – like one's culture and language – accompanies the individual wherever the person goes. Consequently, faith, in this sense, should also be part of the globalization debate as much as other sociocultural and economic topics.

The workplace is one area where intercultural interaction is usually salient. Kenya, for example, is a country rich in cultural diversity constituting 42 tribes and 3 major religious affiliations: Christian, Muslim, and Hindu. The diversity, it could be argued, is far greater than that of areas presently experiencing new waves of immigration in the Middle East and Europe, even though scholarly attention tends to be focused on these areas. This paper takes diversity and interfaith relations in Kenya as its starting point and thus, breaking with the tendency in the literature to focus on European or North American perspectives.

According to the Kenyan 2009 census, Christians constitute about 31.8 million, Muslims 4.3 million, while the Hindu population comes third with a count of 53,393. The wealth of this culture is increasingly extending to the culturally evolving Kenyan workplace. Increase in diversity requires intercultural communication to be examined as a matter of priority so as to understand education across cultural divides in various settings including the workplace. For instance, lack of cultural cohesion saw Kenya break into the 2007/2008 postelection violence (PEV) emanating from cultural divides. This is documented in a PEV video documentary, *Never Again* (Ukweli Video, 2010). The media, according to a PEV analysis, played a key role in fanning the violence, as they incessantly spoke about ethnic cleansing and massacre (Gifford, 2009; Howard, 2008). This violence was repeated, albeit in a subtle way, in the workplace after the 4th March 2013 general elections. Through social media, persons of different tribal affiliations exhibited verbal and nonverbal animosity toward each other (Lando & Mwangi, 2014). Whilst intercultural communication in North America and Europe often focuses on misunderstandings between peoples, it is clear that in conflict zones where there is presence of arms and threat of war, intercultural communication is also a matter of life and death.

In addition to the threat of interethnic and intercultural conflict of a violent nature is also the reality of rapid globalization in Kenya. In an increasingly competitive and globalized marketplace, there lies increased competition for goods and services. Organizations seeking global market presence and significance must embrace diversity and therefore it is imperative for an organization to position itself in ways that will enhance this competitive edge. Resource mobilization is one way to achieve this. The key to sustaining a diverse workforce is maintaining relationships based on mutual trust, respect, and integrity. Failure to maintain these relationships can lead to disunity, poor performance, and eventual losses. A greater understanding of intercultural differences, mutual respect, and communication will lead to a higher probability of achieving business goals.

When cultures in workplaces are mentioned, most people tend to think of it in the narrow sense of race, ethnic background, nationality, or gender, but the notion of culture should also be analyzed in terms of faith or religion. Relations between various religions of the world have often been hostile, yet religion still thrives, particularly in Africa and Asia. Religious conflicts are frequently reported in the news, be it between Christians and Muslims, Jews and Muslims, Christians and Jews, or Muslims and Hindus. Even conflicts within different denomination of the same faith, such as the longtime Catholic and Protestant wars in Northern Ireland, prove the point. As recent as September 2013, the attack on the Westgate mall in Nairobi-Kenya was linked to terrorism and religious intolerance. The attackers referred to the Westgate incidence as Jihad, and human and business losses were disastrous.

Interreligious tension is a matter of grave concern in the world today, and fires fanned by the winds of religious intolerance are not extinguished with ease. If these wars bring nations to destruction, so will interreligious issues bring about conflict in the workplace. As people of different cultures would clash when they come in contact with other cultures, so would people of one faith when they encounter people of a different faith within the organization. Therefore, interfaith dialog is a matter of grave concern, which, if incorporated in an organization, can help achieve organizational goals. Unity is strength, strength is power, and power is competitive edge. Leslie, Larson, and Gorman (1973) assert that the way to resolve religious conflicts is to open up all channels of communication for dialog, negotiation, and creation of values which commensurate with the challenges of the time.

Interfaith dialog: the missing link in intercultural communication studies

Overall, interfaith dialog as a topic is missing in the intercultural communication literature, as well as in readings of organizational culture. The workplace is increasingly becoming more culturally integrated at the same time as becoming more diverse and therefore, communicating across these cultural lines is vital to the coexistence of members within the organization (Littlejohn, 2009). Theories on the interactions of human and intercultural communication and culture within the organization tend to focus on particular elements of culture such as race, gender, ethnicity, or socioeconomic status. Hardly any existing theories of intercultural communication in the workplace focus on religion or faith as an element of culture, yet religion is a vital and universal component of culture. Organizational culture, and particularly religion, contributes to problem solving, cohesiveness among employees, and also greatly influences organizational behavior.

Workplaces present diverse cultural conventions for engaging in work- and nonwork-related activities. However, most people tend to think of workplace culture in the narrow sense of behavioral interaction, yet culture also includes variables of faith or religions such as Catholicism, Islam, Hinduism, or Pentecostalism. The place of work is diverse and dynamic and this study holds religion as a key component in the understanding of workplace culture. Leslie et al. (1973) term religion a 'cultural universal' (p. 548). For a component of culture to be termed universal, it depicts its wide reach and therefore a critical look into its role and impact on intercultural communication, especially in the workplace, is long overdue.

The organization and culture

The key characteristics of an organization are its employees, products, services, and common goals. These elements are unique to each individual organization and give an organization its own distinctive culture, thus differentiating one organization from another. Alvesson (2002) depicts an organization as a social structure that develops meaning from its culture, which in turn guides the behavior, attitudes, and actions of the employees. Thus, just as culture provides 'the rules for living and functioning in the society' (McDaniel, Porter, & Samovar, 2009, p. 12), so it provides the same for and in an organization. Diversity represents the 'multitudes of individual differences and similarities that exist among people' (Kreitner & Kinicki, 2008, p. 37). However, diversity in the workplace is mostly associated with surface level dimensions of cultural interactions based on race, ethnicity, or socioeconomic practices, yet culture exists in other vital areas, such as religion.

The sociocultural tradition theories of organizational communication seek to focus on shared meanings and interpretations that are constructed within the network and the implications of these constructions for organizational life (Littlejohn, 2009). The Standpoint Theory, on the other hand, emphasizes the social group as the main player in the shaping of communication behavior, knowledge, and experiences of an individual to thus satisfy the whole, says Wood (1982). Religion is clearly underrepresented in the study of intercultural communication in the workplace, yet its importance as a contributor to promoting organizational goals is vital. Leslie et al. (1973) define religion as an 'organized set of values, beliefs, and norms focused on alleviating or explaining the problems of human existence' (p. 549). Religion therefore is a major force in the human existence and will always be present especially due to its role in alleviating or explaining human problems, which never cease to be present in all facets of life including organizations. Religious agendas have been the source of significant experiences of history and have caused the world's most vicious conflicts to date, but religious traditions have also laid the foundation for peace and justice. Religion therefore has been, and continues to be, among the most influential elements of culture. Thus, religion is, by nature, a complex element of culture, in the heart of a complex society, whose influence can never be underestimated. Like most organizations, religion is partly defined by the functions it performs.

Despite its underrepresentation, religion, as an element of culture, borders closely with organizational culture in terms of its functions. Leslie et al. (1973) outline the advantages of religion as useful in promoting group cohesion, strengthening the moral order, binding individuals to the social order, providing a source of identity, offering solace in times of trouble, solving problems, and offering mutual trust and motivation. Martin (2002) adds that the functions of organizational culture are broadly intertwined, thus suggesting religion's role as very influential in shaping the culture of an organization. Religion therefore is imperative to the successful running of an organization and consequently, the achievement of its goals.

Religion is one of the increasingly diverse elements of culture in the world today. The world is becoming more religiously diverse and this trend is being exhibited into the workplace with more people revealing an increased desire to embody their beliefs even at work. From adorning oneself with religious artifacts, to praying before meetings, to visibly performing religious rituals such as fasting, religious practices are being exhibited and recognized now more than ever. The influence religion holds in society can thus not be underestimated, and its volatile nature not ignored. According to Green (1952), 'religion is then the supremely integrating and unifying force in human society. But at the same time, it is also a divisive and catastrophic force' (p. 51). Kreitner and Kinicki (2008) stress the significance of religion by referring to it as a 'deep-level' dimension of diversity. The importance of religion as an element of culture is seen in its component as a worldview: religion serves as the foundation of most people's worldview. Pennington (1985) maintains that worldview must be given high priority in the study of culture because it permeates all other components of culture. Thus, we see the significance of religion as a component of culture in its great influence on a person's worldview.

Interfaith dialog in the workplace

Dialog is a process of communication aimed at sharing experiences and learning with another person or group to eventually create and enhance mutual understanding. It operates in a free environment where there would be trust, respect, and openness to exploration of ideas. Interfaith dialog deals with dialog between various religious groups, such as Christian–Hindu, Christian–Islam, or Hindu–Islam, or within similar faiths but different denominations, such as Baptist–Protestant or Anglican–Catholic dialogs.

The focus of religious dialog is on mutual understanding, trust, respect, and achievement of common goals through adherence to mutually identified and agreed upon codes or systems of belief. But interfaith dialog is a particularly difficult form of intercultural communication, especially because of the volatile nature of religious interactions. Historically, various religions have often been hostile and violent to each other. Many societies distrust Islamic fundamentalism and associate it with world terrorism today. Therefore, the religious and interreligious dialog principles of mutual trust and respect are often difficult to achieve. However, interreligious dialogs could also be used for the promotion of peace and coexistence. While delivering a lecture at Fordham University in the aftermath of the 11 September 2001 terrorist attacks in the USA, Cardinal Avery Dulles asserted the importance of interreligious dialog maintaining that:

> in the opening years of the third millennium, interreligious dialogue is not a luxury … it may be required to prevent disastrous collisions between major religious groups. In the present crisis, the religions have a great opportunity to overcome hostility and violence among peoples and to promote mutual esteem and cordial cooperation. (Dulles, 2001, p. 3)

Thus, all of the world's religions have within their scriptures teachings that call for respect, compassion, pursuit of truth, tolerance, and peace.

The study

Interfaith dialog in Kenya is not new at all. More often than not, religious leaders of different faiths – mainly Catholics, Anglicans, mainstream Protestant churches, and Muslims – hold joint functions in order to foster interfaith unity. For example, the Catholic and mainstream Protestant churches organized the first ever Deputy Presidential Debate and Presidential Debate on 14th and 21st February 2013, respectively, at the All Saints (Anglican) Cathedral, Nairobi. The All Africa Conference of Churches, with its headquarters in Nairobi, Kenya, is another ecumenical fellowship body representing about 120 million Christians in 39 African countries working together in their common witness to the Gospel. The global World Council of Churches is yet another example. There are also instances where the mainstream Christian churches collaborate with the Supreme Council of Kenya Muslims on issues of national concern.

Thus, interfaith dialog in Kenya is now well established. However, interfaith dialog at this level is the initiative of the Christian church and Muslim leadership. On few occasions, they come together to pray, but in most cases, the leaders meet to discuss how the various faiths can peacefully coexist and keep the government on check. Yet, in rare circumstances, like the case of Diamond Trust Bank-Kenya (DTB-K) and the Co-operative Bank of Kenya, employees or ordinary people come together and initiate interfaith dialog, where members of different faiths organize themselves and pray for the achievement of organizational goals in addition to their well-being.

Models of interreligious dialog

Dulles (2001) proposed four models in which religions relate to each other. They include: coercion, toleration, pluralism, and convergence. Coercion is the imposing of one faith on others and is most commonly seen in religious persecutions. A common phenomenon is observed in dictatorial states or organizations. Toleration entails the acceptance of the existence of other religions without necessarily approving them. It is based on peaceful coexistence and is essentially the perspective of most democratic nations. Toleration exists within an awareness and acceptance of differences in religion with each religion having an equal right to believe and practice as it does. Pluralism views the existence of different religions as a blessing. It includes an opportunity to observe truth in its various forms and manifestations, creating an environment in which each religion needs to be true to its own beliefs and practices. And finally, convergence is a model of interreligious relationships, which seeks to blend the various religions into one.

Dulles (2001) continues to explain that the different views of religious dialog fall under religious convergence. The theocentric mode of religious dialog contends that religions could agree on the basis of ethnocentrism, recognizing their differences about the means of salvation as culturally relative. The 'soteriocentric' model argues that all religions agree that the purpose of religion is to give salvation or liberation, which they understand in different ways. Therefore, through dialog about liberation, it presumes they could overcome their mutual divisions. The basic premise of these theories is that all religions are human attempts to articulate the divine mystery by which human existence is encompassed. This, however, runs counter to the 'official' historical identity of the religions and meets with resistance on the part of zealous-minded people, who contend that their specific faith is true. Christians hold that central doctrines of their own faith such as Jesus Christ as the Son of God, and the Holy Trinity cannot be sacrificed for the sake of achieving reconciliation, nor will Jews, who adhere passionately to the Law of Moses and the rabbinic tradition, or Muslims, who follow the Koran and look to Muhammad as the greatest and last of the prophets. Therefore, religious convergence hardly provides cohesion among various religions.

Dulles (2001) then suggests several principles that need to be in place for interreligious and intercultural dialog to take place. They include a relationship of mutual respect and knowledge of the other culture as well as one's own culture and tradition, and an environment of authenticity and tolerance. Johnson (1996) classifies religion into two dimensions: religiosity and orthodoxy. Religiosity addresses the intensity and consistency of religious practices, while orthodoxy is the degree to which a person's beliefs center on a guiding authority. Public religiosity therefore describes the religious activities practiced with other people, which may include group prayers, or church attendance. With specific reference to the *Missing Link* section presented earlier in this article, the focus of this study is geared toward religiosity in the workplace, its feasibility in terms of interfaith dialog, and its contribution to achieving organizational goals.

DTB-K and Co-operative Bank of Kenya

DTB-K and Co-operative Bank of Kenya, the two banks selected for this study, have a multireligious workforce constituting Christians, Muslims, and Hindus. As a practice, this workforce meets weekly to pray. To speak frankly and openly of prayer in a scholarly article may perhaps cause some surprise or unease to some readers. The discussion of open and regular practices of faith is not an easy matter for the more secularized contexts of the academy in the west, where prayer is often thought to be a private matter and may even be legislated as such. However, in the Kenyan context, and in the banks we are discussing, this is not the case and the practice is unremarkable in itself. Praying in the workplace is natural, and leading of prayers is rotational among the faiths represented.

This study was conducted on the head offices of the DTB-K and the Co-operative Bank of Kenya. The choice of DTB-K is primarily because of its rich cultural makeup. DTB-K comprises three main religious faiths: Christianity, Hinduism, and Islam. It is one of the few banks in Kenya with such a diverse representation of culture with regard to religion, race, and ethnicity. The bank's staff is made up of employees from various cultural backgrounds with the majority being Africans and Asians. There are Hindu-Asians, Muslim-Asians, and majority native Kenyans being mostly Christian. The focus on the DTB-K Head Office Branch is because it presents the highest multicultural composition of all the other DTB branches in Kenya. On the other hand, the choice of Co-operative bank of Kenya head office is because of its established practice in the steady running of corporate interfaith prayers.

Research findings and discussion

The study was conducted for a period of 15 months, from January 2013 to March 2014. We mainly used questionnaires to collect data (Appendix 1). We also conducted an in-depth interview with the Senior Relational Manager who initiated the interfaith prayers at DTB-K. Other in-depth interviews were conducted with two practicing Hindus.

We sent out 60 questionnaires to DTB-K and another 60 questionnaires to Co-operative Bank of Kenya. The departments that participated in the study were Legal and Shares department, Finance department, Human Resource department, Personal and Business banking, and Managing Directors office. Out of 60 questionnaires sent to DTB-K, 53 were completed and returned. In Co-operative Bank of Kenya, 55 were completed and returned. Thus, we are analyzing 108 questionnaires. Table 1 shows the total number of respondents who took part in the study and other demographical information.

The respondents were both Kenyans and non-Kenyans. There were 64 male and 44 female respondents, meaning more male employees attended the prayers. This is a unique finding because it deviates from the popularly held perception in most parts of Africa that more women than men go to church and pray. But it is also a possibility that the banks simply have more male than female employees, a variable that we did not set out to verify.

In terms of age, the youngest employees who attended prayers were between 21–25 years old and the oldest 41–45, as shown in Table 1. The majority of the respondents were between 31 and 35 years (35 respondents), followed by 36–40 years (23 respondents), and 26–40 years (22 respondents). Thus, middle-aged people attended more. Regarding marital status, 38 (35.18%) were married, 68 (62.95%) were single while 2 (1.85%) did not indicate their marital status. The people who participated in the study were from the lower, middle, and upper management levels. Their religious affiliation is equally diverse – catholic, Protestant, Pentecostal, Baptist, Anglican, Hindu, and Muslims. No Hindu filled in the

Table 1. Demographic data.

	Frequency	Percentage (100%)
Gender		
Male	64	59.3
Female	44	40.7
Total	108	100
Age		
21–25	10	9.3
26–30	22	20.4
31–35	35	32.4
36–40	23	21.3
41–45	18	16.6
Total	108	100
Denomination		
Christians	95	88
Muslims	13	12
Total[a]	108	100

[a]No Hindus answered the questionnaire but two accepted in-depth interviews.

questionnaire, but two accepted oral interviews. They labeled themselves as 'modern Hindus'.

From the in-depth interview with the Senior Relationship Manager of DTB-K, we know that interfaith prayers at DTB-K were her initiative. She initiated the practice of joint prayers with the hope and conviction that it would promote unity and focus the team on a joint purpose of achieving organizational goals. The practice thus began at her corporate department and spread to other departments. She felt that the interfaith dialog would remove self-regarding ambition and the focus on a higher power could unite the team in one direction. The practice then spread to other departments and currently four departments participate in interfaith prayers, which occur every Friday morning. The prayer session initially began with only Christians leading the prayers, but later spread to each religious group leading the others in prayer. According to her, the greatest milestones this practice has initiated are helping all staff focus on a common goal and the promotion of unity in DTB-K.

At the Co-operative bank of Kenya, the majority of the employees are Christians, but of different denominations. The entire bank has a constant practice of praying together once a week at the beginning of the day. Different branches however have different arrangements for the prayers. For instance, the Personal and Business Banking department meets every Tuesday morning for an interfaith prayer service, similar to a real church service.

Findings indicate that inasmuch as the religions represented at the DTB-K have few common teachings, they share similarities such as sacred writings, an authority figure, ethics, and rituals. The work ethic is one such similarity among these religions that cuts across all their sacred teachings. All these religions promote the value of diligent service at whatever capacity of service employees find themselves in. For instance, the Bible instructs Christian workers (employees) to work diligently as servants, with obedience and respect for their earthly masters, and to serve with all one's heart as if one were working for the Lord Himself (Ephesians chapter 6:5–6). The Muslim Qur'an considers idleness, or time wastage in pursuit of unproductive work, as manifestations of lack of faith. Every person is called to pursue work because the existence of every new day is seen as reason to seek sustenance. Thus, the Qur'an instructs Muslims to persistently work whenever and wherever possible (Surah 62:10). Therefore, a person who 'seeks bounty' through hard work is praised. Diligence at work is also emphasized in Islam with examples drawn from the prophet Mohammed whose integrity and honesty while dealing with Khadija bint Khwaylad saw him earn a marriage proposal. Hindu sacred teachings similarly promote diligence at work with the Hindu sacred teachings of the Bhagavad Gita (5:7) linking hard work to leadership by stating 'Work hard and become a leader; be lazy and never succeed.'

The virtues of diligence, integrity, and service are portrayed in all these religious teachings. From these examples we see first of all, that religion plays a significant role in contributing to the work ethic of an individual who in this case represents the employee or employer; second, religion is directly related to organizational behavior, which contributes to the organizational behavior of an organization. Third, the organizational behavior contributes greatly to the attitude of the workforce, the attitude of the workforce in turn determines the end productivity of the organization in that a negative attitude exhibited by the workforce begets a lower productivity level, and vice versa.

The findings commensurate with the earliest work in linking religion and behavior by Social Classist theorist, Marx Weber, who sought to associate the Protestant ethic to the growth of capitalism and industrialization in Western Europe (Pringle & Starr, 2006). Weber saw capitalism as produced by cultural changes especially in religious values and attributed the Protestant Reformation (which held individuals responsible for their own salvation and promoted the work ethic) as laying the groundwork for capitalism (Calhoun, Light, & Keller, 1994). The relationship between religion and behavior was therefore seen in the impact religion had on socioeconomic development.

Further research findings indicate that in both banks under study, all types and levels of employees participate regularly in the interfaith prayers. This is irrespective of their age bracket or positions in the bank. They are all interested, for various reasons, and congregate once or twice a week to pray. One male respondent, aged 25 and working in the Human Resource Department, shared his experience as follows:

> every Monday and Friday I come to work prepared to share in the prayer sessions conducted at our workplace. A Christian prays, then an Ishmael follows suit, with an English translator by his side of course, lest we get lost in the Arabic language that is quite technical but interesting. This experience brings us together, and breaks communication barriers.

Regarding how the prayer sessions are conducted, responses show that a member of the staff from one particular religion leads the prayers, then the others join. The respondents take turns organizing and leading the prayers. As one respondent put it:

> facilitation of the prayers is rotational, and each denomination gets a chance to organize for it. I believe this is good as it sparks a sense of religious responsibility and incorporation.

Question no. 10: 'Do you think the practice of praying together in your organization has contributed to the growth of cohesiveness in the workplace?' elicited similar positive responses across the board. Respondents indicated that interfaith prayers do indeed contribute to the growth of cohesiveness in the workplace. Further, one factor stood out, that is, religion's role in promoting cohesiveness in the organization and consequently providing an avenue to fulfill organizational objectives. A male respondent who works in the Legal and Shares Department stated:

the prayer time is a very solemn time and all the participants take it seriously. We first recite The Lord's prayer, then a short prayer is offered. Thereafter, we pronounce the words of The Grace. When this is done, a Muslim prays and an Ishmael prayer follows immediately after. A totally intertwined but interesting experience, that leaves no faith out.

Eighty-five percent of the respondents believed that praying together created social cohesion, which in turn encouraged teamwork in achieving organizational goals. There was also emphasis on the fact that interfaith prayers bring unity among employees because people have an opportunity to share their personal experiences, which leads to appreciation of one's and other people's religious belief and culture.

With regard to Question 11, 'To what extent do you think working in a multicultural organization and engaging in intercultural activities such as joint prayers contribute to achieving organizational goals?', all data analyzed from the questionnaires and the in-depth interviews seemed to lead in one direction: creation of a common understanding, cohesion and unity that helps in strengthening faith amongst the employees. Relation-ships of trust are also formed among employees as well as with the wider multicultural clientele, that ultimately lead to the reduction of conflict, and the employees become more tolerable and tolerant with individuals of different cultures, races, and religious backgrounds, as they get to learn about different faiths, and exchange ideas on their understanding of the word of God. Further still, a good working environment is created where there is reduced suspicion brought about by religio-cultural myths, and subsequently, open communication and respect among the employees are enhanced.

Asked how impactful they thought interfaith dialog was for the achievement of organizational goals (cf. Q 11), there was consensus that interfaith prayers encourage harmony, appreciation of other religions, and also teaches virtues in achieving organizational goals. Regarding the greatest contributing factor the interfaith dialog has achieved, 83.7% termed the promotion of unity as its greatest achievement, with most respondents citing and appreciating the element of teamwork and unity that the practice provides. Seventy-three percent of the respondents felt that interfaith dialog has taught them to associate better with clients from different cultural backgrounds. This resonates well with Wolf (2012, p. 44) who observes that:

> if religions can be tools of conflict, they can also be fruitful instruments of reconciliation because they teach individuals not to perceive the world from the narrow perspective of their daily lives, but from that of the global world.

Further, 87% of the respondents were of the opinion that the cultural diversity the banks present has led to the growth of a more diverse customer base. The DTB-K bank's clients, for example, currently comprise Kenyans, Asians, Americans, and Europeans, with majority of the clients being Kenyan and Asian-Indians. The staff attributes this to the diverse workforce the bank holds, which is able to relate to the existing and potential culturally diverse customers who access the bank's services. Thus, in their words, interfaith prayers bring about equality, relief from mystical myths, knowledge of other cultures and faiths, as well as appreciation of self and other. Asked whether they would like the practice to continue or not, 88% of the respondents said that they preferred the practice to continue because it tends to eliminate religious conflicts, bring about cohesiveness, be a learning moment for all of the participants, unite the employees in acknowledging belief in a greater being, and thus create peaceful coexistence. In summary, they stated that interfaith dialog enhances commitment and unity of purpose.

Where interfaith dialog fails

While religion is an element of culture commonly associated with cohesiveness, results of this survey reveal that interfaith dialog may not help in achieving organizational goals when members drift to attempting to convert others to a particular faith. This is mainly attributed to the rigidity of different faiths. For one, faiths such as Christianity or Islam are often unwilling to surrender their convictions regarding their belief in God. Religious conversion therefore does not appeal to orthodox believers who are convicted of their doctrines of religion as objectively and universally true.

As earlier stated, no Hindu filled in the questionnaire, but we managed to interview two Hindus. They labeled themselves as 'Modern Hindus', and acknowledged the importance of a god. According to them, they had no problem with the prayers that were conducted in the workplace, and turn up to pray with fellow colleagues of different religious persuasions. But the attempt by some individuals of certain faiths to convert them was a great discouragement and significantly reduced their enthusiasm about interfaith prayers. One of them said:

> although I liked the worship sessions, I backed out when one of our colleagues, (name withheld), proposed that I start accompanying her to her Church, that was Anglican, to be able to learn more about her values and beliefs. Growing up, my siblings and I only went to the temple, where we were free to worship as we desired. I knew what it meant and my father had strict instructions to remain in the faith. I got scared and didn't want to be part of it. I wondered why she proposed that I visit her church, yet I had never asked her to come to our temple.

The other Hindu pointed out that:

> The Hindu religion is not limited to structure and rules, so when the people (Colleagues), and especially the Christians, were telling me about the Laws in their Holy Books, I couldn't keep up. We disagreed on many points such as those, and I just decided to keep off. I felt that my faith was inferior, since I was overpowered by the Muslims, and other protestants, who seemed to laugh every time we had the discussion. But I don't blame anyone, and I still have lunch together with them, when I don't carry my chilies.

While religion is an element of culture commonly associated with cohesiveness, the results of our research revealed that the practice at DTB-K is slowly declining in terms of commitment to attendance because of the attempts, by some members, at converting their peers. This may explain why some members in the two banks have relaxed their attendance in interfaith prayers. In this case, negative interfaith dialog generates conflict.

Conclusion

As Dulles (2001) put it, while interfaith avenues such as prayers encourage interreligious dialog, it seems to generate the greatest results when similar faiths are at play. Interfaith dialog is fruitful only in a relationship of mutual respect and knowledge of the other culture and religion, as well as one's own culture and religion, but only within an environment of authenticity and tolerance in which each participant has full understanding and acceptance of his or her religious heritage, as well as a similar understanding and acceptance of the other. Thus, interfaith dialog among religions must be seen as one that respects various religions, as opposed to differences being seen as points of superiority.

Findings underscore the fact that interfaith dialog is enhanced through a joint commitment to work on common objectives. It is important to note that religion alone is unlikely to cause sweeping social change, but social change without accompanying religious change is implausible (Leslie et al., 1973). A strong culture does improve the organization's chances of becoming successful in the marketplace, with religion as an element of culture playing a pivotal role in the promotion of organizational objectives. A cohesive culture can offer employees a focus of identification or sense of belonging, which may then foster loyalty and values that encourage employees to perform. Subsequently, the overall organizational performance will be enhanced.

In conclusion, interfaith dialog is enhanced through a joint commitment to work, prayer, and common organizational objectives, but not with the aim to convert. If correctly adopted and properly utilized, (positive) interfaith dialog and activities can be a great opportunity to enable institutions achieve organizational goals. This is because in a multireligious setup, it can create in employees a sense of belonging, which may then encourage them to perform. This research presents alternative frameworks for analyzing intercultural communication in the workplace based on faith. By providing a critique of existing models of language and intercultural communication in the workplace, this study could lead to the formulation of a new intercultural communication theory, which includes, as a vital component, religious faith in the workplace.

Acknowledgments

We thank the Centre for Research, Publication and Consultancy of Daystar University for financing this research. The paper was presented at the *IALIC-2013* conference at Hong Kong Baptist University, and we would like to acknowledge a travel grant from IALIC, which made this presentation possible. We are also greatly indebted to the reviewers and editors who tirelessly read through several versions of our work and made valuable recommendations and suggestions for improvements.

Disclosure statement

No potential conflict of interest was reported by the authors.

References

Alvesson, M. (2002). *Understanding organizational culture*. London: Sage.
Baran, S. J., & Davis, D. K. (2009). *Mass communication theory: Foundations, ferment, and future* (5th ed.). Boston, MA: Wadsworth Cengage Learning.
Blommaert, J. (2010). *The sociolinguistics of globalization*. Cambridge: Cambridge University Press.
Calhoun, C., Light, D., & Keller, S. (1994). *Sociology* (6th ed.). Los Angeles, CA: McGraw-Hill.

Dulles, A. (2001). Christ among the religions. *American Magazine, 186*(3).

Gifford, P. (2009). *Christianity, politics and public life in Kenya.* London: Hurst.

Green, A. W. (1952). *Sociology: An analysis of life in modern society* (4th ed.). Los Angeles, CA: McGraw-Hill.

Howard, R. (2008). *My tribe is journalism: Conflict sensitive journalism* (Special ed.). Nairobi: International Media Support.

Johnson, A. G. (1996). *Human arrangements an introduction to sociology: Religious institutions* (4th ed.). London: Brown & Benchmark.

Kreitner, R., & Kinicki, A. (2008). *Organisational behavior* (8th ed.). New York, NY: McGraw Hill/Irwin.

Lando, A. L., & Mwangi, S. (2014). Social media and cell phones are bonding and vilification tools: Exposing Kenya's 2013 postelection violence. In B. A. Musa & J. Willis (Eds.), *From Twitter to Tahrir Square: Ethics in social and new media communication* (Vol. 1, pp. 277–300). Santa Barbara, CA: Praeger.

Leslie, R. G., Larson, R. F., & Gorman, B. L. (1973). *Order and change introductory sociology.* New York, NY: Oxford University Press.

Littlejohn, S. (2009). *Theories of human communication.* Belmont, CA: Wadsworth.

Martin, J. (2002). *Organizational culture: Mapping the terrain. Foundations for organizational Science.* Newsbury Park, CA: Sage.

McDaniel, E. R., Porter, E. R., & Samovar, L. A. (2009). *Intercultural communication: A reader* (12th ed.). Boston, MA: Wadsworth Cengage Learning.

McLuhan, M. (1964). *Understanding media: The extensions of man.* New York, NY: McGraw Hill.

Never Again. (2010). *Video on 2007/2008 post-election violence.* Nairobi: Ukweli Video Productions.

Pennington, U. L. (1985). Intercultural communication. In L. Samovar & R. E. Porter (Eds.), *Intercultural communication: A reader* (4th ed. pp. 30–39). Belmont, CA: Wardsworth.

Pringle, P. K., & Starr, M. F. (2006). *Electronic media management* (5th ed.). New York, NY: Focal Press.

Wolf, A. (2012). Intercultural identity and inter-religious dialogue: A holy place to be? *Journal of Language and Intercultural Communication, 12*(1), 37–55. doi:10.1080/14708477.2011.626860

Wood, J. T. (1982). Communication and relational culture: Bases for the study of human relationships. *Communication Quarterly, 30*(2), 75–84. doi:10.1080/01463378209369432

Appendix 1. The Questionnaire

SECTION A

1. What is your age bracket?

   1. 21–25 | | 2. 26–30 | | 3. 31–35 | | 4. 36–40 | |
   5. 41–45 | | 6. 46–50 | | 7. Over 50 | |

2. What is you gender?

   1. Male | | 2. Female | |

3. What is your marital status?

   1. Single | | 2. Married | | 3. Separated | | 4. Divorced | | 5. Widowed | |

4. In which department do you serve?

   1. Risk | | 2. Human Resource | | 3. Corporate | | 4. Credit | |
   5. Operations | | 6. Other (please specify) | |

5. At what level of management do you serve?

   1. Lower management | | 2. Middle management | | 3. Upper management | |

6. What is your religious affiliation?

   1. Christian | | 2. Muslim | | 3. Hindu | | 4. Other (specify)_____

7. What is your national affiliation?

   1. Kenyan | | 2. Kenyan of Indian decent | | 3. Other (please specify)_____

8. Do you participate in the joint prayer sessions that take place in the workplace?

   1. Yes | | 2. No | |

If NO to Q 8 above, your interview ends here. Thanks very much for your time. If you answered YES to Q 8, please proceed to answer ALL the questions in Section B.

SECTION B Interfaith Prayers

If yes to Question 8 above:-,

9. How often do you attend these prayer sessions?

   1. Very often | | 2. Often | | 3. Rarely | | 4. Very rare | |

10. Do you think the practice of praying together in your organization has contributed to the growth of cohesiveness in the workplace? Kindly explain your answer.
    _____
    _____

11. To what extent do you think working in a multicultural organization and engaging in intercultural activities such as joint prayers contribute to achieving organizational goals?
    _____
    _____

12. Do you think managing a diverse workforce has led to the bank's increase of client base from different cultural backgrounds? Briefly explain your answer.
    _____
    _____

13. In your opinion, has your experience in working in a culturally diverse environment changed your view of people from different cultural backgrounds?
    _____
    _____

Preparing students for the global workplace: the impact of a semester abroad

Jane Jackson

Department of English, The Chinese University of Hong Kong, Hong Kong SAR, China

As the world becomes increasingly interconnected, employers are seeking 'global-ready graduates,' that is, individuals with an intercultural mindset, who can interact effectively and appropriately with people from diverse linguistic and cultural backgrounds. In response, tertiary institutions are creating more opportunities for international experience. This article centers on a mixed-method study that investigated the impact of a semester-long international exchange program on the global-readiness of Chinese university students. Whereas the experimental group experienced gains in intercultural competence, second language self-efficacy, and global-mindedness, the control group (students on the home campus prior to study abroad) regressed slightly. The analysis of the qualitative data revealed multifarious elements that led to these differing outcomes.

摘要：世界各國距離日漸拉近，僱主亦越加要求大學畢業生具環球視野，即擁有跨文化知識，並會學以致用，面對不同母語及文化背景的同事，都能詞句達意，順利並恰當地完成工作。有見及此，各國大專院校加緊投放資源，著力提升學生海外學習經驗。本論文以多重方法論為基礎，探討一個學期的海外交流課程，如何使中國大學生就日後世界性工作，有更充分的準備。量性研究結果顯示，參與該課程的學生(實驗組別)在環球視野、二語自學效率及跨文化溝通上都有顯著進步，而未有參與者(對照組別)卻在有關方面呈輕微倒退。定性資料則顯示，環境及個人因素對交流成果有不同影響。

Introduction

The intensification of globalizing forces and the interrelated world economy are bringing about more diversity in the workplace. Large corporations and even small companies have become increasingly multicultural and multilingual. As more businesses enter the global market and organizations recruit internationally, linguistic and cultural diversity among employees is becoming the new norm in the workplace (Sharifian & Jamarani, 2013; Sorrells, 2013). Migration and global workforce mobility are resulting in more intercultural contact as temporary workers and long-term expatriates intermingle with locals, including immigrants from many parts of the world. In organizations, it is now common for people to work on mixed-gender teams or projects with individuals who have a different linguistic, religious, and cultural background or disability (Guilherme, Glaser, & Méndez-García, 2010; Holmes, 2012; Sorrells, 2012). Clients and customers with diverse backgrounds may also interact with employees in person or *online*. In today's interconnected world, an organization's success increasingly depends on its ability to embrace and manage diversity.

To remain competitive in the international arena or global marketplace, more community leaders are recognizing the need for well-educated, technologically advanced, bilingual (or multilingual) individuals who can thrive in diverse environments (Deardorff & Hunter, 2006). In the global workplace, employees must possess sufficient confidence to initiate and sustain interactions in their second (or third) language. Self-efficacy refers to 'individuals' beliefs about their capabilities to perform well' (Graham & Weiner, 1995, p. 74). Linking this ability construct to motivation in second language use and learning, Ehrman (1996) observes that a greater expectation of good results generally increases motivation and risk-taking (e.g., more willingness to initiate second language interactions). Therefore, enhancing the self-efficacy of second language speakers is essential preparation for workplaces that require bilingualism. Nowadays, there is also more awareness of the need for university graduates to possess global competence, which Hunter (2004, p. 277) defines as 'having an open mind while actively seeking to understand cultural norms and expectations of others, leveraging this gained knowledge to interact, communicate and work effectively outside one's environment.'

More and more governments are pushing publicly funded tertiary institutions to devote extra attention to the preparation of students for the global workplace. The policy-based response of many is internationalization, which Kälvermark and van der Wende (1997, p. 19) define as 'any systematic sustained effort aimed at making higher education more responsive to the requirements and challenges related to the globalization of societies, economy and labor markets.' More specifically, this process entails 'integrating an international, intercultural or global dimension into the purpose, functions or delivery of post-secondary education' (Knight, 2004, p. 11).

As part of their internationalization efforts, many tertiary institutions are creating more opportunities for students to gain some form of international experience (e.g., language and cultural study tours, short-term study abroad programs, semester- or year-long exchanges, service-learning, global internships, etc.). According to the Institute for Statistics of the United Nations Educational, Scientific, and Cultural Organization, in 2010 at least 3.6 million students were enrolled in tertiary education abroad, up from 2 million in 2000 (UNESCO, 2013). The number of students who will be educated transnationally for at least a portion of their undergraduate degree is expected to continue to rise, and more postgraduate students are also being encouraged to gain overseas experience (Bhandari & Blumenthal, 2011). Greater China has become the main exporter of students, with the majority studying in English-speaking countries or in institutions in non-English-speaking countries that offer coursework in this international language, such as Finland, Germany, and the Netherlands (Institute of International Education, 2013; Jenkins, 2013).

Community leaders and government officials often assume that international experience leads to significant advances in such areas as second language proficiency/ self-efficacy, personal growth, global-mindedness, and intercultural competence; how-ever, education abroad scholars are finding that international experience is highly variable, and systematic research is needed to better understand what students actually learn abroad (e.g., Jackson, 2012; Kinginger, 2009; Vande Berg, Paige & Lou, 2012).

This article reports on a pretest, posttest, mixed-method, experimental design study that sought to determine what students gain from a semester-long international exchange program. While this research investigated the 'whole person development' of the parti-cipants, this paper primarily centers on the development of their intercultural competence, second language self-efficacy, and global-mindedness.

Intercultural competence and the Intercultural Development Continuum

In the literature on intercultural communication, one can now find many definitions and models of the complex construct of intercultural competence. The *SAGE Handbook of Intercultural Competence* (Deardorff, 2009), for example, provides a comprehensive review of a number of current understandings, noting that scholars in the field emphasize different elements, depending on such aspects as their disciplinary background, research, and intercultural experiences.

For the part of the study that explored intercultural competence, the Intercultural Development Continuum (IDC) provided the conceptual framework. The IDC, which is described by Hammer (2012) as a 'model of intercultural competence,' is a modified version of the Developmental Model of Intercultural Sensitivity that was devised by Bennett (1986). In the IDC, intercultural competence is defined as 'the capability to shift cultural perspective and appropriately adapt behavior to cultural difference and common-alities' (Hammer, 2013, p. 26). Derived from the analysis of 'real world' experiences of individuals in intercultural situations, the IDC 'describes a set of orientations toward cultural difference and commonality that are arrayed along a continuum from the more monocultural mindsets of Denial and Polarization through the transitional orientation of Minimization to the intercultural or global mindsets of Acceptance and Adaptation' (Hammer, 2012, p. 12).

Denial measures a worldview that simplifies and/or avoids cultural difference. Individuals in this orientation often have very limited intercultural experience and display little interest in learning about other ways of being. Polarization: Defense/Reversal measures a judgmental mindset that views cultural differences in terms of 'us vs. them.' In Defense, 'us' (e.g., one's cultural group) is viewed as superior with little or no recognition of limitations; in Reversal (R) 'them' is superior (e.g., another cultural group is exalted and one's own cultural group is maligned). Minimization (M) measures a transitional worldview that emphasizes cultural commonality and universal values. With limited cultural self-awareness, individuals in this orientation may not pay sufficient attention to deeper level cultural differences (e.g., sociopragmatic norms of politeness, values). Acceptance measures a worldview that can comprehend and appreciate complex cultural differences, while Adaptation identifies the capacity to alter one's cultural perspective and adapt one's behavior so that it is appropriate and authentic in a particular cultural context.

In the last few decades, more than a hundred tools have been developed to measure intercultural competence, and some are linked to a particular model or theory (for reviews of instruments see Fantini, 2009, 2012). The orientations described in the IDC are measured by the Intercultural Development Inventory (IDI) version 3, a cross-culturally validated psychometric instrument that consists of 50 statements (Hammer, 2009a, 2009b, 2012). In addition, open-ended 'contexting questions' prompt respondents to provide details about their intercultural experiences and reactions to them. The IDI results provide a profile of an individual's and/or a group's degree of intercultural competence. Hammer (2013, p. 21) states that the IDI is 'descriptive of a general orientation towards making sense of and responding to cultural differences generally and within particular cultural (group) contexts.' This instrument is now widely used in study abroad research to gauge the impact of stays abroad on the intercultural competence of student sojourners (e.g., Paige & Vande Berg, 2012; Vande Berg, Connor-Linton, & Paige, 2009). It may also be administered to determine the merits of interventions designed to enhance the intercultural competence of education abroad students (e.g., predeparture intercultural communication courses, guided critical reflection during stays abroad, reentry modules; e.g., Engle & Engle, 2012; Jackson, 2013).

The aims of the experimental design study

The purpose of the present study was to determine the impact of a semester abroad on the 'whole person development' of Chinese students from a Hong Kong university who joined a semester-long international exchange program. The developmental trajectories of the international exchange students (the experimental group) were compared with those of their peers who were on the home campus during this time period, prior to joining an international exchange program (the control group). In this pretest, posttest, mixed-method, experimental design study, many elements were investigated; however, due to space limitations, the discussion in this paper centers on the following research questions:

(1) Do students who participate in a semester-long international exchange program experience greater gains in intercultural competence, second language self-efficacy, and global-mindedness than peers on the home campus for the same time period prior to their own exchange experience?
(2) Are they better prepared for the global workplace?
(3) Are there differential gains within groups? What might account for this?

What are the pedagogical implications for future study abroad programs? What steps can be taken to optimize sojourns so that the participants become better prepared for the global workplace?

Method

Participants

The experimental group was comprised of 105 students who joined a semester-long exchange program: 40 (38.0%) went to the USA, 12 (11.4%) to Canada, 10 (9.5%) to Australia, 6 (5.7%) to France, 6 (5.7%) to South Korea, 5 (4.8%) to Singapore, 4 (3.8%) to Mexico, 4 (4.3%) to Denmark, 3 (2.9%) to Finland, 3 (2.9%) to New Zealand, 3 (2.9%) to China, 3 (2.9%) to the UK, and 6 (11.7%) to other destinations. While abroad, nearly all did their coursework in English. For the sojourn, 86 (81.9%) lived on campus, 17 (16.2%) off-campus, and 2 (1.9%) in a homestay.

In the experimental group, there were 66 females (62.9%) and 39 (37.1%) males, with a mean age of 20.74 years and a mean grade point average of 3.31, signifying above average academic performance. All were ethnically Chinese; 80 (76.2%) spoke Cantonese as a first language and 25 (23.8%) Putonghua (Mandarin). All spoke English as an additional language. The students in this cohort came from the following faculties: 53 (50.5%) business administration, 20 (19.0%) social science, 13 (12.4%) arts, 10 (9.5%) science, 5 (4.8%) education, and 4 (3.8%) engineering. When the sojourn got under way, 13 (12.4%) were in their second year of studies, 56 (53.3%) in their third year, 56 (53.3%) in their fourth, and 1 (1.0%) in postgraduate studies. Forty-three (41.0%) had never ventured outside their home country; 62 (59.0%) had some travel experience, which typically consisted of a few days or weeks in Asia. Twenty-two (21.0%) had studied abroad; in most cases, this entailed a micro- or short-term stay (e.g., an English or Putonghua summer immersion program).

The control group consisted of 141 undergraduates who were on the home campus for this semester, prior to participating in an international exchange program. In this cohort, there were 85 females (60.3%) and 56 males (39.7%), with a mean age of 20.16 years and a mean grade point average of 3.35. Similar to the experimental group, all 141 participants were of Chinese ethnicity; 105 (74.5%) spoke Cantonese as a first language and 36 (25.5%) Putonghua (Mandarin). All spoke English as an additional language. Their majors varied; similar to the experimental group, they came from different faculties: 81 (57.4%) business administration, 30 (21.3%) social science, 7 (20.6%), 11 (7.8%) arts, 10 (7.1%) science, and 9 (6.4%) engineering. When the sojourn got under way, 39 (27.7%) were in their second year of study, 88 (62.4%) in their third year, 13 (9.2%) in their fourth year, and 1 (0.7%) in postgraduate studies. Fifty-six (39.7%) had never traveled outside their home country; 85 (60.3%) had some travel experience (e.g., most commonly, a few days or weeks in Asia). One hundred and nine (77.3%) had international education, whereas 32 (22.7%) had studied abroad previously (e.g., a short-term summer immersion program).

Instrumentation

Pretest measures

This experimental design study incorporated both quantitative and qualitative data. All of the participants completed the Pre-international Exchange Survey, an in-house instrument that covered such topics as: reasons for studying abroad; aims, expectations, and level of preparedness for the sojourn; concerns about living and studying abroad; previous international/education abroad experience; intercultural contact; perceptions of intercultural competence; interest in international/global affairs; second language proficiency and use; identity; and family background (e.g., parents' level of education and international experience). While most of the items in the survey were closed, several open-ended questions were also included to gather more insight into the respondents' experiences and perceptions. In the pretest phase, the IDI version 3 was administered to both cohorts (experimental and control) to provide a measure of their intercultural competence on entry.

Prior to their stay abroad, 22 students in the experimental group took part in semi-structured interviews that were conducted in Cantonese, Putonghua, or English, depending on the preference of the interviewee. The average length of these interviews was 80 minutes. Topics included: aims and expectations for the sojourn, intercultural contact, intercultural communication skills, global-mindedness, perceptions of intercultural competence, identity, previous international experience and education abroad, level of preparedness for life/study abroad, second language proficiency (self-assessment; TOEFL/IELTS scores), social networks, readiness for the global workplace, and language use, as well as other issues of relevance to the international exchange experience that the interviewees wished to discuss.

Posttest measures

At the end of the semester, the participants (experimental and control groups) were invited to complete the Post-international Exchange survey to gather information about their sojourn experiences/learning. This instrument primarily consisted of closed questions with a few that were open-ended. To facilitate the assessment of their learning, the instrument included many items that were similar to those in the Pre-international Exchange survey. Topics included: reasons for studying abroad; aims, expectations and level of preparedness for the sojourn; assessment of goals achieved; challenges faced while living and studying abroad; benefits of previous international experience; second language proficiency and use; perceptions of intercultural sensitivity/competence and global-mindedness; social networks, identity; readiness for the global workplace; and recommendations for the preparation of future exchange students. Both cohorts were also re-administered the IDI version 3.

The 22 students in the experimental group who were interviewed prior to going abroad were re-interviewed in the language of their choice. This time, the average length of the post-sojourn interviews was 90 minutes. Topics included: their overall impression of their international experience/learning; academic and intellectual development; sojourn activities and travel; intercultural contact and adjustment; intercultural communication skills; level of preparedness for sojourn/re-entry; global-mindedness; second language development and usage; personal/social/academic/cognitive/professional/intercultural development; identity (change); social networks, reentry challenges and adjustment; current intercultural contact and future plans; readiness for the global workplace; and recommendations for the preparation and support of future exchange students/returnees. Similar to the pre-sojourn interview, the participants were invited to talk about additional issues related to their sojourn or reentry that interested them.

Data analysis

NVivo 10, a qualitative software program (Bazeley & Jackson, 2013), aided the organization, coding, and triangulation of the quantitative and qualitative data (e.g., interview transcripts, open-ended survey questions, pre- and postsurvey results, responses to IDI 'contexting' questions). The pre- and Post-international Exchange Surveys were processed using SPSS to enable a comparison of the intercultural/second language learning and global-mindedness of the participants before and after the semester. Pre- and post-IDI profiles for the full cohorts, as well as for individual participants, were also prepared (Hammer, 2012). This facilitated a pre- and postcomparison of the actual and perceived levels of intercultural competence of each participant, as well as the groups as a whole.

To better understand the impact of the semester-long sojourn on the global-mindedness, second language proficiency, and intercultural competence of the experimental group, the transcripts of the 22 pre- and post-semi-structured interviews were subjected to thematic content analysis along with responses to open-ended questions in the in-house surveys and IDIs (responses to 'contexting questions'). The qualitative data linked to their pre- and post-IDI scores and other surveys were then triangulated and analyzed.

When processing the qualitative data (interview transcripts, open-ended survey questions, responses to IDI 'contexting questions'), I employed a thematic, 'open coding' approach (Bazeley & Jackson, 2013), rather than limit myself to preconceived notions and categories. As I developed more understanding of the relationship between items, new categories emerged and others were modified. The surveys and interview transcripts included the code numbers of the participants, making it possible to group together all of the data for each individual. This facilitated the development of rich case studies of interviewees as well as whole group profiles.

Findings

Overview

While the instruments gathered data on multiple issues, this section largely focuses on the development of the participants' intercultural competence, second language self-efficacy, and global-mindedness. The IDI scores for the pre- and posttests were analyzed and are presented for both experimental and control groups. The results for both groups are then compared to offer insight into the impact of the stay abroad. Key findings in the analysis of qualitative data (pre- and post-sojourn transcripts of interviews with 22 students in the experimental group, open-ended surveys, IDI 'contexting questions') are then presented in relation to their intercultural/second language learning and global-mindedness. Due to space limitations, this article includes only a few excerpts from the database (e.g., quotes from interviews).

Pretest IDI group profiles of intercultural competence

All of the participants completed the IDI at the beginning of the semester. In the following sections, the findings for the experimental and control groups are presented, followed by a comparison of group results.

The experimental group

The perceived orientation (PO) of a group indicates where the group as a whole 'places itself' along the IDC (either denial, polarization (defense/reversal), minimization, acceptance, or adaptation; Hammer, 2009a, 2009b, 2012, 2013). The PO of the Experimental group was 116.02, in the beginning of the acceptance range, which indicates that they believed they were very interculturally competent.

The development orientation (DO) provides an indication of 'the group's primary orientation toward cultural differences and commonalities along the continuum *as assessed by the IDI*' (Hammer, 2009b, p. 5). The DO is the perspective that the group is most apt to draw on in intercultural encounters. Similar to the PO, the DO can be denial, polarization (defense/reversal), minimization, acceptance, or adaptation (Hammer, 2009b, p. 5). This cohort's DO was 76.88, in polarization: defense/reversal.

The orientation gap (OG) is the difference between the PO and the DO. According to Hammer (2009b), a difference of 7 points or more indicates a meaningful difference. The experimental group's OG was 39.14, signifying a great overestimation of their intercultural competence.

The IDI profile also provides an indication of what Hammer (2009a, p. 5) refers to as trailing orientations (TO), 'orientations that are "in back of" the group's DO on the intercultural continuum *that are not "resolved."*' When embroiled in an intercultural conflict, for example, trailing issues may pull individuals back from their DO for coping with cultural difference. In other words, they may temporarily draw on an earlier orientation to make sense of the intercultural situation. The analysis of the TO indicated that all of the experimental group's worldviews were in transition.

Leading orientations (LO) indicate the next step to take in the enhancement of intercultural competence, in terms of the intercultural continuum. As their DO on entry was polarization: defense/reversal, this group's LO were minimization, acceptance, and adaptation.

The control group

On entry, the PO of the control group was 118.11 (acceptance), while their DO was 82.47 (on the cusp of minimization). Therefore, the OG was 36.64, slightly less than that of the experimental group, but still a significant overestimation of their intercultural competence.

Similar to the experimental group, the analysis of TO revealed that none of their worldviews were fully resolved. As the control group's DO on entry was minimization, the group's LO were acceptance and adaptation.

Pretest IDI results: a comparison of experimental and control groups

In summary, on entry, both groups were in an ethnocentric stage of development (the cusp of minimization and polarization: defense/reversal); both significantly inflated opinions about their levels of intercultural sensitivity/competence, rating themselves in acceptance. As for TO, the IDI profiles for both groups revealed that none of their worldviews were fully resolved. The LO for both groups were minimization, acceptance, and adaptation. Thus, the overall IDI group profiles were quite similar on entry.

Posttest IDI group profiles of intercultural competence

At the end of the semester, both the experimental and control groups again completed the IDI. The results for both groups are presented followed by a comparison of pre- and postscores for each cohort.

Experimental group

After the semester-long exchange program, the PO of the experimental group was 118.08 in acceptance, while their DO was 82.86, on the cusp of minimization, the transitional phase. The OG was 35.22. As for TO, reversal was resolved, while the other worldviews were still in transition. As the DO had advanced to minimization, the LO were acceptance through adaptation.

In terms of the PO, a comparison of the experimental group's pre- and post-IDI scores revealed a slight increase in their self-perception of their intercultural competence (moving from 116.02 to 118.08), with both scores in the acceptance range. There was an increase in their DO from 76.88 in polarization: defense/reversal to 82.86, in the low end of minimization, a gain of 5.98 points. Further, the number of TO was reduced with reversal resolved. The LO had shifted to acceptance and adaptation.

Control group

At the end of the semester, the PO of the control group was 117.05 (acceptance), while their DO was 80.67, in polarization: defense/reversal. The OG was 36.38; similar to the experimental group, this indicates a great overestimation of their level of intercultural competence. As for TO, none of their worldviews were resolved. Their LO were minimization, acceptance, and adaptation, as in the pretest.

A comparison of the pre- and posttest results of the control group revealed that they still held significantly inflated self-perceptions of their intercultural competence (a PO of 118.11 on the pretest and 117.05 on the posttest), with both scores in acceptance. In terms of their DO, there was a slight regression (from a pretest score of 82.47 to a posttest score of 80.67, with both scores indicative of an ethnocentric stage of development). The OG stayed almost the same (pretest 36.64; posttest 36.38), indicating a consistent great overestimation of their intercultural competence. The TO remained unresolved but the LO changed from acceptance and adaptation to minimization, acceptance, and adaptation.

Posttest IDI results: a comparison of experimental and control groups

Both cohorts retained a very inflated perception of their degree of intercultural competence. While polarization: defense/reversal was no longer a trailing issue for the experimental group, for both cohorts, all other worldviews remained in transition. In terms of actual intercultural competence, the control group regressed slightly (a reduction of 1.8 points in DO). In contrast, the experimental group as a whole shifted in the direction of greater intercultural competence (moving from a DO of 76.88 to 82.86, a gain of nearly 6 points), suggesting that they had become better prepared for the global workplace, as the semester abroad had had a positive impact on their 'intercultural worldview.'

To put the IDI results in perspective, it is helpful to refer to the outcomes of the Georgetown Consortium Research Project, a large-scale study which administered pre- and post-IDIs to nearly 1300 US-American students in 61 study abroad programs. Only one group received some form of intervention (cultural mentoring while abroad). The sojourners who did not engage in cultural mentoring, on average, gained only 1.32 points in their DO, while those on the home campus advanced by just 0.07 points, revealing little or no gain in intercultural sensitivity for these cohorts. Interestingly, the students who experienced the intervention gained 12.47 points in their DO, a significant enhance- ment of their intercultural competence, pointing to the benefits of guided, critical reflec- tion for student sojourners (Vande Berg et al., 2009, Vande Berg et al., 2012).

The qualitative data

The analysis of the qualitative data (e.g., application essay, interview transcripts, open- ended survey responses, IDI 'contexting questions') revealed that those who attained a higher level of intercultural competence on the post-IDI took fuller advantage of orienta- tions, extra-curricular activities, and 'buddy systems' organized by their host university. Early in their stay, this enabled more contact with other international students and locals and helped ease their adjustment in the alien environment. As they were willing to initiate interactions in the host language and try new things, this, too, facilitated their intercultural/ second language learning and the diversification of their social networks.

These returnees provided richer accounts of their experiences abroad (e.g., intercultural interactions) and displayed more awareness of linguistic and cultural norms in the host environment (e.g., sociopragmatic norms of politeness, local cultural scripts for apologies and refusals) than their more monocultural peers. On reentry, these individuals were more interested in global affairs and their survey responses showed that they either read about international events or listened to international newscasts more frequently than before the sojourn. In post-sojourn interviews, some claimed that they had taken steps toward global citizenship, an important element in global-readiness for the workplace:

> I think in order to be a global citizen, one should have a global view. You first need to understand cultural differences. Then, respect the disparity. Apart from recognizing and respecting the different behavior and habits of international students, I realized that I could learn a lot from them, too. I think I made progress in terms of becoming a global citizen as I've become more open, more bold, and more confident than before, and more interested in international affairs. I now know more about western cultures and foreign people so I know what to talk with them about. (Female Professional Accountancy major who sojourned in the USA)

> I think a global citizen should respect different cultures and recognize universal values rather than stick to a certain country's ideology. You should have a global perspective and be interested in what is happening in the world. As for myself, I feel that I've become more global-minded. (Male Risk Management Science major who sojourned in the USA)

Buoyed by their international experience, these individuals recognized the merits of intercultural competence and fluency in more than one language, as evidenced in their post-sojourn interviews:

By the end of my stay abroad, I noticed some improvement in my intercultural communication skills. When interacting with people from different cultures, I've always thought that we should put away our stereotypes and be sincere. The exchange experience provided me with the opportunity to practice this rule and reinforce such consciousness. This rule effectively guided my behavior. After all, it's inevitable that you might have prejudice towards others if you make judgments based on your own cultural norms. (Male Professional Accountancy major who sojourned in the USA)

Because there were so many things that I had to face by myself in the U.S., I became a more independent and stable person. Though my English is still far from enough, I've improved a lot and now I can communicate confidently with foreigners. (Male Risk Management Science major who sojourned in the USA)

I think local companies will be quite willing to employ a person like me, as I now have international experience and can communicate more easily with people from different cultural backgrounds than students who have no international experience. I can communicate in three languages: Putonghua, English, and Cantonese, and that's also important for the workplace here. (Female Professional Accountancy major who sojourned in the USA)

With intercultural, international experience, most had become more self-reliant and much more confident in their ability to communicate their ideas and emotions in their second (or third) language. Compared with their pre-sojourn selves, these returnees had become much more willing to interact with individuals who had a different linguistic and cultural background, a key requisite for the global workforce. In their post-sojourn interviews they remarked:

Academically, I've become more professional. More importantly, I've became more confident as I got along with people from other cultural backgrounds when I was abroad. My English language abilities also improved. As I've experienced the hurdle of trying to find conversation topics when facing Europeans, I now find it much easier and more relaxing when I communicate with others. Everything seems much easier for me now as my interpersonal communication skills were enhanced in Canada. I became more capable of asking questions to keep a conversation going. Now, I'm better at finding topics to talk about with different groups of people. I've become more extroverted. I feel a real psychological and mental change in me. (Male Professional Accountancy major who sojourned in Canada)

Soon after I came back to Hong Kong, I met an exchange student on campus, who asked me directions. I pointed out the building he wanted and then chatted with him. I felt very happy. In the past, I would have told him the directions but no more. After having been abroad, I am more accepting of foreigners and more willing to be in contact with them. (Female Math major who sojourned in the USA)

In a new environment, I had to accept new and different things. I tried to learn more about other people and other cultures. I learned how to accept others and be less self-centered. Over time, I became more active in communicating with people from other cultural backgrounds. I no longer wait to express myself until others ask. I find it easier to communicate with people from different cultures. I can speak several languages with people from different cultural backgrounds in the same situation, and now it feels natural. (Male Government and Public Administration major who sojourned in Korea)

On their home campus, many of the returnees who had acquired a higher level of intercultural competence offered to help orientate new international students on campus and joined the International Student Association to have more opportunities to develop intercultural friendships. After the sojourn, these individuals perceived themselves to be better prepared for the global workplace. In their post-sojourn interviews, many expressed the desire to work in a multicultural environment either at home or abroad.

> I'm now thinking more about the possibility of working and living in different countries. It's because of this exchange experience that I have this kind of thought. I've become more confident interacting with foreigners and now I'd like to work for an NGO (non-governmental organization). I'm noticing more about international institutions and those that can offer the opportunity to work overseas. Before going on exchange, I didn't have any plans to work abroad. (Male Sociology major who sojourned in Finland)

> My overseas experience helped me to figure out what I want to do in the future. I'd like to work overseas and try new things like public relations. My communication skills have improved a lot, I think. I really want to work overseas because of this exchange experience. (Female Psychology major who sojourned in South Africa)

> I'd like to look for jobs or internships in Hong Kong that are somehow related to Korea. I have a deeper understanding of that country now and have confidence in developing my career in this way. Ideally, I'd like to work for an international company in Hong Kong. After this exchange experience, I've become more open to different career paths. (Male Government and Public Administration major who sojourned in Korea)

In stark contrast, the student sojourners who made the least gains in intercultural competence returned home without achieving their goal of developing meaningful intercultural friendships. Less open to unfamiliar ways of being, they did not take an active role in orientations or extra-curricular activities at the host university and tended to cling to conationals. As they spent nearly all of their free time with Chinese peers, this reduced the degree and quality of their exposure to the host culture and language. In their post-sojourn survey and interview, they displayed limited interest in international affairs. Most of these returnees did not consider themselves global citizens and saw no reason to change.

> A global citizen should have a worldwide vision, that is, he or she should understand and care about international affairs. I do not care much about the world condition. I have a much stronger incentive to know more about China and Hong Kong as I am living in this environment. I do not have much interest in affairs or incidents that happen outside China. (Male Professional Accountancy major who sojourned in the USA)

Interestingly, in contrast with those who developed a higher level of intercultural competence and global-mindedness, these returnees had no plans for further international experience and, in many cases, appeared to be more determined to have less intercultural contact.

> Before going on exchange, I thought about working or living abroad. However, the exchange experience made me realize that the western world is not like what I'd imagined. After comparing life in both places, I want to settle down in Hong Kong or China. After all, I had not been to foreign countries before and I was not sure which place was more suitable for me. Now I realize which is better and therefore I've abandoned my earlier ideas. It's much easier to communicate with other Chinese. (Male Integrated Business Administration major who sojourned in Canada)

> I'm now more motivated to learn about the Hong Kong insurance market, as I've decided I get a job here after graduation. After seeing England and America, I don't have a strong desire to go to other cultures. I don't really want to work there because the Chinese are a minority and you will encounter much resistance and many annoying things. I won't have these problems in Hong Kong. Another reason is that the living style in America is not suitable for me. The public facilities and living space are good enough, but I don't like the

food. I am quite picky about that. Although some may like the relaxing lifestyle of Americans, I'm an ambitious person and think youngsters should work hard when they're young. (Male Professional Accountancy major who sojourned in the USA)

When I was young I thought about working or living abroad. My imagination of America at that time was all good, but after my two visits I've changed my idea. America is not as good as I imagined. Also, my parents play a bigger role in my life now and I want to stay close to my family. If I get a job in Hong Kong and my company offers me the chance to go back to Beijing I'll take it because my home and family are there. Although China has many problems, it has great potential as an emerging economy. Also, America has a lot of problems, too. Personally, I think China is a good place. From my observation of the ABCs (American-born Chinese) that I encountered in the USA, Chinese people are more conservative and traditional in thinking, and I prefer this. Now I'm very clear about my short-term future plans. At least, I don't feel confused any more. (Male, Business Administration major who sojourned in the USA)

Significantly, these returnees still made little or no effort to interact with international students on their home campus. They quickly returned to familiar routines and their tight circle of co-national friends, raising doubts about the benefits of their semester abroad.

Summary and discussion of key findings

A comparison of the pre- and post-IDI scores for the experimental and control groups suggests that the semester abroad positively impacted the students' intercultural development and readiness for the global workplace. A review of the Pre- and Post-international Exchange Survey results and interview transcripts, however, revealed some interesting variations in the developmental trajectories of the student sojourners. Those who experienced the greatest gains in intercultural competence according to the IDI demonstrated more interest in global issues and expressed a stronger desire for further international experience and intercultural relationships. More confident in their second language skills, they indicated more willingness to initiate conversations with people who have a different linguistic and cultural background. As well as enhanced self-efficacy in their second language, these individuals generally perceived themselves to be more 'global-ready,' that is, they felt better prepared to work in a multicultural environment.

Interestingly, before and after the semester, both cohorts significantly overestimated their intercultural competence, which may be due to a range of factors, including the desire to maintain a positive self-image (e.g., Fischer, Greitemeyer, & Frey, 2007; Kruger, 1999) and biased reference points (Alicke & Govorun, 2005). This finding may help explain why few students recognized the merits of an intercultural communication course prior to international experience. While abroad, most of the participants in the experimental group experienced intercultural misunderstandings and sometimes found it difficult to adjust to unfamiliar ways of being, especially in the first few weeks. Back on home soil, some regretted their limited participation in the host environment and acknowledged that they had not achieved their goal of establishing meaningful connections with host nationals. When prompted to reflect on their sojourn, some interviewees stated that they better understood the potential benefits of an intercultural communication course prior to education abroad; most recommended it for future exchange students.

In the experimental group, a complex array of internal and external factors influenced the development of intercultural competence, second language self-efficacy, and global-mindedness. Variations in expectations, sojourn goals, attitudes toward the host language and culture, degree of openness, willingness to communicate in the host language, and personality characteristics (e.g., degree of extroversion) led to differing developmental trajectories. While agency played a pivotal role, external elements also influenced how the sojourns unfolded. Some receiving institutions provided orientations for new arrivals and made an effort to integrate local and international students throughout the semester by way of innovative informal activities and coursework, whereas other institutions provided little or no support. Some exchange students found host nationals welcoming, whereas others found it difficult to break into tight social circles that had formed years earlier.

Housing arrangements also proved to be an influential factor. Some student sojourners shared a room on campus with either a host national or an international student who spoke another first language. This helped some of the newcomers to diversify their social network, gain practice in using the host language, and feel more at home; others, however, spent very little time with their roommate, citing cultural differences as a barrier. Those who opted to live with other students from Hong Kong or Mainland China (e.g., in an off-campus apartment) tended to have social networks that were not diverse. Unless they made an effort to participate in extra-curricular activities with students from other cultural backgrounds, they gained little opportunity to use their second language in informal social situations and had limited, informal exposure to the host culture.

The findings indicate that simply being present in the host environment for a semester does not magically lead to intercultural competence, more interest in international affairs, advanced second language proficiency, and more readiness for the global workplace. While the experimental group, as a whole, experienced gains in intercultural competence, there were individual variations within this cohort, and the analyses of the qualitative data, in particular, pointed to multiple internal and external elements that contributed to diverse outcomes. Similar to other recent studies of education abroad learning, the results illustrate the idiosyncratic nature of student sojourns (e.g., Kinginger, 2009; Vande Berg et al., 2012) and underscore the benefits of systematically gathering both qualitative and quantitative data in education abroad research.

It is also important to note the limitations of this study. Although an objective measure of intercultural competence was employed in this research, much of the data were in the form of self-reports, which rely on the honesty, openness, and memories of the participants. Interviewees, for example, were encouraged to recount their international, intercultural experiences and disclose their perceptions of and reactions to intercultural encounters. On these occasions, they were presenting their *versions* of events and experiences, which may have been incomplete and inaccurate. As noted by Pavlenko (2007, p. 180), 'narratives constitute, rather than reflect reality' and care must be taken when interpreting data of this nature. While the participants in the present study appeared to candidly reveal short-comings and missteps, caution must be exercised when interpreting these first person accounts.

Conclusion

As we move further into the second decade of the 21st century, international education has the potential to build dramatically the intercultural competence of the next generation of global leaders. This vision can be realized by recognizing (a) that the immersion assumption cannot support the development of intercultural competence and (b) that intercultural competence is teachable, learnable, and achievable if learning interventions are appropriately designed based on the developmental mindset of the student. (Hammer, 2012, p. 134)

The results of the present study lend support to the observation of Hammer (2012) and many other interculturalists (e.g., Engle & Engle, 2012; Vande Berg et al., 2012) who recognize that studying abroad does not necessarily lead to intercultural competence and readiness for the global workplace. Accordingly, more education abroad researchers are advocating systematic intervention at all stages of international education: pre-sojourn, sojourn, and reentry (Paige & Vande Berg, 2012; Vande Berg et al., 2012). Carefully designed, research-inspired intercultural communication courses can help students develop the skills and mindset necessary to nurture meaningful intercultural relationships and bring about deeper levels of engagement in the host environment. Intercultural education (e.g., pre-sojourn modules, sojourn coursework, reentry debriefings) should take into account the students' levels of intercultural competence, global-mindedness, and second language proficiency/self-efficacy. Curricula and related activities will be most effective when relevant and appropriate for the participants (Bennett, 2004; Hammer, 2013; Stuart, 2012).

As the number of education abroad students is rising significantly in many parts of the world, it is difficult for institutions to provide sufficient face-to-face intercultural communication courses for all participants, and brief predeparture orientations that largely focus on logistics (e.g., security, the transfer of credits) are inadequate. In these situations, while perhaps not ideal, online support can play a useful role in the enhancement of education abroad learning by promoting ongoing critical reflection and meaning-making. Developed by the Center for Global Education, the *Global Scholar* website now provides online courses for study abroad students at all phases: pre-sojourn, sojourn, and post-sojourn (Rhodes, 2011). Derived from intercultural principles and theory, this site integrates materials from the University of Minnesota's innovative 'Maximizing Study Abroad' project (Paige, Cohen, Kappler, Chi, & Lassegard 2006) as well as the *What's Up with Culture?* website (La Brack, 2003). While *the Global Scholar* is primarily targeted at American students, *iStudent 101: Online learning for international students*, a new site, has been designed with international students in mind (see *http://istudent101.com*).

To enhance the global-readiness of international exchange students, much more work needs to be done in various contexts to better understand the developmental trajectories of student sojourners and determine the most effective and appropriate interventions. In particular, ethnographic investigations of student sojourners in different education abroad programs and host environments would help us to better understand and support second language, culture, and disciplinary learning. Detailed case studies of successful interventions (e.g., intercultural transition courses, blended intercultural communication courses with on-site instruction and online learning) are needed to enrich our field. By sharing accounts of successful practice, we can help more students optimize international experience and become better prepared for the competitive, interconnected world in which we live and work.

Funding

The investigation of the learning of semester abroad exchange students from the Chinese University of Hong Kong has been supported by General Research Fund grants [grant number #4280012], [grant number 4440713] from the Research Grants Council of Hong Kong and Teaching Development Grants [grant number #4170338], [grant number #4170356] from the Chinese University of Hong Kong. It would not have been possible without the participation of the exchange students. I am also grateful to the local and international students in my *Intercultural Transitions* course whose insights provided direction for the reshaping of interview protocols and surveys.

Disclosure statement

No potential conflict of interest was reported by the author.

References

Alicke, M. D., & Govorun, O. (2005). The better-than-average effect. In M. D. Alicke, D. A. Dunning, & J. I. Krueger (Eds.), *The self in social judgment* (pp. 85–108). Hove: Psychology.

Bazeley, P., & Jackson, K. (2013). *Qualitative data analysis with NVivo* (2nd ed.). Thousand Oaks, CA: Sage.

Bennett, J. M. (2004). Turning frogs into interculturalists: A student-centered developmental approach to teaching intercultural competence. In R. A. Goodman, M. Phillips, & N. Boyacigiller (Eds.), *Crossing cultures: Insights from master teachers* (pp. 312–342). London: Routledge.

Bennett, M. J. (1986). Towards ethnorelativism: A developmental approach to training for intercultural sensitivity. *International Journal of Intercultural Relations, 10*(2), 179–196.

Bhandari, R., & Blumenthal, P. (2011). Global student mobility and the twenty-first century silk road: National trends and new directions. In R. Bhandhari & Blumentahl (Eds.), *International students and global mobility in higher education* (pp. 1–24). New York, NY: Palgrave MacMillan.

Deardorff, D. (Ed.). (2009). *The SAGE handbook of intercultural competence*. Thousand Oaks, CA: Sage.

Deardorff, D. K., & Hunter, W. (2006). Educating Global-ready graduates. *International Educator, 15*(3), 72–83.

Ehrman, M. E. (1996). *Understanding second language acquisition*. Oxford: Oxford University Press.

Engle, L., & Engle, J. (2012). Beyond immersion: The American University Center of Province experiment in holistic intervention. In M. Vande Berg, R. M. Paige, & K. H. Lou (Eds.). *Student learning abroad: What our students are learning, what they're not, and what we can do about it* (pp. 284–307). Sterling, VA: Stylus.

Fantini, A. (2009). Assessing intercultural competence: Issues and tools. In D. Deardorff (Ed.). *The SAGE handbook of intercultural competence* (pp. 456–476). Thousand Oaks, CA: Sage.

Fantini, A. (2012). Multiple strategies for assessing intercultural communicative competence. In J. Jackson (Ed.). *The Routledge handbook of language and intercultural communication* (pp. 390–405). London: Routledge.

Fischer, P., Greitemeyer, T., & Frey, D. (2007). Ego depletion and positive illusions: Does the construction of positivity require regulatory resources? *Personal and Social Psychology Bulletin, 33*, 1306–1321. doi:10.1177/0146167207303025

Graham, S., & Weiner, B. (1995). Theories and principles of motivation. In D. Berliner & R. Calfee (Eds.), *Handbook of educational psychology* (pp. 63–84). New York, NY: MacMillan.

Guilherme, M., Glaser, E., & Méndez-García, M. C. (Eds.). (2010). *The intercultural dynamics of multicultural working*. Bristol: Multilingual Matters.

Hammer, M. R. (2009a). The intercultural development inventory: An approach for assessing and building intercultural competence. In M. A. Moodian (Ed.), *Contemporary leadership and intercultural competence: Exploring the cross-cultural dynamics within organizations* (pp. 203–217). Thousand Oaks, CA: Sage.

Hammer, M. R. (2009b). Intercultural development inventory version 3 (IDI) education group profile report. Retrieved from http://idiinventory.com/pdf/idi_sample.pdf

Hammer, M. R. (2012). The intercultural development inventory: A new frontier in assessment and development of intercultural competence. In M. Vande Berg, R. M. Paige, & K. H. Lou (Eds.),

Student learning abroad: What our students are learning, what they're not, and what we can do about it (pp. 115–136). Sterling, VA: Stylus.

Hammer, M. R. (2013). *A resource guide for effectively using the intercultural development inventory (IDI)*. Berlin: IDI, LLC.

Holmes, P. (2012). Business and management education. In J. Jackson (Ed.). *The Routledge handbook of language and intercultural communication* (pp. 464–480). Oxford: Routledge.

Hunter, W. D. (2004). *Knowledge, skills, attitudes, and experience necessary to become globally competent* (Unpublished Ph.D. dissertation). Lehigh University, Bethlehem, PA.

Institute of International Education. (2013). *2013 Open Doors Report*. Retrieved from http://www.iie.org/Research-and-Publications/Open-Doors

Jackson, J. (2012). Education abroad. In J. Jackson (Ed.). *The Routledge handbook of language and intercultural communication* (pp. 449–463). London: Routledge.

Jackson, J. (2013). The transformation of 'a frog in the well: A path to a more intercultural, global mindset. In C. Kinginger (Ed.). *The social turn in study abroad research* (pp. 179–204). Amsterdam: John Benjamins.

Jenkins, J. (2013) *English as a lingua franca in the international university.* London: Routledge.

Kälvermark, T., & van der Wende, M. C. (1997). *National policies for internationalization of higher education in Europe.* Stockholm: National Agency for Higher Education.

Kinginger, C. (2009). *Language learning and study abroad: A critical reading of research.* Basingstoke: Palgrave Macmillan.

Knight, J. (2004). Internationalization remodeled: Definition, approaches, and rationales. *Journal of Studies in International Education, 8*(1), 5–31. doi:10.1177/1028315303260832

Kruger, J. (1999). Lake Wobegon be gone! The 'below-average effect' and the egocentric nature of comparative ability judgments. *Journal of Personality and Social Psychology, 77*, 221–232. doi:10.1037/0022-3514.77.2.221

La Brack, B. (2003). *What's up with culture?* Retrieved from http://www2.pacific.edu/sis/culture/

Paige, R. M., Cohen, A. D., Kappler, B., Chi, J. C., & Lassegard, J. P. (2006). *Maximizing study abroad: A student's guide to strategies for language and culture learning and use* (2nd ed.). Minneapolis: University of Minnesota.

Paige, R. M., & Vande Berg, M. (2012). Why students are and are not learning abroad: A review of recent research. In M. Vande Berg, R. M. Paige, & K. H. Lou (Eds.). *Student learning abroad: What our students are learning, what they're not, and what we can do about it* (pp. 29–58). Sterling, VA: Stylus.

Pavlenko, A. (2007). Autobiographic narratives as data in applied linguistics. *Applied Linguistics, 28*, 163–188. doi:10.1093/applin/amm008

Rhodes, G. (2011). *Global scholar: Online learning for study abroad.* Retrieved from http://www.globalscholar.us/

Sharifian, F., & Jamarani, M. (2013). Language and intercultural communication: From the old era to the new one. In F. Sharifian & M. Jamarani (Eds.). *Language and intercultural communication in the new era* (pp. 1–19). New York, NY: Routledge.

Sorrells, K. (2012). Intercultural training in the global context. In J. Jackson (Ed.). *Routledge handbook of language and intercultural communication* (pp. 372–389). London: Routledge.

Sorrells, K. (2013). *Intercultural communication: Globalization and social justice.* Thousand Oaks, CA: Sage.

Stuart, D. K. (2012). Taking stage development seriously: Implications for study abroad. In M. Vande Berg, R. M. Paige, & K. H. Lou (Eds.). *Student learning abroad: What our students are learning, what they're not, and what we can do about it* (pp. 61–89). Sterling, VA: Stylus.

United Nations Educational, Scientific and Cultural Organization (UNESCO). (2013). *Global flow of tertiary-level students.* Retrieved from http://www.unesco.org/new/en/

Vande Berg, M., Connor-Linton, J., & Paige, R. M. (2009). The Georgetown Consortium Project: Interventions for student learning abroad. *Frontiers: The Interdisciplinary Journal of Study Abroad, XVIII*, 1–76.

Vande Berg, M., Paige, R. M., & Lou, K. H. (2012). Student learning abroad: Paradigms and assumptions. In M. Vande Berg, R. M. Paige, & K. H. Lou (Eds.). *Student learning abroad: What our students are learning, what they're not, and what we can do about it* (pp. 3–28). Sterling, VA: Stylus.

The impact of international students on the university work environment: a comparative study of a Canadian and a Danish university

Jane Vinther[a] and Gordon Slethaug[b]

[a]Institute of Language and Communication, University of Southern Denmark, Odense, Denmark;
[b]Department of English Language and Literature, University of Waterloo, Waterloo, ON, Canada

Increasingly students want to go abroad to study – to further their knowledge of English, experience a new culture and cultivate skills. Universities have been actively courting these students, sometimes without regard to their impact on responsibilities of heads of department, secretaries and support staff. Much is written on the intercultural aspects of the international teaching and learning environment, but almost nothing has appeared on the impact of international students on the university work environment, so it is necessary and opportune to discover what is being done, where problems lie and what could be improved. Based on a survey of lecturers and frontline administrative staff, this paper explores workplace perceptions of different cultural discourses, intercultural practices and relations among international students, academics and administrative staff in two universities in Canada and Denmark chosen to explore differences between Europe and North America. For the most part, academics and support staff all think that internationalization has brought many benefits to the university: intercultural diversity and awareness, strong work ethic and study habits, intellectual curiosity and a more interesting social environment. They also note problems of proficiency in English, culture clashes inside and outside the classroom and higher dropout rates, depression and anxiety.

Studerende i stadig større tal vælger at tage til udlandet for at studere – bl.a. for at opnå bedre engelskkundskaber, opleve en ny kultur og opdyrke andre færdigheder. Disse unge studerende er blevet efterspurgte hos universiteterne, men ofte er det sket uden nærmere overvejelse omkring påvirkningen på ansatte som undervisere, sekretærer, studieledere og studievejledere. Der er forsket meget i interkulturelle aspekter af internationalisering af undervisning og læringsmiljø, men der findes mindre dokumentation for, hvorledes det stigende antal internationale studerende påvirker universitetets arbejdsmiljø. Denne artikel baserer sig på en spørgeskemaundersøgelse blandt undervisere og administrativt personale, og har til formål at undersøge de forskellige kulturelle diskurser, praksis og relationer mellem studerende, akademikere og administratorer på to universiteter i henholdsvis Canada og Danmark til illustration af problemstillinger i henholdsvis Europa og Nordamerika. Den fremherskende holdning er, at internationalisering har bragt mange fordele med sig: interkulturel diversitet, en styrket arbejdsetik og gode studievaner, intellektuel nysgerrighed og et mere interessant socialt miljø. Modsat påpeges der også problemer med niveauet i engelskkundskaberne, kultursammenstød både i og uden for undervisningen, stigende frafald, depression og angst.

Introduction: divergent stakeholders and discourse groups

The university workplace contains numerous stakeholders who do not necessarily share the same discourse communities or apply the same discursive strategies. The first division is between external and internal stakeholders, i.e., government policy-makers and civil servants on the 'outside' and university administrators, lecturers/researchers and support staff on the 'inside'. In its own category are the students who benefit from these stakeholders' efforts, but who often have little involvement and say in the decision processes. As illustrated in this study, the work environment of the lecturers and support staff who serve international students is highly complex and requires communication across various discourse groups even while being impacted by globalization, the development of the mass-university and the administrative decisions of policy-makers. Based on questionnaires administered to faculty and staff at a Danish and a Canadian university, this paper analyzes the ways in which frontline faculty and staff within the university perceive the impact of internationalization and how they are trying to remain faithful to ideals of quality while managing the challenges of everyday multilingual and intercultural interactions.

This paper will first characterize the two universities in Denmark and Canada that are the objects of this study. It will then discuss the qualitative methodology on which the findings are based. Next, it will analyze the work environment as historically tied to national and local values but increasingly under the test of globalization and internation-alization. It will explore the concerns but largely positive responses of faculty and staff to the increasing diversity of the student population and the internationalization of the classroom. There is clearly significant benefit in the international classroom, but because of varying expectations and different backgrounds and discourses of the students and faculty/staff, cultural clashes do arise, especially around language and communication issues. Because Denmark and Canada both share in educational values that first arose in Enlightenment Germany, students who come from outside this frame of reference and educational scaffolding may have difficulties, but intercultural communication and dialogue can be of assistance, so that faculty and staff can celebrate the rising of the international university, even though not all of the necessary building blocks are in place.

The study

Universities under study

The Canadian university is a top-ranked research and teaching institution with nearly 40,000 undergraduate and graduate students and 4000 full-time employees on four campuses with many links to business and industry and with far-flung global relation-ships. It is one of the top receivers of international students in Canada with more than one in three of its students from over 100 countries in Asia, Africa, Europe and all of the Americas (North, Central and South). International students who come only for study represent 35% of the graduate students and 12% of the undergraduate students, but there are many others taking out citizenship who are not counted as 'international'. Most go into science, mathematics and technology-related programmes, though most faculties and departments have some international students.

The Danish University is one of the largest in Denmark with more than 27,000 students and 4000 employees on six campuses. It has both undergraduate and graduate programmes with most students taking a BA and MA, though the Ph.D. portion is more limited in scale than in the Canadian institution. International students come from some 40 countries from Europe, Asia, North and South America and the Middle East, but, because tuition is free for students from the EU, many originate from Europe − 25% come from Germany. The proportion of international students is around 20% – 5000 international students in 2013. This Danish institution has comprehensive programmes in arts, science and engineering, though less practically oriented than in the Canadian university. The satisfaction of internationals students resulted in an 'Award for Excellent International Student Satisfaction' with a score of 9.1 out of 10 (http://www.studyportals.eu/).

Methodology

Universities keep records of the flow of international students, but not of faculty and staff perceptions of this enterprise, so that little is known about the impact of international education on the work environment. Consequently, a questionnaire consisting of 10 open-ended questions was administered to those directly responsible for dealing with international students in many different faculties from application to graduation stages. These questions (see Appendix 1) concentrated on:

- perceived *benefits and/or problems* of international students
- their *academic achievement*
- their *social integration*
- *staff behaviour* when dealing with international students
- ways internationalization *pushes and pulls* programmes and administrative decisions

Responses varied from three pages to 10, and respondents could sign their names (this was not required, but most did), enabling follow-up, if necessary. Most had never before been polled about the international dimension of their work and were delighted to voice opinions about their very demanding positions. The authors of this study both had access to the total results, analyzed the results independently, and then compared their findings. The strength of this qualitative study was its ability to discover faculty and staff opinion in depth, but the weakness was that some faculty and staff chose not to complete the questionnaire because it seemed too demanding.

Though decisions about international education may have been taken at governmental levels, each university has to plan and pay for its own implementation, meaning that slightly different groups of professionals were targeted in each university because of different work cultures. Denmark has seen the establishment of international offices in each university, with pedagogical and administrative adjustments placed on individual faculties and departments, including the head, faculty members and secretaries. Consequently, the survey undertaken addressed mainly faculty members and secretaries dedicated to particular study programmes. In Canada, by contrast, most universities follow their own lights with only a few governmental guidelines, and individual faculties, departments and centres are able to admit and assist international students as they see fit. Hence, the Canadian survey addressed faculty and staff members who provided assistance in programme planning, course requirements, scholarships, English-language instruction, housing, health care, transportation and employment.

In Canada invitations to participate were hand-delivered to particular departments and centres, and the questionnaire was filed through Survey Monkey. In Denmark the questionnaires were electronically delivered and collected internally. Eight faculty and staff members responded in Denmark (all but one in English), while 19 responded in Canada (all in English). Altogether, these respondents consisted of: heads of departments who handled administrative issues for international students; faculty members and secretaries in charge of coordinating graduate and undergraduate programmes; 'regular' faculty members teaching international and local students; faculty members in English as a Second Language (ESL) programmes; and administrative assistants in charge of recruitment, student advisement and employment.

The work environment
National, local and international

Though employees are expected to 'leave their beliefs' at the door when entering the workplace, many argue that workplace and national cultures are closely related (De Mooij, 2011; Scollon, Scollon, & Jones, 2012), especially in the field of education. Hofstede asserts that nations 'are the source of a considerable amount of common mental programming of their citizens' (1997, p. 12), but others like McSweeney (2002), challenged this view, indicating that in an increasingly global world, this nation/work/ education link is dubious. Though Hofstede did not back down (2002; Minkov & Hofstede, 2012), Rizvi (2011, pp. 693, 697) claims that the 'shifting social imaginaries of people' are 'broadly linked to the processes of globalization', so that it is increasingly possible to separate nation and work:

> Driven largely by developments in information and communication technologies, globaliza- tion has given rise to new forms of transnational interconnectivity. It has implied that while people continue to live in particular localities, these localities are increasingly integrated into larger systems of global networks.

Despite advancing globalization and differences in enculturation and acculturation processes, they are similarly embedded and imbricated in culture physically and psychologically, whether in the marketplace or in higher education. Equally, though the internationalizing of education is shifting identities to the global stage, university culture – whether Western, Eastern or one of the many variations within and between them – is still embedded and adapted to national culture, though the national 'platform' may be fraught with regional, ethnic and gender differences. Still, as Keeling notes of the internationalizing education strategies in the EU (2006, p. 203):

> The Bologna Process is an intergovernmental commitment to restructuring higher education systems which extends far beyond the EU and the Lisbon Strategy is part of the Union's wider economic platform that extends beyond the higher education sector. In combination, these European-level actions are supporting and stabilizing an emergent policy framework for the EU in higher education.

While these policies are meant to reshape European higher education generally, each university must provide the means and structures to accomplish this goal within national contexts, but with less attention paid to the internationalization of curriculum or employees.

While formal academic structures (e.g., international offices) to accomplish these means are increasingly globally congruent, each institution has its own formal and informal power structures to accomplish these goals. The actual means by which this process is accomplished has real consequences for local staff, faculty and students, affecting interactional relationships, work and study conditions and operative discourses. Putting pressure on this internal process is the rapid escalation in the number of students that move across borders and continents to educate themselves, simultaneously embodying globalization and coping with its consequences.

Increasing international student enrolment and workplace pressures

The university administration, lecturers, frontline staff, home and international students – all run into problems because internationalization, multilingualism and multiculturalism as vision and practice have yet to be realized. A chorus of scholars (Gu & Schweisfurth, 2006; Leask, 2009; Ryan & Viete, 2009; Turner & Robson, 2008; Zheng, 2013) have noted that administrators only think of international competition and student enrolment, while curriculum and university operations have been largely ignored, leaving international students to make most of the adjustments (Coverdale-Jones, 2013; Ryan, 2010). What Cortazzi and Jin describe as the required 'cultural synergy' (2013, p. 100) and learning interchange between international students and receiving institution, and among the various academic and organization functions/discourses on campus, has yet to be realized.

Olcott (2009, p. 74) points to a dilemma facing universities and higher education by highlighting the schism between universities' acceptance of a rapidly growing number of international students and failure to provide funds for curriculum, academic development and support systems. Internationalization, then, fails to meet Knight's requirement (2004) that all university activities and operations have an 'international dimension'. Consequently, the discourse in good part remains simultaneously national (policies, funding and culture) and local (implementation and adjustment) but not fully international, the result being that the formal structures and support systems as well as curriculum planning and development are not well prepared for the new international reality.

As internationalization impacts on each university, disparate interest and discourse communities are often poised against each other, and staff and lecturers may experience a conflict between professional ideals and organizationally imposed expectations. To some extent, faculty and staff all adjust to time, place and function, but such discordant demands are unsustainable in the long run. This is particularly true when lecturers and staff are overburdened in having to serve too many students too quickly, and when the teaching community is subjected to changes that they feel compromise the traditional independence of teaching and learning.

In considering how actions and discourses relate, Foucault argued, 'it seems to me that "what is to be done" ought not to be determined from above by reformers, be they prophetic or legislative, but by a long work of comings and goings, of exchanges, reflections, trials, different analyses' (1991, p. 84). In effect, he argues against top-down control and for dialogue among those who initiate changing conditions and those who have to live with them, but neither of them are considering the financial dimensions to this localization. In the international university work environment, a number of internal top-down directives of change are guided by external principles and pressures rather than in-house conversations. As a result, heads of departments, individual professors and staff members must be inventive and flexible in finding ways to cope with daily problems of rapid internationalization. The strength and speed of this internationalization seems to have taken most universities by surprise.

Study results

Responses to increasing diversity

In the process of internationalizing universities, English-speaking countries such as Australia, Canada, the UK and the USA were the first to experience the global educational flow, but Canadian and Danish respondents indicate little distinction in recognizing and understanding the cultural and educational implications of the 'stranger' in the international university – though philosophies of the workplace differ. In Denmark some lecturers feel the pressure of maintaining traditional ideals of independent and autonomous learning and character formation within a liberal education tradition in the face of pressures from industry and government to provide work-related programmes for international and local students. In Canada, where universities take in stride the need to reconcile the training of minds and the cultivating of skills for the marketplace, staff members providing basic services and lecturers wanting to be true to their academic conviction while responding to the workplace are often overwhelmed by the escalating scale and complexity of international education.

Of course, the international students also experience the clash of discourses. In the Canadian institution under study, some 40% of students out of nearly 40,000 were born and raised outside of Canada and need support to study and live that goes well beyond the classroom. Although the Canadian university has scaffolding in place to find accommodation, choose courses, understand regulations, negotiate the health system, etc., little has been done to integrate international students academically and socially. These outside needs also characterize those coming to Denmark because, as one secretary noted, 'some students are very young and it is their first time of being away from home, so some struggle with basic things in everyday life (cooking, cleaning, etc.), and this can have an effect on their studies'. In Denmark these international students are expected to fend for themselves, although help with accommodation is provided.

In both the Danish and Canadian institutions, the rapid increase in volume of international students means that, to a considerable degree, success is measured in student workloads, dropout rates and completion times. To some extent, this concern is understandable because, as Lux notes, in Germany the dropout rate for international students is significantly higher than for home students (2013, p. 83), most likely because of language issues and problems with adaptation. In any case, this concern for the 'business' of international students' enrolment and academic progress means that personal formation and construction of identity are largely ignored. In this focus on numbers and progress, both home and international students suffer, but the international students doubly so because they are unlikely to have networks that can help them manoeuvre through the system and readily participate in the various discourses.

Pressure on universities to reshape programmes

Because international students can represent a strong mass (30% in mathematics in the Canadian university, and 50% in a work-related academic option in the Danish university), their presence can alter programmes and class dynamics. One Danish programme administrator asserted that 'certainly numbers (more so than particular destinations) push/pull programme administrative decisions'. As one Danish lecturer remarked:

> Some programmes have a high (sometimes more than 50%) percentage of international students as full-degree students (i.e., not exchange students) and this alters the whole concept of 'home' degree programmes. The realities of the multicultural and multilingual classroom (and university) have yet to be fully appreciated.

None of the academics or staff at either the Canadian or Danish university asserts that the presence of international students has forced fundamental revisions of academic programmes, but increasingly scholars advocate curriculum and organizational changes that consider the needs of the international students (Coverdale-Jones, 2013; Knight, 2004; Rizvi, 2011; Ryan & Viete, 2009). A Canadian faculty member responsible for administering a graduate programme noted the presence of many students from Iran who were as diverse in interest and background as the Canadians and speculated that:

> I suppose if we increased those numbers we'd want to spend more time looking into the educational system in Iran as a way to know what preparation they had so we could better offer them the best opportunity for success and build on their existing preparation. In general I think if the university committed to taking increased numbers of international students it would need to do a far better job of creating structural means of ensuring those students' success in terms of language learning (if needed) [and] integration.

There have been some small concessions in this respect at the Canadian university: revamping courses and requirements in the use of the English language, scheduling classes around Muslims' Friday prayers, and scheduling special class sections for women with head coverings. This is not curriculum reform, but it suggests a dialogue on student needs.

Valuing international students

Though the rapid escalation in the number of international students may put pressure on programmes and bring complications, international students do confer benefits and bring diversity to the university environment. Both the Danes and Canadians found them among the most adventurous, strong and qualified students. As one of the Danish lecturers noted, 'the best students get to go abroad', and another observed that 'International students bring a welcome diversity to the classroom context. They can introduce perspectives unknown to Danish students – lived intercultural experience and competence'.

Although Chinese students were reputed to be demanding (according to one Dane), Chinese and Middle Easterners not observant about time (according to many Danes and Canadians), Africans and Middle Easterners hierarchical and male-oriented (according to several Danes and Canadians) and Asians and southern and eastern Europeans careless about citation conventions in writing (according to many Danes and Canadians), faculty and staff were almost invariably affirmative of students' willingness to cooperate, try to do the right thing, and ultimately be thankful. A Canadian international employment coordinator said:

> They are patient, understanding and fun to work with; they are the reason why I have a job; interesting to talk to about coming to Canada, and seeing snow for the first time, or experiencing our heat, what they thought it would be like here in Canada.

This coordinator did notice, however, that:

> some from masculine, hierarchical cultures did not want to deal with women, and the answer we give them, isn't good enough because we are female. They continue to ask different people in our dept. the same question, until they feel they finally have the right answer (they have spoken to a male in a senior position).

A secretary from Denmark also mentioned that problems sometimes occur from 'cultural differences that clash with Danish rules, regulations and bureaucracy', and a faculty member found that the intellectual independence characteristic of Danish students did not always fit well with international students. According to Zhang and Xu (2007) and Tan and Weidman (2013), even the syllabus can pose a major cultural challenge for non-

Westerners because they do not realize the weight that it carries in the classroom and the need to follow it meticulously.

A Canadian undergraduate coordinator added that international students 'are highly invested in their studies' and set a high bar for the local students. Most are hard workers, and one Danish instructor said their 'work habits … are more intense than what Danish students are used to – which can be really beneficial and inspiring'. One scheduler in a popular work-oriented programme in Denmark particularly lauded the Germans who, he said, 'are a joy to administer – they are focused, intelligent, polite and respectful'.

The classroom and social environment

Although there are clearly home students and international students, the lines are becoming blurred. Because of globalization in general as well as the rising economies of Asia and Africa, war, social unrest and adverse economic circumstances, large numbers of people are on the move as immigrants, refugees or citizens of more than one country. As a result, they become 'home students' without the cultural background and understanding of higher education systems. For that reason, we will assume that the term 'international student' applies to all who have their pre-university qualification from a country other than their tertiary place of study. This is something Germans call *Bildungsausländer* (Lux, 2013, p. 83). Even so, in Canada it is increasingly common for mainland and Hong Kong Chinese students to spend their last high school years in Canada to be able to attend a Canadian university. So, even the above definition holds true only in the majority of cases.

International students often feel lonely (Lux, 2013, p. 86; Slethaug & Vinther, 2012) in their new environment, regardless of wanting to seek educational challenges outside their own cultural context. This tendency has multiple causes: lack of friends and family relations, insufficient knowledge of the local language, wish to stay within their own cultural framework and alienation when exposed to academic environments operating on different levels of explicitness, teaching methods, class management and levels of autonomy and self-regulation. On this issue, Lux (2013, p. 84) remarks that Chinese students in Germany live together and form small ghettos, apparently not wanting to form relationships with home students or even international students of different background. One of the Danish instructors corroborated that 'the international students tend to group together with people from their own country or with other international students'. Consequently, those who go abroad to study often find it hard to build international relationships given a tendency to keep personal relationships apart from those in the classroom. The flip side of this observation is that in Germany international students 'complain that their German peers (and teachers) show little interest in them' (Lux, 2013, p. 86). This scenario plays out in Denmark as well where few staff are appointed to care for these students because, as one Danish lecturer indicated, 'social integration of international students may not be seen as the responsibility of the department'. In Canada, these appointments do exist, but the academic and administrative staff are often frustrated by their lack of ability to help all the needy students, especially because of linguistic difficulties, financial shortfalls or general inability to adapt. One Canadian staff member said that it is 'often difficult to get those who struggle to accept that and seek assistance before it is too late to help'.

Language issues and academic and social integration

Central to the success of international students is their ability to speak the language of instruction, but studies have shown that many international students consider 'English language as the biggest challenge and barrier' (Tan & Weidman, 2013, p. 123), and, as one Canadian staff member from engineering noted, 'there can always be social clashes and language barriers that are hard to cross'. For both Canada and Denmark, the operative language for international students is English, except in Canadian French-speaking universities or Danish-medium courses of study. In Canada all English-medium lecturers must be proficient in English, which is a factor in the international students' selection of that country's universities. This is generally the case, although Canadian instructors and staff both commented that some professors in engineering and mathematics, for example, might be better speakers of the native languages of their students than of English per se. Ironically, this was a factor in attracting particular ethnic students to the instructor's classes, though it drove others away.

In Denmark there is potentially a three- or four-sided language problem in that none of the international students, home students, lecturers or administrators is necessarily a native or expert English speaker. To counter this perceived problem, the Association of Danish Universities created a 'Code of Conduct' (Danish Universities Website, 2010) insisting on an adequate level of English for lecturers. However, Danish universities cannot inaugurate remedial English courses for students because the Danish government does not finance remedial work. One staff member in Canada noted that:

> It is important to make English language tutoring and classes available to these students. But more particularly, speaking and comprehensive writing classes, since this will drastically improve their ability to communicate not only in the academic English world but in their day to day lives on campus.

This has been implemented at this university in Canada.

Although Slethaug (2007, p. 10) pointed out that when no one is 'native' to the modus operandi of the classroom, it is truly cross-cultural and 'everyone is an outsider because when teachers and students are from various countries [and/or language systems], there is no inside space that can be taken for granted', but when this happens, the international student is often singled out for blame or lack of expertise:

> Dichotomized between the international student group and the domestic student group, the deficit model of internationalisation regards international students as less able to contribute to the learning environment because of their English language proficiency levels. A review of the literature of models of internationalisation in Canada, Australia, and the United Kingdom, for example, strongly suggest that these models subscribe to the ethnocentric worldview. (Patel & Lynch, 2013, p. 226)

In Denmark classes may easily run two to three hours, and yet another language issue arises because informal exchanges with lecturers and home students take place in Danish in breaks and even during class, adding to the feeling of insecurity for international students who will not know if they missed something essential.

Frontline staff members at the Canadian institution also commented that admonitions to international students often went unheeded because they did not understand English well enough to know what they should do and were afraid to lose face by asking. This was serious enough in classroom matters but doubly serious when students were trying to negotiate the Canadian health or legal system, or applying for jobs both during and following degree programmes.

In addition to the classroom and societal problems for those who lack English skills, in Denmark the Danish language is the preferred mode of communication for home students among themselves, which may create a feeling of exclusion, loneliness and estrangement for international students who may be struggling with English but have no knowledge of Danish. As one responding head of department mentions, social integration may be the biggest challenge in international education in Denmark, because Danes are noted for having a 'coconut' shell because of their diffidence to strangers. Surveys by anthropologist Dennis Nørmark (2012) show that Danes are not for short-time relationships, but once a relationship happens, they are friends for life. If they know that people will be around for only two to three years, they are reluctant to engage in social relations. It is paradoxical that class articulation and oral participation are expected of lecturers and students, but outside class, Danes are not used to involving themselves with everyone. In Denmark this can be a result of the traditional homogeneity of the population, though this is changing (Oxford Research, 2010). From the official university position, however, this is a social rather than academic problem and as such beyond its purview. Indeed, it runs through the responses from both Denmark and Canada that neither lecturers nor departments see socialization as their responsibility.

This isolation may not just be a Danish or Canadian problem. Studies from the USA (Lee & Rice, 2007; Sherry, Thomas, & Chui, 2010, p. 35) have shown that universities expect international students to adapt, but students do not easily form friendships outside class. Similarly, as Slethaug and Manjula (2013) have indicated about international students in Malaysia, social integration with home students and the local population is a worldwide problem without an easy solution. Nevertheless, respondents overwhelmingly indicate that in most cases students get along well, and friendships do develop, though not so frequently as desired. One easily implemented initiative would be to offer instructors seminars in intercultural communication (Ladegaard, in press) and involve them in the social side of internationalization inside and outside the classroom. Professional identity and self-image may be obstacles to this solution, but it would assist work in the classroom and facilitate engagement among faculty and students.

Study results: clash of norms, expectations and consequences for communication
Different discourse communities: following the system

At the present time, incoming international students are prepared for many linguistic, cultural and organizational differences, but may not be prepared for the total variance in discourses between their home cultures and those of Northern European and/or North American academic and organizational contexts. As one Canadian graduate coordinator noted, 'Cultural diversity is always an asset in any environment but with diversity comes conflict and cultural differences which can result in problems with communication, personal interactions, policy implementation, etc'.

These differences are evident inside and outside the classroom in expectations from lecturers, staff and counsellors based in good part on the belief that each person is responsible for his/her own autonomous development and ability to cope with the 'system'. The academic discourses for teachers and students alike in both the Northern European and North American contexts arise from the Enlightenment views of Germany's Wilhelm von Humboldt, who believed that learning should not be rote but rather should focus on independent, autonomous critical thinking for both teacher and student. It is ultimately the student who is responsible for his/her education (Vinther & Slethaug, 2013). These expectations can especially pose problems for those from communally oriented cultures.

This notion of the autonomous and independent student responsible for his/her education is inherent in the set-up of services and communication systems though manifested differently in Denmark and Canada. In each case, values, norms and tacit understandings all work towards a particular formation of standards and systems. As one Canadian administrative assistant in graduate studies noted, students may be surprised and also not wholly comfortable with new cultural ways, however well intentioned:

> I find international students are not as aware of university procedures as others, sometimes due to a language barrier. I have also found that international students are often not familiar with the type of friendly natured relationships that we have in our university. Often in their home universities there is quite a distance between students and faculty members, or even admin staff, whereas here we are very welcoming, warm, and friendly which often comes as a surprise and takes some getting used to by our students.

From Danish and Canadian perspectives, friendliness from a staff member may be expected, but other cultures may find it foolish and compromising. As one Danish instructor mentioned, 'the informality of the Danish system can be misinterpreted (friendly teachers perceived as buddies = passed exams with good marks)'.

Also, because the student may have been raised in a culture where it is impolite to question authority or to show ignorance of procedures, faculty and staff may not understand how they have violated the students' own cultural discourses even by smiling a lot. A supervisor of student accounts in Canada asserted that 'it's hard to tell if they truly understand procedures and directions they're to follow', causing intercultural communication issues and financial and academic hardship. These are common kinds of cultural clashes and communication problems that accompany such acculturation, but staff members in Canada noted that depression, anxiety and psychological problems are much higher among international students than local ones. This was not an observable result in the data from Denmark, however. But, acculturation takes place at any institution or workplace – it has been experienced by every adult when taking up or changing employment positions. There is a big difference, though, between becoming acculturated to different tasks in one's own culture and attempting that when totally immersed in a foreign one. The success of the individual in mastering the new reality will depend on the availability of understanding and support, in addition to clear guidelines and manuals – though unfortunately these are not always crystal clear, if they exist at all.

Different discourse communities: the classroom and society

Universities tend to assume that all students can understand procedures, organizational and academic systems and diverse discourses, so the content of induction ceremonies and official webpages is supposedly enough. The official Danish universities' 'Study in Denmark' webpage (Danish Universities Association Home Page, 2014) describes the classroom as comprising 'innovative teaching methods and an informal learning environment designed to promote creativity, self-expression, analytical and critical thinking'. However, these features as well as 'open debate during class' and 'active participation and problem solving rather than passive listening' will not distinguish the Danish environment in any marked way from other Western universities. Indeed, missing is any indication of the Danish emphasis on directness, which international students often mention as a trait in teaching and conversation that they were not prepared for. To some degree in Canada, directness and culturally taboo topics can be problematic as well. As one female faculty member mentioned, international students:

> found that class discussion might feel more fraught because of underlying differences in communication style (some students are more direct than others for cultural reasons), perceptions of acceptable or taboo subjects, and comfort with the course material (e.g., I have found some of my graduate course material is sensitive for some students, international or otherwise but perhaps more markedly so for those from more conservative cultural backgrounds). This can lead to productive, if tense, discussion, but can also sometimes take up more class time in directions I hadn't anticipated and which I'm not sure further the course goals.

Another characteristic which may give rise to asymmetric behaviours and priorities is the fact that Danes often choose study programmes out of personal interest, as opposed to the Canadians' tendency to seek particular skills and steady employment as goals [Danmarks Erhvervsforsknings Akademi (DEA), 2013, p. 11–13]. This, however, may be changing in Denmark, too, for Danish humanities' programmes have declined in enrolment compared to those in business. For many years, Canadian universities have embraced the interface between the practical and the theoretical, incorporating practical fields like engineering and business along with traditional arts and science. In addition, subjects like English, Fine Arts and Communications share equally in well-paid work-study programmes across the country, so that Canadian faculty and staff have added responsibilities for their students.

Communication issues and consequences

Unquestionably, there is some slippage in communication and comprehension in this new internationalization of universities. As Ting-Toomey said, 'intercultural conflict typically starts off with miscommunication. Intercultural miscommunication often leads to misinterpretations and pseudo-conflict' (2003, p. 373). Intercultural miscommunication and different university procedures and discourses can be especially problematic for international students, an impediment to teaching and learning outcomes, and burdensome for staff in their complicated dealings with international students. As one Canadian staff member mentioned, 'there can always be social clashes and language barriers that are hard to cross'. Another commented that with many students coming from China, 'one challenge is participation in the classroom. Language preparation was a challenge, but we have had a strong program in place for 21 years to ensure ESL students have the skills they need to be successful in their program', while another attributed some such social and academic difficulties to a lack of funding: 'the international students typically can't afford to live on the amount of money we give them and they struggle financially which in turn causes them problems socially'.

Cultural intelligence, dialogue and different student groups

Plum, Achen, Dræby, and Jensen (2008) align their construct of cultural intelligence to Gardner's (1993) theory of multiple intelligences and advocate them to promote intercultural cooperation and understanding. Their concept has three dimensions: emotional, knowledge-based and pragmatic. These dimensions are similar to the physical, emotional and intellectual spaces that Slethaug (2007, p. 63) argues operate together in the classroom environment for all students. These dimensions interact in the multicultural workplace whenever individuals or groups from different cultures work together. Too little attention has been given to this area, but Plum et al. argue that cultivation of cultural intelligence (instead of affective factors alone) will make for better communication and decision-making.

The pragmatic side of cultural intelligence involves the students' understanding that the system of the host country constitutes a framework of power and that the university has the obligation to assist in negotiating this for the international students cannot sense this dynamic in the same way as the local students. The 'construction' of the classroom is thus an ongoing dynamic, shared equally by a responsible and responsive university and international students.

Two opposite types of strategies in the 'construction of the classroom' for international students are offered by our respondents: one says change nothing and be your usual friendly self; the other says be flexible and tolerant but maintain academic standards. One respondent advises recognition of the mutual support that academic and social integration provide. Others point out that lecturers need to be knowledgeable about customs and traditions in other countries and thus be better able to support international students. That could involve not only intercultural training of various sorts, but also the lecturers' self-reflection on their teaching methodologies: 'teachers must also be cognizant of the effect of the teaching methods they use, overt and covert messages that are delivered, and their powerful influence on learners' (Patel & Lynch, 2013, p. 227). This emphasis on self-awareness and engaging conversationally with students also applies to frontline staff who have to deal with international students on a minute-to-minute basis. Many at the Canadian institution note that such dialogue is important but also the need to stand back for a few minutes to examine the situation to see what can be improved at the moment and over time.

Similarly in the classroom, lecturers need to examine their views and the students about knowledge acquisition versus knowledge production. Lecturing places an emphasis on the acquisition of information rather than the co-construction of knowledge advocated in 'The Teaching Style in Denmark' (Study in Denmark, 2014), and international students need to understand the prevailing modes and ways to feel comfortable with them. One feature of an active and participatory style is the ability to listen, critique, learn from critique and engage in conversation and cooperation with peers. A supportive development for lecturers would be the possibility of incorporating a diversity of assessment methods in coursework to ensure a broad basis for everyone to find a method of assessment that they are comfortable with. Frontline staff in Canada say something similar: that the international students they counsel need to listen carefully, ask questions fully and critique the conversation until they know what to do; but they also indicate that there should be overcoding so that there are multiple ways by which students can come to understand the same material.

The culture in universities reflects standards and expectations nationally and internationally. Katz notes that in Canada 'managers prefer workers who step forward with new ideas and ways to solve problems and show what they know by sharing that knowledge with co-workers' (2000, p. 152), and problem-solving is frequently advocated as a tool and goal in the Canadian classroom. In Denmark no programme can achieve academic certification without first hearing and incorporating such comments from the businesses, industries or public authorities that are the potential employers of the graduates. The description of student life and educational philosophy from the 'Study in Denmark' website reflects a workplace culture documented in the Danish *Expat Study*:

Corresponding to the fact that many expats [in Denmark] experience a culture characterised by trust and self-management also means that it is expected that the employee takes initiative and decisions. In Danish work culture it is expected that the employees create and initiate their own tasks and the areas of expertise the individual wishes to develop. (Oxford Research, 2010, p. 32)

This quote illustrates general ideals which are also recognized classroom ideals, but while some international students are enthusiastic about it, others misinterpret approachability and informality to mean lax standards, as mentioned above.

Conclusion

Clearly, Danish and Canadian universities are becoming globalized, and this study has explored how faculty and staff perceive themselves as part of this intercultural and international process. While many acknowledge hitches when cultures and discourses clash in university classrooms and offices, most embrace the new reality and reflect on improved teaching techniques, course content and organizational practices. By reflecting on new international opportunities and means and goals as well as foundations rooted in local and national cultures, faculty, staff and students alike can acknowledge cultural differences and move forward in ways that will incorporate meaningful traditions and workplace improvements.

In our survey we see more similarities than differences between the situation in Denmark and Canada. In both countries, academics indicate some uncertainty as their classrooms become more diverse, English proficiency declines, enrolments shoot up, the emphasis shifts to the business world and curriculum comes under review to better incorporate international students. They are also uncertain how to combine traditional academic goals and proficiencies with new thinking about incorporating international and home students in and out of the classroom. The support staff in international offices and programme secretaries also experience new challenges but seem to find it easier to deal with as it does not fundamentally shift their self-image or pedagogical role. If there is a significant difference about perceived responsibilities and roles in the Danish and the Canadian university, it is that the Canadian staff members (as opposed to faculty) are much more involved in international students' lives, recognise it to be the case, and are happy about that.

Disclosure statement

No potential conflict of interest was reported by the authors.

References

Cortazzi, M., & Jin, L. (2013). Creativity and criticality: Developing dialogues of learning and thinking through synergy with China. In T. Coverdale-Jones (Ed.), *Transnational higher education in the Asian context* (pp. 97–117). Houndsmills: Palgrave Macmillan.

Coverdale-Jones, T. (2013). Introduction: The widening context of transnational higher education. In T. Coverdale-Jones (Ed.), *Transnational higher education in the Asian context* (pp. 1–12). Houndsmills: Palgrave Macmillan.

Danish Universities Association Home Page. (2014). *Teaching style in Denmark*. Retrieved April 24, 2014, from http://studyindenmark.dk/study-options/the-danish-way-of-teaching-1

Danish Universities Website. (2010). *Code of conduct for offering Danish university programmes to international students*. Retrieved April 24, 2014, from http://dkuni.dk/Internationalt/~/~/media/EAF3BA3FFA4A4A23A7511EF8D2EE17B0.ashx

Danmarks Erhvervsforsknings Akademi (DEA). (2013). *Motivation og Studieintensitet Hos Universitetsstuderende. En Spørgeskemaundersøgelse i Danmark, Sverige, Tyskland og England* [Motivation and study intensity of university students. A questionnaire survey in Denmark, Sweden, Germany, and England]. Copenhagen: Author.

De Mooij, M. (2011). *Consumer behavior and culture: Consequences for global marketing and advertising*. Los Angeles, CA: Sage.

Foucault, M. (1991). Questions of method. In B. Burchell, C. Gordon, & P. Miller (Eds.), *The Foucault effect: Studies in governmentality—with two lectures by and an interview with Michel Foucault* (pp. 53–86). Chicago, IL: Chicago University Press.

Gardner, H. (1993). *Multiple intelligences: The theory in practice*. New York, NY: BasicBooks.

Gu, Q., & Schweisfurth, M. (2006). Who adapts? Beyond cultural models of 'the Chinese learner'. *Language, Culture and Curriculum, 19*(1), 54–73. doi:10.1080/07908310608668754

Hofstede, G. (1997). *Cultures and organizations: Software of the mind*. New York, NY: McGraw-Hill.

Hofstede, G. (2002). Dimensions do not exist: A reply to Brendan McSweeney. *Human Relations, 55*, 1355–1361. doi:10.1177/0018726702055011921

Keeling, R. (2006). The Bologna process and the Lisbon research Agenda: The European commission's expanding role in higher education discourse. *European Journal of Education, 41*, 203–223. doi:10.1111/j.1465-3435.2006.00256.x

Knight, J. (2004). Internationalization remodeled: Definition, approaches, and rationales. *Journal of International Studies, 8*(5), 5–31.

Ladegaard, H. J. (in press). Personal experience and cultural awareness as resources in teaching intercultural communication: A Hong Kong case study. In G. E. Slethaug & J. Vinther (Eds.), *International teaching and learning at universities: Achieving equilibrium with local culture and pedagogy*. New York, NY: Palgrave Macmillan.

Leask, B. (2009). Using formal and informal curricula to improve interactions between home and international students. *Journal of Studies in International Education, 13*, 205–221. doi:10.1177/1028315308329786

Lee, J., & Rice, C. (2007). Welcome to America? International student perceptions of discrimination. *Higher Education, 53*, 381–409. doi:10.1007/s10734-005-4508-3

Lux, M. (2013). Challenges and measures related to the integration of Chinese students in Germany —The activities of a German foundation. In T. Coverdale-Jones (Ed.), *Transnational higher education in the Asian context* (pp. 82–94), Houndsmills: Palgrave Macmillan.

McSweeney, B. (2002). Hofstede's model of national cultural differences and their consequences: A triumph of faith—A failure of analysis. *Human Relations, 55*(1), 89–117. doi:10.1177/0018726702055001602

Minkov, M., & Hofstede, G. (2012). Is national culture a meaningful concept? Cultural values delineate homogeneous clusters of in-country regions. *Cross-Cultural Research, 46*, 133–159. doi:10.1177/1069397111427262

Nørmark, D. (2012). *Cultural intelligence for stone-age brains: How to work together with Danes and others not like you*. Copenhagen: Gyldendal.

Olcott Jr., D. (2009). Global connections—local impacts: Trends and developments for internationalism and cross-border higher education. In T. Coverdale-Jones & P. Rastall (Eds.), *Internationalising the university: The Chinese context* (pp. 72–84). London: Palgrave-Macmillan.

Oxford Research. (2010). *The expat study*. Copenhagen: The Oxford Research A/S and The Copenhagen Post. Retrieved November 17, 2013, from http://ec.europa.eu/ewsi/UDRW/images/items/docl_18218_429629354.pdf

Patel, F., & Lynch, H. (2013). Glocalization as an alternative to internationalization in higher education: Embedding positive global learning perspectives. *International Journal of Teaching and Learning in Higher Education, 25*, 223–230.

Plum, E., Achen, B., Dræby, I., & Jensen, I. (2008). *Cultural intelligence—The art of leading cultural complexity*. London: Libri.

Rizvi, F. (2011). Theorizing student mobility in an Era of globalization. *Teachers and Teaching: Theory and Practice, 17*, 693–701. doi:10.1080/13540602.2011.625145

Ryan, J. (2010). Chinese learners: Misconceptions and realities. In J. Ryan & G. Slethaug (Eds.), *International education and the Chinese learner* (pp. 37–56). Pok Fu Lam: Hong Kong University Press.

Ryan, J., & Viete, R. (2009). Respectful interactions: Learning with international students in the English-speaking academy. *Teaching in Higher Education, 14*, 303–314. doi:10.1080/13562510902898866

Scollon, R., Scollon, S. W., & Jones, R. H. (2012). *Intercultural communication: A discourse approach* (3rd ed.). Somerset, NJ: Wiley-Blackwell.

Sherry, M., Thomas, P., & Chui, W. H. (2010). International students: A vulnerable student population. *Higher Education, 60*, 33–46. doi:10.1007/s10734-009-9284-z

Slethaug, G. (2007). *Teaching abroad: International education and the cross-cultural classroom*. Hong Kong: Hong Kong University Press.

Slethaug, G., & Manjula, J. (2013). Interpreting Malaysian results in international education assessments. In T. Coverdale-Jones (Ed.), *Transnational higher education in the Asian context* (pp. 195–215). Houndsmills: Palgrave Macmillan.

Slethaug, G., & Vinther, J. (2012). The challenges of multi-lingualism for international students in Denmark. In J. Ryan (Ed.), *Cross-cultural teaching and learning for home and international students: Internationalisation of pedagogy and curriculum in higher education* (pp. 82–94). Abingdon: Routledge.

Slethaug, G., & Vinther, J. (Eds.). (in press). *International teaching and learning at universities: Achieving equilibrium with local culture and pedagogy*. New York, NY: Palgrave Macmillan.

Study in Denmark. (2014). *The teaching style in Denmark. Home page of the association of Danish universities*. Retrieved August 22, 2014, from http://studyindenmark.dk/study-options/the-danish-way-of-teaching-1

Tan, T., & Weidman, J. C. (2013). Chinese graduate students' adjustment to academic demands in American universities. In T. Coverdale-Jones (Ed.), *Transnational higher education in the Asian context* (pp. 118–131). Houndsmills: Palgrave Macmillan.

Ting-Toomey, S. (2003). Managing intercultural conflicts effectively. In L. A. Samovar & R. Porter (Eds.), *Intercultural communication. A reader* (pp. 373–384). Belmont, CA: Thomson Wadsworth.

Turner, Y., & Robson, S. (2008). *Internationalizing the university*. London: Continuum.

Vinther, J., & Slethaug, G. (2013). The Danish educational tradition: Multiple heritages and international challenges and 'conversation'. In L. Jin & M. Cortazzi (Eds.), *Researching intercultural learning* (pp. 58–77). London: Palgrave Macmillan.

Zhang, Z., & Xu, J. (2007). Understanding Chinese international graduate students' adaptation to learning in North America: A cultural perspective. *Higher Education Perspectives, 3*(1), 45–59.

Zheng, L. (2013). Insight into UK China articulation programmes and internationalisation: What has changed in the last few years? In T. Coverdale-Jones (Ed.), *Transnational higher education in the Asian context* (pp. 32–48). London: Palgrave Macmillan Press.

Appendix 1. Questionnaire

Questions:

(1) What country are you in, what is your job and what is your function in dealing with international students?

(2) In your opinion, what are the perceived benefits and/or problems that international students bring to your university or particular unit?

(3) What are the issues that departmental/programme staff must deal with concerning the academic achievement of international students?

(4) What are the issues that departmental/programme staff must deal with concerning the social integration of international students?

(5) Do you change your behaviour when dealing with international students? If so, how, and how might it impact your attitude to the job?

(6) What are the ways in which numbers of students from particular international destinations may push and pull programmes, learning, perceptions and administrative decisions within departments and have lasting effects?

(7) What countries do your international students typically come from? Are any of the issues from one country easier/more difficult to deal with than from others? If so, what are the reasons?

(8) What advice would you give to staff dealing with international students?

(9) What advice would you give to international students coming to your programme?

(10) Do you have any further comments?

'The cultural stuff around how to talk to people': immigrants' intercultural communication during a pre-employment work-placement

Prue Holmes

School of Education, Durham University, Durham, UK

This paper reports on a small in-depth study of 16 immigrants' intercultural communication experiences as they enter the workforce in New Zealand through a volunteer work-placement scheme. The key research questions are: What intercultural communication challenges do immigrants face during work-placement with (1) co-workers and (2) employer(s)? How is intercultural communication facilitated/constrained in intercultural encounters in the workplace? The findings highlight how cultural, social, economic, political and contextual factors support immigrants' intercultural communication and work experience in their respective organisation. The outcomes provide important feedback to employers, immigrant communities, funders and other voluntary organisations, community workers, and politicians on the value of work-placement programmes and the intercultural communication challenges immigrants face when entering the workplace.

本研究以跨国移民为调研对象, 选取了十六位由某志愿服务组织引荐到新西兰工作的移民, 对他们的跨文化交流经历进行了深入的调研。本文主要探索了他们在工作期间与同事、老板进行跨文化交流时遇到的挑战, 以及在跨文化的工作环境下如何促进或阻碍跨文化交流。根据研究结果, 本文概述了文化、社会、经济、政治及环境等因素如何助力移民的跨文化交流和工作。这为雇主、移民团体、相关的慈善基金会和志愿服务组织、社区工作者、以及执政者提供了重要的反馈信息, 从而为更好地发挥这些移民工作实习项目的价值, 并为移民减少跨文化交流带来的挑战提供借鉴。

Introduction

Migration for purposes of work or another way of living (for better or worse) usually requires that those immigrants find employment to facilitate, at a basic level, survival, but more positively, settlement into the community and broader society. Working within what is often a different linguistic, cultural, ethnic, religious, geographical, historical, national and local context often requires new forms of interaction, both for the incomer and those already established at the site of the encounter. This situation requires that interlocutors must (re) negotiate and (re)evaluate their ways of communicating, identifications and positions of power to accommodate new and sometimes different communication practices within the workplace. Yet, the nature of these workplace intercultural communication experiences, especially from the perspectives of immigrants themselves as they have been supported through a work-placement programme, has been little investigated or reported in the literature.

This study aims to address that gap by investigating the intercultural challenges immigrants face in the workplace (via a work-placement programme), and the communication practices that facilitate and/or constrain intercultural communication in this context from a social constructionist perspective. I begin by reviewing the literature on immigrant employment and workplace intercultural communication, focusing on the New Zealand context where the study is situated. The research questions shape the empirical data collection and methodology. The findings from the study and their conclusions and implications are then presented.

Many cross-cultural research approaches in business and organisational research have typically drawn on essentialist theories and approaches that seek to generalise understanding to specific cultures or nation states (e.g. Hall, 1976; Hofstede, 2001; Triandis, 1995) (see Holmes, 2012, for a critical discussion of these models in business communication education). By contrast, I draw on social constructionism (Berger & Luckmann, 1966) and concepts linked to intercultural communication to interpret the individual lived experiences of migrants as they interpret their communication and interactions with workplace colleagues. In addition, I favour a critical-interpretive approach that foregrounds immigrants' voices from a position of powerlessness, especially as they search to establish themselves through employment in a new country. This approach resonates with Holliday's (2012, p. 38) notion of critical cosmopolitanism that asserts 'the potential independence of social action' where culture is described as a 'negotiated process', expressed in dialogue among individuals and where these individuals have the possibility of 'being able to change existing orders'. In this sense, culture is a set of meaningful practices influenced by language, religion, history, geography, political and national ideologies (Hall, 1996; Shi-xu, 2001) that the immigrants bring with them, and which are negotiated in intercultural communication in the workplace. Culture is also messy, shifting and uncertain, constructed and reconstructed by different people with new and different ideas moving within and across communities and groups (Holliday, 2012). Therefore, to understand immigrants' workplace intercultural communication experiences, approaches that offer context-specific analyses rather than differences between national cultures or universalised competences within (inter)national groups, and that acknowledge multiple identities and particular competences among individuals and local groups are important (Lund & O'Regan, 2010). Thus, I present an insider perspective, through the voices of immigrants, of their intercultural encounters in the workplace with their colleagues.

An intercultural encounter is defined as:

> an encounter with another person (or group of people) who is perceived to have different cultural affiliations from oneself …. [Intercultural encounters] may involve people from different countries, people from different regional, linguistic, ethnic or religious backgrounds, or people who differ from each other because of their lifestyle, gender, social class, sexual orientation, age or generation, level of religious observance, etc. (Barrett, Byram, Lázár, Mompoint-Gaillard & Philippou, 2013, p. 7)

However, this definition denies the similarities and shared realities that interlocutors from different backgrounds may experience, whether regional, religious, ethnic, social class, gender, linguistic, historical, migratory or relating to memories (Holmes & O'Neill, 2012). Parts of the definition also resonate with a structuralist approach in identifying individuals with particular countries, a problematic attribution, especially in the context of migration for employment as it risks that others may essentialise an individual based on what they know about people from that country. In the workplace context, it is also important to acknowledge that intercultural communication occurs among individuals who may have 'starkly different material, economic, social and cultural resources at their disposal' (Piller, 2011, p. 173). Where immigrants are concerned, they are likely to have unequal access to discourses of interpersonal communication and associated small talk, and to discourses of power and positioning within organisations. Intercultural encounters in the workplace are therefore useful sights to understand intercultural communication and how individuals might (re)negotiate and (re)construct their communication styles and identity.

Immigrants and the New Zealand workplace

The literature on labour market marginalisation of ethnic minority people is well documented in Europe (Zegers de Beijl, 2000), and internationally (Fugazza, 2003). Research in the New Zealand context reveals the nature of intercultural communication in the workplace. For example, research undertaken by the Department of Labour (DOL, 2004) reports that immigrants enjoy positive experiences in the workplace, and concomitantly, more positive settlement when their language, skills and qualifications complement those of other people in the New Zealand labour force. Yet, 30% of the 7137 immigrants (excluding refugees) who responded to the DOL (2004) survey, having resided in New Zealand for approximately 6 months, were unemployed; 25%, particularly those from North and South-east Asia, reported incidents and feelings of discrimination in the workplace. Other research conducted by the Electricity Supply Industry Training Organisation (ESITO, 2008) suggests that immigrants leave their employment for reasons of discrimination; lack of respect, recognition and professional growth; and job satisfaction expectations not being met. Where language is concerned native-speaker fluency was often expected; and New Zealand English was often prioritised by both employers and employees in terms of accent, a preference for a local/New Zealand variety of English, and colloquialisms (Henderson, Trlin, & Watts, 2006; North, 2007). These factors affect migrants' employment prospects and also create potential inter-cultural communication difficulties in the workplace.

English language issues are also linked to immigrants' ability to connect with non-immigrants in their communities, to fit in, and mix. Extensive research by the Language in the Workplace team at Victoria University of Wellington has identified that migrants may be rejected from employment for their perceived inadequate language skills instead of attributing such communicative styles to socio-linguist nuances. For example, Holmes and Riddiford (2009) in their qualitative study of immigrants' communication practices in the workplace observed that migrants are competent in managing technical, task-oriented interactions, but some problems arose in small-talk.

Butcher, Spoonley, and Trlin (2006) found that migrants did not regularly experience specific acts of discrimination from their New Zealand neighbours who, while civil to immigrants, appeared to make little effort to communicate with or learn about them, their background, culture or language. Findings from the Connecting Diverse Communities Project (2006), a New Zealand Government initiative directed at building (immigrant) capacity and developing connections in communities, however, noted that some immigrants felt the need to continue to identify strongly with their country of origin as part of the process of integrating into the new culture, while simultaneously wanting to establish meaningful contact with people in the host community. Further, the report found that New Zealand citizens expected that people from other cultures should be the same as everyone else, or at least, not be too different. And Johnston, Gendall, Trlin, and Spoonley's (2010) research noted that despite policy shifts towards a multicultural society, New Zealanders still demonstrated a resistance towards immigrant arrivals, especially from Asia and the Pacific Islands. In fact, in terms of barriers to workplace employment, cultural fit versus cultural differences, English language skills, communication, and interpersonal skills, and accent were rated as the leading barriers to workplace employment (Podsiadlowski, 2007).

In conclusion, research on immigrant employment suggests that immigrants' workplace experiences may not always be positive; at worst, immigrants face unemployment and continual rejection in job applications. The outcome may be a downward spiral of isolation and disadvantage for immigrants, and a society of diverse communities living alongside one another, but isolated in their own groups and failing to connect – a failed multiculturalism (Cantle, 2012).

This study reflects on the potential for immigrant workplace inclusion and exclusion by investigating the intercultural communication among immigrant employees, their employers and local staff as facilitated through an immigrant work-placement programme. As evidenced in the literature, the success of immigrant work-placement programmes has overarching implications for their longer-term engagement and settlement in the community and wider society. Given this situation, the following research questions emerged:

RQ1: What intercultural communication challenges do immigrants face during work placement with (1) co-workers, and (2) employer(s)?
RQ2: How is intercultural communication facilitated/constrained in intercultural encounters in the workplace?

The research methodology

Acknowledging that many studies of immigrant employment patterns and experiences have relied on quantitative surveys (see, e.g. the New Zealand literature conducted by governmental bodies cited above), my concern was to provide thick descriptions of how immigrants experienced intercultural communication in the workplace with their co-workers and employers. Insider perceptions of immigrants' everyday social interaction may shed light on their intercultural communication experiences and how they make sense of these. The study was informed by the overarching theory of social constructionism (Berger & Luckmann, 1966, p. 15) which gives primacy to everyday conversations as the process in which knowledge is 'developed, transmitted and maintained' in social interaction. Through open-ended interviews participants could 'look more deeply at self-other interaction' which Ellis and Bochner (2000, p. 740) argue can be 'emancipatory', allowing participants to reflect on self and other through exploration, questioning, emotional involvement and self-discovery. Further, the research enabled immigrants' voices to be heard by others, thus opening up spaces for deeper understanding.

The context of the study is a volunteer 3-month work-placement programme, supported by government funding, for immigrants who had been living in New Zealand from 3 months to 6 years and who had not yet found employment. The programme included a series of preliminary workshops to introduce immigrants to New Zealand workplace culture, e.g., job searching, immigration law, curriculum vitae writing, interview techniques, and social and legal matters (including the role of the Treaty of Waitangi as a founding document for bicultural/bilingual New Zealand). The workshop sessions were administered and taught by the programme coordinator and included invited speakers. The immigrants on the programme then undertook paid or voluntary employment, usually in a small business.

Of the 16 participants in the study, only one had previous work experience as a volunteer for 3 months. Twelve were females and four males; they were aged between 26 and 55 years. They came from Chile, China, Columbia, Fiji, India, the Philippines, the Republic of Congo, Sri Lanka and the United Kingdom (UK). The programme coordinator, from the UK, had lived in New Zealand for 9 years. Five employers were also interviewed to establish their perceptions of how immigrants experienced their work placements. Three employers had experienced employing immigrants, and two had previously hired immigrants from this programme.

The interviews, transcriptions and coding were conducted by a paid research assistant, herself an immigrant and international student from Germany. Like all the participants (except the UK participant), she was using another language, English, in the research process which helped to bridge the power distance likely to be found in native-speaker-researcher and non-native-speaker-participant interviews. To ensure that she worked in ethical and transparent ways, and in order to establish rapport, develop familiarity and gain trust, the research assistant attended some of the workshops offered by the programme coordinator. The programme coordinator helped to establish the authenticity and importance of the research to participants as she both confirmed and endorsed the research assistant's researcher role by emphasising the study's importance in developing an insider understanding of immigrants' intercultural communication experiences in the workplace. These shared experiences with participants enabled the research assistant to develop rapport and empathy with them, and to support the less fluent and more apprehensive participants in the interview context.

The in-depth, open-ended interviews lasted for 45–90 minutes. The research assistant invited participants to choose where to be interviewed in order to enable them to feel comfortable about the interview process: four chose a secluded space in their workplace, two were interviewed in their own homes and the remainder were interviewed in a room on the premises of the work-placement programme. The researcher transcribed and coded the interviews thematically, drawing on the six-step process identified by Braun and Clarke (2006). This involved familiarisation with the data transcription, reading and rereading the data, noting down initial ideas, and searching for themes, and then naming and defining themes. In the presentation and analysis of the data, identity markers of language or nationality have been excluded to avoid essentialist, stereotypical interpreta-tions based on participants' nationalities. Such markers may disguise the complexity of their (cultural) identities (Holliday, 2010), the linguacultures they have come to inhabit through transcultural migration (Risager, 2012) and deny their own discursive construc-tions of their identity (Piller, 2011).

Like all research involving humans, this study is subjective. As Charmaz and Mitchell (2001) note, both research subjects and researchers hold worldviews. The participants reflected on their own predispositions, socially constructed communication practices, beliefs and attitudes which were illuminated to them as they engaged with colleagues in the workplace. These subjective experiences are their own, specific to their identity and local workplace experience, and therefore may not be transferable to all other immigrant employment contexts (Lincoln & Guba, 2000).

An analysis of the interview data revealed the following two key themes: negotiating informal and non-hierarchical intercultural relationships, and constructing collegial relationships through intercultural communication.

Negotiating informal and non-hierarchical relationships

Hierarchies are present in the organisational structure of most workplaces, including the small businesses where these immigrants were placed. While employees respect and manage hierarchical relationships, the communication among and across individuals and groups tends towards informality and equality, e.g., through the use of first names, ignoring titles and reciprocal communication (Holmes & Stubbe, 2003). In the following example, the degree of informality, signalled by the 'yelling' at the employee, with the expectation that the yelling would be reciprocated, created complications regarding the employer–employee hierarchy and the expected response:

> If you have such a respect or hierarchy in an organisation then they treat you in some different way as well. They will never scream at you because they know you cannot do it back. But here, your boss could yell at you, so you have to yell back. Sometimes you have to adapt.

And the consequences:

> If you cannot get rid of this hierarchy in your mind, then your New Zealand supervisor would treat you as less significant because that is the way you present yourself.

One participant expressed feelings of discomfort when her boss praised her work:

> I don't feel comfortable when [my supervisor] says …. I'm not used to praises because in [my country] we don't really do that. If you get something done you give it to your boss and he will say 'alright'. But [my supervisor] would say really nice things like 'perfect, very good' [also in front of others]. I don't feel comfortable because in our culture we don't do that and I just don't know how to respond.

The employer was also aware of her discomfort as he had created an open exchange with her in weekly meetings where she was able to explain her attitudes and feelings around being praised. The employer explained:

> In some of those weekly meetings she said that she felt uncomfortable because I kept on saying 'good job, well done, I like this'. She was not used to that. Her boss would never ever say, 'good'. There was always something wrong. It took her maybe two or three weeks to get used to that.

The employer's attempt to make her feel valued and develop her confidence by praising her work was misunderstood by this participant, instead, resulting in feelings of awkwardness. In their home countries, immigrants can gauge the social position of others through language, background and the unspoken. But in New Zealand, they are likely to be unaware of these sociocultural-linguistic cues, or if they are aware, how to use them to their advantage. Holmes (2006), in her research on gender in the workplace, noted that compliments are complex; when the speaker is in a higher status position, giving compliments may reinforce their position rather than lessening it, while also helping to create a sense of team among employees. As the example illustrates, this immigrant needed time to absorb and give meaning to the employer's praise.

Working autonomously, without the need for constant checking, also had to be negotiated. One participant commented on how she thought it important to check her work with her boss to avoid making a mistake:

> I do it correctly because I don't want to get a bad image. I always double-check everything. It is very stressful to do that, but I do that because I don't want to make a mistake because I want to be permanent.

By contrast, her employer found this need for constant feedback unusual and slightly irritating:

> She had been used to negative feedback and being told to check everything with her boss. I wonder if she slowly understands now that we prefer that she wouldn't check everything, but rather that she did it. She is extremely intelligent so she is not going to make big mistakes. From my perspective, it is slightly irritating to have someone check.

This participant's personal anxiety about her performance was linked to her desire to secure future employment, yet her need to have her work checked contradicted her employer's expectations that employees show independence, initiative and autonomy. Her anxiety is also indicative of what is at stake in the placement – the possibility of employment, leading to greater acceptance and integration into the community (Ward & Masgoret, 2006), and well-being and security.

Constructing collegial relationships through intercultural communication

A second major theme centred on the ways in which participants sought to build relationships with colleagues during and after work: through communication in tea breaks, engaging in small talk and a preference for face-to-face communication over email.

Tea breaks. These offer an opportunity for developing relationships, but joining the conversation required an ability to use the informal language register and familiarity with colleagues' topics of interest. Participants discussed the awkwardness and unfamiliarity of communicating in the New Zealand social idiom, and feelings of being excluded because they could not follow:

> There are words they are using, bad words, swearing, but then it looks like they are happy using it. They are smiling while they are talking. So I feel that they are not talking against me. But sometimes if they are serious talking, you have this kind of feeling that they are talking about me.

And another participant:

> With the group, outside the office, in the fresh air, they have this kind of group segregation, informal conversation. You find sometimes that not to listen to their swearing kind of things. I don't want to join their conversation anymore. So I better segregate, just commune with the nature. Because if you are going to join them, then you should use the words they are using, but I am not used to that.

These examples illustrate that conversational English outside of desk work proved challenging. Some participants had used English in the workplace in their own country, which they described as 'formal' English. For some participants who had been used to socialising with compatriots in their immigrant communities, the workplace highlighted the differences in communication styles. However, the coordinator explained the importance of sharing organisational rituals such as tea breaks as a way of socialising and promoting acceptance among local staff:

> It is actually counterproductive for you settling in the workplace if everybody else is having morning tea and you stay at the desk working. People won't think here 'Oh, they are a really hard worker'... they might start to think 'Oh, why have they not wanted to mix with me and have morning tea?' In New Zealand ... the social side of work and having morning teas is actually an important part of life. But migrants think 'If I stay and work, work, work, it's going to make me look good', and I say, 'Well, actually, it might not give the best impression. It might give the impression that you don't want to mix!'

These participant experiences illustrate the tensions around language codes and practices. As Scollon, Scollon, and Jones (2012) remark, language is constructed around discourse systems in organisations (and in the community). Immigrants entering a new workplace may not necessarily share the same linguistic resources and knowledge, and may need to learn this discourse system; in doing so, they must attend to the micro- and macro-contexts of the interaction. Piller (2011, p. 159) argues that 'language choice and understanding are a matter of what is "acceptable", what our language ideologies allow us to accept, within a particular social space or institution'. As these examples show, the responsibility to conform to the language codes and practices – which often have to be learned and negotiated 'on the job' – is on the immigrants, thus placing them in an unequal power relationship with those already there.

Engaging in small talk

Tea breaks necessitated the ability to engage in small talk. Some participants noted unfamiliarity with the practice of tea breaks and the self-disclosure it sometimes involves:

> [In my home country] everything is quite straight-forward. People don't do a lot of small talk. They don't do tea break, and most time we keep our life professional.

Another participant described the sense of time wasting it implies, preferring direct communication:

> It is taking forever to find out what people are actually trying to talk about. Here it is small talk first, and then they are coming to the point later on, and when they do it is 5 minutes talk. I guess sometimes my co-workers feel that I am quite straight-forward because I just I don't want to do the small talk first. I always say, 'Have you done that? Do you have that? Do you have this?'

A further challenge emerges when certain knowledge is privileged, specific to the New Zealand experience and context, which resulted in feelings of exclusion from the conversation:

> If you are talking about sports, we would know about cricket, about hockey, about more traditional things. We wouldn't know about bungee jumping and jump off which cliff. We

wouldn't know the terms, we wouldn't know how to do it. Even when they talk about horse riding I don't know that. Many people have, but I haven't. … You don't have so many things you can talk about.

These examples illustrate how small talk contexts potentially caused awkwardness and embarrassment for participants as their colleagues talked fast, used colloquial terms and spoke in a register they described as 'Kiwi English'. However, as the coordinator concluded earlier, immigrants are not always aware of the importance of small talk which provide opportunities for intercultural encounters, language learning, and integration into the community and larger society (Henderson et al., 2006; Johnston et al., 2010).

The cultural stuff around how to talk to people

A participant used this phrase to describe the cultural complexities associated with email as opposed to face-to-face communication. While small talk and tea break communication required certain informality, participants felt that, in contrast, emails were 'cold' and 'serious':

> When managers write emails here it seems like it is very very cold. But when you talk they seem very nice. They will say, 'How are you?' And all that.

The lack of non-verbal, contextual, affective cues available in emails created challenges in gauging their tone; consequently, face-to-face conversations seemed more manageable:

> I am still trying to understand when people are really serious, when they really mean it. When they are trying to be rude and I should respond on email and be colloquial or should I just talk to them. So that is something I still can't make out. On emails you don't know the person, don't know his background, his culture, or what day he is having.

An employer also commented on some immigrants' uncertainty around tone in emails:

> In an email she said to somebody, cold, somebody we never had any communication with in the past. It was a bit, it was really abrupt and kind of 'Please make an appointment!' and I was like, 'Oh my God, you don't do that, you have to try and build a relationship … not slam the door, so of course, that person never replied. [Employer]

The coordinator described situations where immigrants failed to realise that their formal email came across as 'quite demanding, just because that is the background they come from' (Co-ordinator). She also described situations where interns had sent her emails asking her the meaning of the email. These examples illustrate the complex sociocultural cues embodied in emails which, like other forms of workplace communication, need to be understood and learned.

Intercultural communication as disempowerment

The final theme concerns how participants found communication could sometimes leave them feeling disadvantaged, resulting in feelings of detachment and of being an outsider. Collier (2005) discussed the mismatch between an avowed identity, the identity an individual chooses to project, and an ascribed identity, the identity that others give to an individual. Similarly, some participants experienced this mismatch between the identity they avowed in the workplace in their own country which was at odds with the identity they wished to project in the New Zealand workplace, as illustrated by these two participants' comments:

> In my home country I am a different person. I am just talking, talking, but here I do my thing. I am a silent person. But it is a little bit hard.

> I was always accustomed to talking English very fluently and pronouncing properly. I used to talk like locals and in [my country] I was the native speaker who could speak very fluently English, so when I got here and people couldn't understand. It was very frustrating.

The linguistic competence participants experienced in their own country and workplace became 'incompetence' in the New Zealand workplace. They felt a lack of linguistic resources to express their thoughts and ideas in real-time communication, and an inability to grasp the illocutionary force of the message:

> I really like to talk, but if they ask some questions or talk about something, I can only give some simple word and they might think, 'ah, you don't like to talk with me', but that is not true.

> You feel a little bit stupid. You are used to understand everything in your first language. And then sometimes they treat you like, they look at you like 'aw, must be stupid'.

> Here [in New Zealand] 'thank you' and 'how can I help you', to express yourself, what you want to say. You want to help, you have to express it. In [country] it is not like that. In [country] everyone will know from my accent. Everybody will know from what words I have chosen. But here, English is not so much rich with the words.

Another participant, affirming the above experience, noted that 'English is not emotional'. Even understanding the appropriate non-verbal communication required, for example, in greetings – whether to shake hands, hug, kiss, shake hands or none of these – could create feelings of awkwardness, as one participant who had been living in New Zealand for 3 years commented:

> Every time I have to say hello you have that minute where you don't know how to say hello. I think it is still every time.

In conclusion, the intercultural communication experiences and challenges reported here by all participants (immigrants, employers and coordinators) suggest that introducing immigrants to the workplace through a voluntary internship programme may not lessen or eliminate communication issues. However, through the supportive environment of the workshops, and the mediation and support offered by the coordinator, immigrants could begin to put these intercultural communication experiences into perspective, share and deconstruct them with others on the programme, and acquire important workplace (communication) skills. Henderson et al.'s (2006) quantitative study of migrants in the workplace reported how language proficiency was important in affecting employment prospects for professionally qualified immigrants like those in this study. And similarly, their results indicated that their immigrant respondents perceived communication with clients or customers, either face-to-face or by telephone, and with colleagues at work as problematic. However, in foregrounding a critical cosmopolitan approach (Holliday, 2012), responsibility for communication lies with both migrants, in ensuring that their voices are heard, and employers and co-workers in acknowledging the multiple discourses and communication styles in the workplace. This study has shown that the values and communication rules informing immigrants' discourse systems (showing respect and diligence, not voicing opinions too loudly) may be different from what is expected in the New Zealand workplace. Then who judges which is the correct way? The findings in this study suggest that the responsibility to learn lies with the incoming immigrants.

Further, these insider perspectives on social interactions and communication illustrate the kind of support and training that would benefit immigrants, their co-workers and employers in reflecting on their own intercultural awareness and communication. Guilherme, Keating, and Hoppe (2010, p. 79) argue for the need for intercultural responsibility in the workplace, that is, that 'members-in-action [must] demonstrate that they are aware of the particularities of collaborating with their co-workers, either in an inter- or intra-national context, recognising that their identities have been socially and culturally constructed based on different ethnic elements and influences'. Intercultural responsibility requires that all members are responsible for 'developing full and reciprocally demanding professional relationships' with one another.

The work-placement programme: preparation for intercultural communication

The work-placement programme, in helping to prepare immigrants for intercultural communication in the workplace, is a step in the direction of developing intercultural responsibility in the workplace. Participants commented that workshops 'clarify[ied] and confirm[ed] certain things about the workplace', and 'workshops really helped a lot ...we found other people who are in the same boat, so you don't need to disappear'. These shared experiences enabled immigrants to feel less isolated. One participant summed up the value of the programme in providing a point of difference, highlighting immigrants' assets and the opportunities these can create for employers:

> One of the advantages that companies can take from this programme is to use that kind of local skills like my experience, my skills, my networking in my region to improve the commercial performance of companies ... the opportunity to open markets, to use another skills that people from here don't have. ... They [migrants seeking employment] must think about which skills make them different than other people here. Aren't afraid to offer that.

In facilitating immigrants' access to the workplace, the programme helps to address discrimination displayed towards immigrants in the job market (Butcher et al., 2006; Connecting Diverse Communities Project, 2006; Fugazza, 2003; Henderson et al., 2006; Johnston et al., 2010). The participants in this study were skilled, educated and held professional qualifications from their own countries. But without 'word of mouth' connections or recommendations, they were disadvantaged, usually because they did not have 'New Zealand experience'. As one participant commented, 'in New Zealand, it is more who is your reference, who have you gone through, which is a very important part. It is called social networking here, which places migrants at a disadvantage because we don't know anybody here'. One of the goals of the work-placement programme is to sidestep these discriminatory practices by establishing alternative routes into employment.

The programme also showed the potential value of the multicultural workplace, e.g., facilitating employers to develop self-awareness and criticality of their own communication, which potentially impacted on other employees in the company:

It did make me stop and think about communication and reflect on [how I interact with immigrants] in a serious way. I hadn't done that for a long time. That was really a quite strong sense of being mindful of how many ways there are to miscommunicate and how many meanings there are to things that seem quite simple. ... It challenges your own work processes and makes you reflect about those things. It is good learning for the company as well.

The programme also demonstrated the important role of the coordinator as coach and mentor for immigrants, and mediator between them and employers. Participants held the coordinator in high esteem: 'Having someone in between is really relieving, so you feel more confidence and for the mind', and another reported that 'she sees things objectively'. Where communication is concerned, the coordinator encouraged participants to 'be assertive ... and speak your mind out'. The coordinator was perceived to be objective, to not have any vested interests in the businesses concerned. Therefore, participants could put trust in her, as someone who would not betray them.

Conclusions

This study sought to address two questions: What intercultural communication challenges do immigrants face during work-placement with co-workers and employers (RQ1)? How is intercultural communication facilitated/constrained in intercultural encounters in the workplace (RQ2)? Concerning the first question, the findings illustrated the immigrants' fears and concerns in managing informal communication and relationships in tea breaks, small talk situations and in workplace practices concerning email. Notwithstanding these concerns, participants experienced largely positive interactions, perhaps attributed to the programme itself, the important work of the coordinator (as a point of contact, a trouble-shooter, a mediator), and the employers' support. Concerning the second question, while immigrants tried to communicate sensitively, and for the most part, responsibly, in intercultural encounters, they felt a sense of vulnerability in supervisor/employee relationships, e.g., in seeking affirmation rather than working autonomously. They also indicated a need for support and affirmation from co-workers. Participants' responses in interviews showed a respect and gratefulness towards employers and the work-placement programme. They also felt that they offered a point of difference, a contribution confirmed by employers who sought to support their acceptance and integration. However, whether this feeling was reciprocated by co-workers is unclear.

From the immigrants' perspectives, co-workers appeared less sympathetic to the intercultural communication challenges they faced, suggesting that more needs to be done to encourage and support new (immigrant) colleagues, through tolerance, sensitivity and respect towards language and difference and a willingness and openness to see similarities as well as differences, and to address sociocultural and sociolinguistic inequalities where English is the dominant language (Blommaert, 2005). Such intercultural encounters point to the importance of ethical communication that challenges preconceived ideas of the other, of culture: of 'taking the risk of meeting the other qua other' (Ferri, 2014, p. 19). Ferri argues that ethical communication emphasises the interdependence of self and other, but simultaneously, an awareness of one's potential to silence others through positions of power.

In conclusion, the work-placement programme provided a valuable resource in initiating immigrants into the workplace, and in helping them to manage and make sense of intercultural encounters with co-workers and employers. Yet, these outcomes were not straightforward. Several studies show that immigrants enjoy positive experiences in the workplace, and concomitantly, more positive settlement when their language, skills and qualifications complement those of other people in the New Zealand labour force (Butcher et al., 2006; DOL, 2004; ESITO, 2008; Henderson et al., 2006). However, unless immigrants have the opportunity to show these abilities in the workplace, this outcome is unlikely. The intergroup miscommunication and differing practices and values around communication in the workplace, evident in this study, indicate the need for reciprocal intercultural learning among immigrants, co-workers and employers, a responsibility that must be shared, rather than placing the onus on incoming immigrants.

Several implications emerge in supporting immigrants into work. First, governments should focus on internal linguistic-sociocultural issues linked to discrimination in the workplace rather than casting intercultural communication as a problem brought about by immigration or individual immigrants (Colic-Peisker & Tilbury, 2007). Denial of equal opportunities in employment may result in the affected group being unable to attach themselves to mainstream society, resulting in a vicious circle of poverty and crime (Zegers de Beijl, 2000).

Second, globalisation has increased the spread of lingua-cultural flows of different groups of people establishing their language communities around the world (Risager, 2012). The result is that multilingualism in the workplace is becoming increasingly common in cities experiencing immigration, as described by Otsuji and Pennycook (2011) in their study on metrolingualism in Sydney, Australia, raising questions of social inclusion. Piller (2011) argues that language ideologies and regimes in support of English (where it is the official language, e.g., in Australia) serve to discriminate against, and thus, disempower speakers of other languages, with the result of lessening their opportunities for employment. This is especially the case in societies where English is the dominant and official language – despite the presence of other official and minority languages. New Zealand, and the city where this study was conducted, is no exception to these global flows, lingua cultures and language regimes. Thus, the resuscitation of languages education and a greater emphasis on intercultural education are imperative in bringing about a 'languaging subject' who is attentive towards the hybrid and shifting nature of the self and the socially constructed nature of language (Phipps & Gonzalez, 2004). This move is urgent at all levels of society, e.g., in government, health, education and business.

Third, these findings show that training models of intercultural competence that 'focus on the results or ends that an individual can achieve' (Crosbie, 2014, p. 92) are limited in understanding the complexity of intercultural encounters and practices in the workplace. Phipps (2014) argues that such models, including models of intercultural dialogue, have resulted in 'an industry of difference-creation, difference management and difference training as "solutions" to problems in intercultural dialogue' (Phipps, 2014, p. 120). Crosbie suggests that a capabilities approach (drawing on the work of Nussbaum and Sen) focuses attention on the freedom and agency that individuals have to be and act. Thus, educating individuals to engage interculturally and responsibly involves enabling them to 'critique different social discourses and practices, and to envision a life of flourishing based on notions of hospitality and social translation' (Crosbie, 2014, p. 105). The findings from this study show, in varying degrees, these processes at work (e.g. in the support of the coordinator and employers towards the immigrants, and in the immigrants' attempts to communicate with co-workers in work breaks). However, there is scope for further theorising of these concepts in future research in the context of workplace intercultural encounters.

Finally, governments must also show intercultural responsibility by implementing policies and practices, and including intercultural education programmes for all, that support immigrant entry into the workplace. Investment in schemes like this work-placement programme will help immigrants in contributing socially and economically to society. Community centres and non-governmental/non-profit agencies have a role to play in providing employment services, as do potential employers. Immigrants, too, need to recognise the value of work-placement programmes and lobby for their presence in the community.

Although this is a small, exploratory study of intercultural encounters among immigrant, employers and employees in the workplace, the findings may transfer to other contexts of immigrant employment. Future research involving a larger in-depth study that explores the perspectives of co-workers, employers and work-placement programme coordinators would enrich understanding of immigrants' intercultural communication issues in the workplace, and therefore, how work-placement programmes could be developed. Further studies of attitudes towards multilingualism and intercultural communication among all groups of immigrants (beyond professional groups) are required. The data for this study were generated by a non-native speaker who interviewed other non-native speakers in English; however, the role and language practices of the researcher (and the researched) in eliciting, collecting and analysing the data needs deeper investigation. Implications for settlement, identity negotiation and workplace intercultural responsibility among all concerned warrant further investigation. Finally, intercultural encounters in the workplace offer a valuable context for further theorising of the concepts of capability, ethical communication and intercultural responsibility.

Acknowledgements

The contributions of many have made this study possible. I thank the immigrant interns, employers and coordinator for their support and time in contributing to this study. I sincerely thank the student researcher, Vera Spratte, for her careful work with the participants and data management and student researcher, Charlie Gillard, for his literature review contributions. I thank Dr Hongbo Dong, Durham University, for the translation of the abstract into Chinese.

Disclosure statement

No potential conflict of interest was reported by the author.

Funding

This research was funded by the Summer Research Scholarship Scheme (2009–2010), University of Waikato, Hamilton, New Zealand.

Note on contributor

Prue Holmes is a reader in the School of Education, Durham University. She is the pathway leader of the MA Intercultural Communication and Education, and she researches and supervises doctoral students in intercultural communication and its links to education, languages, competence and dialogue. She is Co-Investigator on the AHRC-funded project 'Researching Multilingually at the Borders of Language, the Body, Law and the State', and on the Erasmus Mundus-funded project 'Intercultural Education Resources for Erasmus Students and their Teachers'. She is a chair of the International Association for Languages and Intercultural Communication (IALIC).

References

Barrett, M., Byram, M., Lázár, I., Mompoint-Gaillard, P., & Philippou, S. (2013). *Developing intercultural competence through education*. Directorate of Democratic Citizenship and Participation, Council of Europe, Strasbourg, France.

Berger, P., & Luckmann, T. (1966). *The social construction of reality*. New York: Doubleday.

Blommaert, J. (2005). *Discourse: A critical introduction*. Cambridge: Cambridge University Press. doi:10.1017/CBO9780511610295

Braun, V., & Clarke, V. (2006). Using thematic analysis in psychology. *Qualitative Research in Psychology, 3*(2), 77–101. doi:10.1191/1478088706qp063oa

Butcher, A., Spoonley, P., & Trlin, A. (2006). *Being accepted: The experience of discrimination and social exclusion by immigrants and refugees in New Zealand*. New Settlers Programme, Massey University.

Cantle, T. (2012). *Interculturalism: The new era of cohesion and diversity*. Hampshire: Palgrave Macmillan. doi:10.1057/9781137027474

Charmaz, K., & Mitchell, R. (2001). Grounded theory in ethnography. In P. Atkinson, A. Coffey, S. Delamont, J. Lofland, & L. Lofland (Eds.), *Handbook of ethnography* (pp. 160–174). London: Sage.

Colic-Peisker, V., & Tilbury, F. (2007). Integration into the Australian labour market: The experience of three "visibly different" groups of recently arrived refugees. *International Migration, 45*(1), 59–85. doi:10.1111/j.1468-2435.2007.00396.x

Collier, M.-J. (2005). Theorizing cultural identifications: Critical updates and continuing evolution. In W. B. Gudykunst (Ed.), *Theorizing about intercultural communication* (pp. 235–256). Thousand Oaks, CA: Sage.

Connecting Diverse Communities Project. (2006). *Ministry of Social Development*. Retrieved from http://www.msd.govt.nz/about-msd-and-our-work/work-programmes/initiatives/connecting-diverse-communities/

Crosbie, V. (2014). Capabilities for intercultural dialogue. *Language and Intercultural Communication, 14*(1), 91–107. doi:10.1080/14708477.2013.866126

Department of Labour (DOL). (2004). *The New Zealand settlement strategy*. Wellington: Department of Labour.

Electricity Supply Industry Training Organisation (ESITO). (2008). *Skilled migrant research report*. Gary Nicol Associates. Wellington, New Zealand. Retrieved from http://www.immigration.govt.nz/NR/rdonlyres/A8824CC5-E588-4B50-A517-227F1AAB0548/0/Chapter1IntroductiontotheLongitudinalImmigrationSurveyNewZealand.pdf

Ellis, C., & Bochner, A. (2000). Autoethnography, personal narrative, reflexivity: Researcher as subject. In N. Denzin & Y. Lincoln (Eds.), *Handbook of qualitative research* (2nd ed., pp. 733–768). Thousand Oaks, CA: Sage.

Ferri, G. (2014). Ethical communication and intercultural responsibility: A philosophical perspective. *Language and Intercultural Communication, 14*(1), 7–23. doi:10.1080/14708477.2013.866121

Fugazza, M. (2003). Racial discrimination: Theories, facts and policy. *International Labour Review, 142*, 507–541. doi:10.1111/j.1564-913X.2003.tb00542.x

Guilherme, M., Keating, C., & Hoppe, D. (2010). Intercultural responsibility: Power and ethics in intercultural dialogue and interaction. In M. Guilherme, E. Glaser, and M. Méndez García (Eds.), *The intercultural dynamics of multicultural working* (pp. 77–94). Clevedon: Multilingual Matters.

Hall, E. T. (1976). *Beyond culture*. New York: Doubleday.

Hall, S. (1996). Introduction: Who needs 'identity'. In S. Hall & P. Du Gay (Eds.), *Questions of cultural identity* (pp. 1–17). London: Sage.

Henderson, A. M., Trlin, A. D., & Watts, N. (2006). *English language proficiency and the recruitment and employment of professional immigrants in New Zealand*. New Settlers Programme, Massey University.

Hofstede, G. (2001). *Culture's consequences: Comparing values, behaviours institutions and organizations across cultures*. London: Sage.

Holliday, A. (2010). Complexity in cultural identity. *Language and Intercultural Communication, 10*(2), 165–177. doi:10.1080/14708470903267384

Holliday, A. (2012). Culture, communication, context and power. In J. Jackson (Ed.), *The Routledge handbook of language and intercultural communication* (pp. 37–51). Oxon: Routledge.

Holmes, J. (2006). *Gendered talk at work*. Oxford: Blackwell.

Holmes, P. (2012). Intercultural communication and business education. In J. Jackson (Ed.), *The Routledge handbook of language and intercultural communication*. London: Routledge.

Holmes, J., & Stubbe, M. (2003). *Power and politeness in the workplace: A sociolinguistic analysis of talk at work*. Harlow: Pearson Education.

Holmes, J., & Riddiford, N. (2009). Talk at work: Interactional challenges for immigrants. In V. Bhatia, W. Cheng, B. Du-Babcock & J. Lung (Eds.), *Language for professional communication: Research, practice & training* (pp. 217–234). Hong Kong: The Hong Kong Polytechnic University.

Holmes, P., & O'Neill, G. (2012). Developing and evaluating intercultural competence: Ethnographies of intercultural encounters. *International Journal of Intercultural Relations, 36*, 707–718. doi:10.1016/j.ijintrel.2012.04.010

Johnston, R., Gendall, P., Trlin, A., & Spoonley, P. (2010). Immigration, multiculturalism and geography: Inter-group contact and attitudes to immigrants and cultural diversity in New Zealand. *Asian and Pacific Migration Journal, 19*, 343–369.

Lincoln, Y., & Guba, E. (2000). Paradigmatic controversies, contradictions, and emerging confluences. In N. Denzin & Y. Lincoln (Eds.), *Handbook of qualitative research* (2nd ed., pp. 163–188). Thousand Oaks, CA: Sage.

Lund, A., & O'Regan, J. (2010). National occupational standards in intercultural working: Models of theory and assessment. In M. Guilherme, E. Glaser & M. C. Méndez García (Eds.), *The intercultural dynamics of multicultural working* (pp. 41–58). Clevedon: Multilingual Matters.

North, N. (2007). *The employment of immigrants in New Zealand: The attitudes, policies, practices and experiences of employers*. Palmerston North: New Settlers Programme, Massey University.

Otsuji, E., & Pennycook, A. (2011). Social inclusion and metrolingual practices. *International Journal of Bilingual Education and Bilingualism, 14*, 413–426. doi:10.1080/13670050.2011.573065

Phipps, A. (2014). "They are bombing now": The meaninglessness of 'Intercultural Dialogue' in times of conflict. *Language and Intercultural Communication, 14*(1), 108–124. doi:10.1080/14708477.2013.866127

Phipps, A., & Gonzalez, M. (2004). *Modern languages: Learning and teaching in an intercultural field*. London: Sage.

Piller, I. (2011). *Intercultural communication: A critical introduction*. Edinburgh: Edinburgh University Press.

Podsiadlowski, A. (2007). *Facilitating migrant entry and integration into the New Zealand workforce*. The New Zealand Federation of Ethnic Councils.

Risager, K. (2012). Linguaculture and transnationality: The cultural dimensions of language. In J. Jackson (Ed.), *The Routledge handbook of language and intercultural communication* (pp. 101–115). London: Routledge.

Scollon, R., Wong Scollon, S., & Jones, R. (2012). *Intercultural communication: A discourse approach* (3rd ed.). Oxford: Wiley-Blackwell.

Shi-xu. (2001). Critical pedagogy and intercultural communication: Creating discourses of diversity, equality, common goals and rational-moral motivation. *Journal of Intercultural Studies, 22*, 279–293. doi:10.1080/07256860120094000

Triandis, H. (1995). *Individualism and collectivism*. Boulder, CO: Westview Press.

Ward, C., & Masgoret, A.-M. (2006). An integrative model of attitudes towards migrants. *International Journal of Intercultural Relations, 30*, 671–682. doi:10.1016/j.ijintrel.2006.06.002

Zegers de Beijl, R. (2000). *Documenting discrimination against migrant workers*. Geneva: International Labour Office.

Virtual team management: what is causing communication breakdown?

Jane Lockwood

Department of English, City University of Hong Kong, Kowloon Tong, Hong Kong, China

The combined effects of business offshoring, of flexible work practices and of rapid improvements in technology have resulted in workplace virtual communication becoming increasingly prevalent for business meetings. However, business leaders report them to be more challenging than face-to-face ones. Most global teams are located where diverse offshored work teams are using English as a lingua franca, and despite common business complaints that they are fraught with communication breakdown, the precise causes appear to be highly complex. This paper reports on a training needs analysis carried out in a large globalized workplace for a programme entitled 'Communicating in Virtual Teams'. Multiple sources such as surveys, interviews, document reviews and meeting observations were used to better understand the causes of virtual team communication breakdown. Whilst the analyses revealed different kinds of language and cultural misunderstandings, deeper problems of marginalization and identity confusion within global teams were also reported. This paper argues that without addressing the underlying struggles caused by offshoring, a training programme runs the risk of only addressing the surface communication problems of technology, leadership and meeting skills and even language and culture issues, which can arguably be seen as 'masking' deeper employee concerns and struggles.

在商业离岸外包, 灵活的工作方式, 以及快速发展的科技的共同作用下, 用于商务会议的工作场合虚拟交流越来越流行。然而, 商业领袖们称虚拟交流比面对面交流更富挑战性。频频的商业投诉显示虚拟交流充满了交流障碍, 即便如此, 绝大多数多元化的离岸工作团队仍然位于将英语作为通用语的地区。这其中的确切原因十分复杂。本论文报告了在一间大型全球化的工作场所中进行的培训需求分析的结果。该培训需求分析是为一个名为'虚拟团队中的交流'的项目而作的。为更好地了解引发虚拟团队中交流障碍的原因, 本研究使用了多个资料来源, 如问卷, 访谈, 文件检阅, 和会议观察。数据分析结果显示出各种语言和文化的误解, 同时, 也报告了全球性团队中的深层问题——边缘化和身份困惑。本文认为培训项目如不解决离岸外包导致的潜在挣扎这个问题, 将有可能只解决了一些趋于表面的交流问题, 包括技术, 领导和会议技巧, 乃至语言和文化的议题。可以认为这样的做法是'掩盖'了深层次的员工的忧虑和挣扎。

Introduction

In the last decade increasing amounts of work are being sent offshore to developing countries, such as India, the Philippines, Costa Rica and Vietnam. It is estimated that by

2020, the market for this Business Processing Outsourcing (BPO) industry will triple in size from USD 500 billion to USD 1.5–1.6 trillion (NASSCOM, 2009). A well-known English speaking multinational company reported in 2013 that 45% of its international employees are now scattered around Asia, and a large-scale study across global multinational companies recently reported that 80% of its respondents were part of teams with members based in different locations (RW CultureWizard, 2010). This has resulted in fundamental shifts in the way people work globally and has meant rapid organizational change. In 2010, a multinational financial company called MetroFin, a pseudonym for the purposes of this study, initiated a call for a one-day 'Communicating in Virtual Teams' training course provider. The course would address the communication needs of on- and offshore frontline managers of virtual teams. The aim of the training needs analysis (TNA) was to understand how managers and teams communicate and work in virtual teams, both on- and offshore, and identify key gaps and difficulties to be addressed by a well-targeted training course. The company that won this training project was a BPO communications consultancy group which I founded when I lived and worked in Manila 10 years ago. As a full-time academic now, I was permitted by the company and the client to shadow and participate in the TNA, and use the data for research and publication purposes. The identity of the company would obviously need to remain confidential.

Understanding the problems for training, through a TNA, is a key educational step in the development of a successful course (see for example, Belcher & Lukkarila, 2011). As with an ethnographic study, many voices in this process need to be elicited and heard, and this requires investigating the problem via multiple sources for triangulation purposes. MetroFin is used as a case study to explore how challenges in virtual team communication are evidenced and understood in its workplace. This particular workplace aims to be a significant player in the financial services business in Asia with offshore worksites recently established throughout the region. For example, since 1989, MetroFin has established an offshored workforce of over 500 staff in Bangalore alone with 360 high-level information technology (IT) jobs sent there from its onshore location starting from 2002. Recent MetroFin workplace texts, such as their vision and corporate values statements champion 'multi-diversity' and 'flexibility' as global workforce practices and promote the importance of knowledge and skills sharing across the region. However, both on- and offshore managers and teams appear to be experiencing challenges in realizing this new vision, and their efforts appear to be made more difficult when working and communicating virtually. The following research questions are therefore explored in this article:

(1) Are there problems related to virtual team communication at Metrofin revealed in the TNA?
(2) If so, what are these problems and their characteristics?
(3) How might these inform the training development for a MetroFin course to enhance virtual team communication?

In order to answer these questions, first I provide an overview of the current and relevant literature in the fields of business management, intercultural communication, linguistics and critical discourse analysis (CDA) as they relate to workplace settings in general, and specifically where studies have been completed, to virtual communication work teams. I then examine samples of key internal and external documentation that encapsulate the MetroFin corporate values, including extracts from the original Request for Proposal

(RfP); the RfP scopes the business view of the virtual communication problem. I report in detail on the TNA where manager and team member surveys were carried out and followed up by interviews. The final discussion suggests the causes (e.g. power struggles, identity confusion and job losses) of virtual team communication failure, as revealed in the TNA, and offers insights for training. I caution that treating the symptoms for virtual team failure (e.g. technology, meeting skills and perceived intercultural and language gaps) will not directly address the underlying problem of disempowerment and distrust over offshoring. This has important implications for training design and implementation. I will first explore current studies that have been carried out in communication in virtual and co-located work teams and their relevance to this study.

A review of the literature

VTM Studies in the business literature

Much has been written in the business management and organizational behaviour literature about the impact of leadership, meeting skills, team characteristics, technology and the notion of 'trust' when managing and working in virtual teams; however fewer studies have explored the intercultural and linguistic issues of working in this context.

Studies in the business management and organizational behaviour fields have sought to explore the question of how virtual teams operate, what problems they experience and how they can be improved to meet business requirements. These studies are wide-ranging and have focused on issues such as leadership style and management skills in virtual teams (Chutnik & Grzesik, 2009; Kayworth & Leidner, 2002; Walsh, 2011), the nature and composition of specific virtual teams (Hertel, Geister, & Konradt, 2005), technologies for virtual teamwork (Klitmøller & Lauring, 2013) and the notion of 'trust' (Olsen & Olsen, 2012) as possible locations for improvement. Many of the studies stress the importance of 'mindfulness' in virtual leadership where relationship building and management is difficult without the affordances of regular face-to-face contact. Leaders therefore have to do what they normally do but be 'more vigilant, purposeful and intentional about mitigating differences (e.g. culture, time and geography); about using effective leadership practices and about leveraging technology to build virtual work spaces that surpass 'real' ones' (Walsh, 2011, p. 2).

Other studies have looked specifically at the nature and work of different virtual teams, for example, simple reporting work completed on a project versus collaborative knowledge-building and problem-solving. Understanding the differences in the nature and work of virtual teams is viewed as critical in deciding how best to manage and lead virtual work. Paulus, Kohn, and Dzindolet (2011) suggest that creative teams are highly interdependent and therefore need to meet and be managed responsively on a needs basis; they further report that team characteristics such as size, diversity, inter-disciplinarity, turnover, cohesion and task structure impact virtual management and communication to achieve optimal results. In other words, there is no prescribed way of managing teams as such; the complexity of the work being done, however, is key to understanding how and when such teams should meet and how they should be managed. This view is particularly pertinent to this study where some MetroFin teams do highly collaborative knowledge-building and problem-solving work as part of IT projects, whilst others regularly report to their onshore managers on routine operational progress. The expectations for meeting participation and input, and meeting management, are therefore somewhat different.

Hertel et al. (2005) take a different approach by summarizing recent research into the management of virtual teams in terms of the kinds of key activities that are evident in the 'lifecycle' of virtual team management; those being, preparation, launch, performance management, team development and disbanding. It is proposed that each part of this cycle presents unique and varied management and participation challenges, and therefore, different communication skills for virtual teams.

Leadership and trust are two dominant themes in the business management studies. Kayworth and Leidner (2002) suggest:

> (that leaders) require a capability to deal with paradox, contradiction and uncertainty by performing multiple leadership roles simultaneously; act in a mentoring role and exhibit a high degree of understanding (empathy) toward team members; assert their authority without being perceived to be overbearing and inflexible and being effective at providing regular, detailed and prompt communication with their peers in articulating role relationships and responsibilities among virtual team members. (Kayworth & Leidner, 2002, p. 40)

Whilst such suggestions would also be equally valid in the leadership and management of co-located meetings, these leadership characteristics are seen as critical in virtual communication where face-to-face and chance meetings in corridors do not happen. The notion of 'trust' is discussed extensively in this literature with a distinction drawn between what researchers call 'swift trust' and 'earned' trust (Javenpaa & Leidner, 1998). Swift trust can be defined as that kind of immediately ascribed trust founded on expertise or authority. However, such immediate trust, they argue, is fragile and different from 'earned' trust which is developed over time with timely, predictable and well-considered responses and demonstrated work follow through by leaders. Such leadership virtues of trust, openness and dependability are proposed as key qualities in virtual team management but few studies have explored the communication and intercultural issues inextricably connected with such behaviours. Furthermore, many communication strategies are offered in this literature (see for example, Gibson & Cohen, 2003) but without a good understanding of how virtual communication using English as a lingua franca is impacted by corporate change and strategies, and how intercultural differences and second language impacts listening and speaking, such strategies may not be effective. This study contributes to this understanding by revealing how a group of key stakeholders at Metrofin see both the causes and the problems of virtual team communication when using English as the lingua franca, and how they may be mitigated (or not!) in communications training.

Intercultural differences have been explicitly raised as possible challenges when managing diverse virtual teams. Daim et al. (2012) found in their study that the problematic handling of cross-cultural differences was:

> a significant differentiator in effective cross functional communication and leveraging benefits as the virtual teams comprise ethnically diverse members. (Daim et al., 2012, p. 203)

Other studies (see for example Dekker, Rutte, & Van den Berg, 2008; Henderson, 2005) have explored the issue of intercultural difference as a contributing factor to virtual team management communication using Scollon and Scollon (2001) and Hofstede (1994) approaches respectively to explore face loss in multicultural virtual teams and power distance. They concluded that perceptions of appropriate communication behaviours within the virtual teams differed across culture and that all members of virtual teams need to become aware of behaviour and communication expectations. Two further intercultural studies in the business management field have demonstrated the possible business opportunities of the intercultural composition of virtual teams. Janssens and Brett (2006) suggest that superior outcomes in global virtual teams are achieved when the qualities of different cultures are combined. Shenkar (2011), on the other hand, in his study is critical of the void/gap metaphor in the international business studies where businesses assume something called cultural distance. He proposes replacing 'distance' with 'friction'. This new metaphor, he suggests:

> is not merely semantic as it implies focusing on the interface between transacting entities rather than the void between them. (Shenkar, 2011, p. 9)

Whilst there is broad agreement that there are key differences and challenges in managing and participating in virtual teams as opposed to co-located teams, many of these business management and intercultural studies conclude that further investigation in the nature of language in the communication exchange in these meetings is needed.

> Multinational companies are multilingual and each one will need to deal with the language barriers it encounters when expanding into countries that do not share its home country language. It is therefore surprising that language diversity has attracted so little attention in the field of international management and business. This is all the more remarkable as research into the role of language in organisations is well established. (Harzing, Köster, & Magner, 2011, p. 279)

However, I argue in this paper that assigning communication failure solely to ethnicity or language problems masks more fundamental problems of misalignment around corporate offshoring strategies resulting in job loss and a sense of professional disempowerment and confused identities in the on- and offshore business.

Interestingly, the notion of 'trust' in this literature is reduced to a personal frontline management issue where attributes and behaviours of managers of virtual teams are the key focus of these studies. There is however, I would argue, an equally important issue of organizational trust where corporate values may be seriously misaligned with corporate practices and implementation policies. This is alluded to in the interview data findings discussed later in the article where offshoring is seen on the one hand as encouraging 'diversity, knowledge sharing and flexibility' and, on the other hand, as resulting in onshore redundancies. As well, later on in the data, offshore managers reported aspirational frustrations in not being able to 'live the corporate values' because of onshore management styles. Both can be seen as organizational distrust resulting in management misalignment. The impact of organizational distrust could provide an important area of further research in virtual team management and communication training.

Linguistic and CDA studies in workplace settings

Insights from linguistic and critical discourse theories may be highly relevant in understanding the root causes of communication difficulty in this virtual work context. Such studies, some using CDA, pursue themes of power relationships and workplace identity building. The changing nature of work in post-industrial times is variously described as capitalist reorganization (Foley, 1994); 'fast capitalism' (Gee, 1994), new capitalism and new work order (Gee, Hull, & Lankshear, 1996), and neo-liberal capitalism (Harvey, 2005). However:

> the common message coming from domains as varied as cultural theory, organization studies, management theory, sociology, literacy theory, and adult education, is that we are in the midst of significant organizational change. (Iedema & Sheeres, 2003, p. 317)

Insights from critical discourse analysts, such as Jan Blommaert and Chris Bulcaen (2000) and Ruth Wodak (1989, 1995), have investigated the intricate relationship between power and language seeking to analyze 'opaque as well as transparent structural relationships of dominance, discrimination, power and control as manifested in language' (Wodak, 1995, p. 204). They have become increasingly interested in how the new globalized economy has impacted communication in the workplace (see for example, Cameron, 2000; Iedema & Wodak, 1999; Rhodes, Scheeres & Iedema, 2008) and on how new managerial requirements impact the construction of employee identities, through language use, at work. Of particular relevance to this article are the notions of 'textualization', 'commodification' or 'metadiscursive regimes' around new work practices. These have been the subject of a number of studies (see, for example, Darville, 1995; Jackson, 2000; Iedema & Sheeres, 2003; Park, 2013) where contemporary workplace discourses are reflected in corporate documentation and new practices:

> where workers across a variety of sites are being confronted with having to renegotiate their knowing, their doing, and their work identity. (Iedema & Sheeres, 2003, p. 316)

These notions are of high relevance to this study where MetroFin promotes new ways of 'doing and being' (e.g. valued behaviours reflecting flexibility, multidiversity, collaboration and innovation) in its corporate literature. Such corporate 'textualisations' realize its aggressive strategic direction where offshoring product development and working collaboratively in virtual teams is fast becoming the norm. These metadiscourses of 'diversity management', 'flexible work management' and 'being excellent' can be seen to be part of the neo-liberal capitalist workplace (Iedema & Sheeres, 2003; Park, 2013) where:

> the ideal neoliberal subject does not begrudgingly participate in work, but displays initiative, responsibility, and flexibility, willingly taking risks and engaging in projects of endless self-improvement instead of relying on past achievements, welfare, or solidarity. (Park, 2013, p. 560)

These new roles and identities are highly valued within MetroFin, and how they can be supported through training is at the heart of this study. If there is resistance and misalignment around these values and directions, which a critical stance would suggest, then it would seem logical that these would need to be confronted and addressed before participants, whether they be onshore or offshore, would be receptive to developing skills and strategies for improved communication in a training course.

Studies have also been carried out in the global service industry (see, for example, Heller 2003, 2010) where the 'workforce has become the wordforce' (Park, 2013, p. 560) and English is a key commodity. Linguistic analyses of the virtual communication in call centre work (see, for example, Forey & Lockwood, 2007) have identified second language customer services representatives struggling to communicate with native-speaker customers to meet the expectations of Western onshore management. Whilst there is scope for similar linguistic analyses of virtual team exchanges to reveal particular locations of communication difficulty, this article has been limited to how informants in the MetroFin case study TNA perceive difficulties in communicating in this new work order as part of the TNA.

The value of these intercultural and linguistic insights into workplace communication may contribute to an improved understanding of the root causes of communication difficulty where language, culture, power and identity are key concepts in realizing the new metadiscourses of the changing globalized world of capitalism. Without this, training packages may simply be treating the symptoms of the problem without addressing the deeper issues.

The MetroFin case study
The methodology

Multiple sources were used in the needs analysis phase of this project, which took place over a period of 12 weeks. These included reviews of internal and external documentation, key stakeholder surveys and interviews and the observation and recording of VTM meetings. Given that company documentation encapsulates values, changes and strategic direction, it is important to understand how Metrofin is positioning itself for change and growth in the future, and what attendant problems (e.g. alignment around these) may be emerging. This is directly relevant to the first research question. In order to triangulate the findings, survey and follow up interviews with key stakeholders on- and offshore were conducted and analyzed. Two live virtual team meetings were observed and six onshore virtual team meetings at MetroFin were recorded and transcribed; these will be analyzed in a future study of how language is specifically used in the management of virtual team meetings.

The MetroFin TNA findings

MetroFin has been undergoing rapid change in the last 10 years where offshored project and operational teams have been expanding and 'matrix' reporting lines have become normal business practice. 'Matrix' reporting in global workplaces can best be described as a situation where employees are often working in multiple teams and reporting to multiple managers, thus superseding the old, and perhaps more predictable work order of one-line reporting. These changes are reflected in the new workplace texts that promote work values such as collaboration, knowledge sharing, teamwork, flexibility and diversity. An analysis of these texts is important in this study because they reflect MetroFin's core values and strategic priorities. As outlined in the previous section, such textualizations present managers and employees with new work practices and aspirations, around which workplace employees may find themselves misaligned. If this is the case, then communication will be impacted and what may appear to be a surface linguistic or intercultural misunderstanding may in fact be masking much deeper issues of identity threat and power play. Samples of these texts are exemplified and discussed in the next section.

The MetroFin corporate documents - The website

Diversity is consistently highlighted in the website where it also says in the 'values' statement document:

> We believe in the inherent strength of a vibrant, diverse and inclusive workforce where the backgrounds, perspectives and life experiences of our people help us to forge strong

connections with all our customers, innovate and make better decisions for our business. Our people have the opportunity to learn and progress with us, regardless of gender, age, ethnicity, cultural background, disability, religion and sexual orientation and professional background. (website accessed 5 April 2014).

Not only does this website highlight diversity, in all its forms, as a key aspirational characteristic of Metrofin, but it also states that this will add value to the business though innovation and better decision-making. Metrofin acknowledges that this will provide opportunities for learning and business improvements. Understanding how these employees engage with these values is key to evaluating the level of alignment and where the workforce may be supported through training. Some of the challenges are stated in the proposal document below and are further illuminated through the surveys and interviews.

The MetroFin corporate documents – RfP

The MetroFin RfP revealed a number of work team and management problems which are specified the VTM programme requirements as follows:

> MetroFin has a global structure with a matrix overlay and flexible work practices which means that many teams operate in situations where they are not physically co-located and where management practices need to be shaped to support the delivery of business outcomes in virtual teams. The skills and practices need to build on managing this diverse context and specifically manage the challenges and opportunities of virtual team management in a broad cross-cultural context.

Major challenges threatening work communication are revealed in the above statement. First the 'matrix overlay' where employees and managers have to deal with multiple reporting lines; second, 'flexible work practices' where employees may work only part-time and at home putting pressure on regular communication. Third, given that most teams will be multicultural in composition, first language and cultures will not necessarily be shared. These factors in themselves are possible barriers to smooth communication, but given that most of the teamwork is carried out virtually, the problems of relying on voice rather than face-to-face meetings may well exacerbate this work context. These issues relate directly to my first two research questions that probe the kinds of problems revealed in this part of the TNA for virtual workplace communication. This document further describes uncertainty, lack of trust and inappropriate micromanagement as current risks in the new work context and these in themselves perhaps set an agenda for training priorities and contributes to answering my third research question.

> Managerial practices need to be transitioned to a new way of working in a global setting; there is uncertainty in the new world about how to succeed in this context, especially with the increase in offshoring of teams. We are not fully leveraging opportunities to learn and gain insights into improved processes from these changing work contexts. There is evidence that the effectiveness of management in remote or virtual contexts is diminished when people do not recognize the shift required, or are not given enough space to think about the challenges and address them specifically. Employee survey data has highlighted micro-management, lack of trust, confused accountabilities stemming from lack of clear direction and poor relationship building in the remote and virtual team environment (RfP, 2013, p. 3).

This extract of the RfP is revealing in that MetroFin declares its failure to date in implementing its new work practices. Interestingly, there is a recognition of the time and space needed for alignment around the new business strategy of offshoring and virtual teamwork, and this brings into question the efficacy of offering a one-day course.

The survey findings

A virtual team survey comprising 38 questions was sent out to 100 MetroFin team members and managers both on- and offshore probing areas to do with technologies, communication and culture and meeting behaviours. Given that this survey was formally part of the TNA, there was an almost 100% response. Managers were mostly domiciled onshore, with 7% in India, whilst the participants were more scattered across the region with 21% of respondents offshore. There was a noticeable trend in the findings where the onshore managers reported more positively on the use of virtual team technologies, on communication and intercultural behaviours and on the use of management meeting skills, than participants offshore. Onshore managers felt, on the whole, that their virtual teams were going well. This finding was in stark contrast to their offshore team counterparts who appeared to feel disempowered, marginalized and frustrated in the virtual meetings run by onshore managers. This is evidenced in the survey where 25% of team members reported that they felt 'unvalued' in meetings whereas onshore managers gave a nil response for this question; the survey data further revealed that participants felt top down delegation, lack of strategic focus and micro-management to be prevalent in the management style.

Key differences in the data further pointed to how 'silence' in meetings was construed by onshore managers as an indicator of lack of confidence and nothing to say, whereas onshore managers and members viewed 'talking a lot' as a positive attribute while the participants did not, as shown below in Table 1.

Critically, managers also attributed this to 'taking the initiative' (53%), a work practice highly valued in MetroFin. There may be cultural explanations for this finding to do with western work practice expectations that warrant further investigation. These findings are pertinent to the first research question and suggests gaps in communication that may relate to perceptions of power as well as cultural sensitivities when dealing with onshore authority.

The Interview findings

The onshore managers interviewed were from a variety of departments and the offshore managers were local employees, typically at supervisor level. Pseudonyms for the managers are used for the purposes of confidentiality.

The interview data have revealed deep tensions in MetroFin's strategic direction in offshoring.

Table 1. Question 22. If a team member talks a lot it is interpreted as (% for YES to that option).

	Manager (%)	Participant (%)
Important information to share	47	37
Dominating	33	37
Disrespectful	20	29
Taking the initiative	53	24

Interview 1. Head of learning and development – Sally (onshore)

Sally is Head of Learning and Development at MetroFin and emphasized MetroFin's commitment to flexible work practices where employees not only may elect to work part-time, but also work from home if they were employed onshore. However, working from home was not encouraged in the offshore context for legal, health and safety reasons. She further explained that the offshoring strategy required enhanced onshore managerial capability in working with diverse teams across MetroFin's 'regional hub' and this was the rationale for the 'Communicating in Virtual Teams' course. She said:

> Managers are expected to maintain team focus and productivity in an era of redundancy and hub strategy. When MetroFin talks about change management, it is seen as a euphemism for redundancy. We find that on-shore managers often dominate on the phones where knowledge sharing and collaborative problem-solving practices should be happening. We don't know quite why collaboration is not happening; are they afraid Bangalore can do their jobs just as well? Team respect and open communication is sorely lacking and we want improvements here as a result of the VTM course.

Lack of trust, lack of meeting skills management, intercultural communication breakdown and technology instability were all reported by Sally as key challenges in managing virtual teams. However, it was clearly stated that the issue of redundancy should not be opened up for discussion as part of this programme although she agreed that this may be a major source of resistance and misalignment. This is an interesting comment and suggests that an analysis of authentic virtual team meetings may be an important area of further study where the language used would reflect such tensions and power struggles.

Interview 2. IT project manager – Sam (onshore)

Sam was generally positive about his team on- and offshore, and describes himself as a 'good communicator'. He reported however that knowledge sharing through technology did not happen as 'the onshore guys see it as losing their control'. This was an interesting observation given the discussion above, and perhaps this kind of 'passive resistance' could be a key challenge in effective management practices (and indeed training) in the future. He further reported that he did not feel that MetroFin technology supported the company's collaborative processes:

> We're being asked to collaborate with our teams but our technology does not support this ... telespace is hard to book so we rely on phones, concalls and emails. We need faster and more reliable communication technology.

Much has been written in the business management studies about the impact of technology where work teams are collaborating virtually (see, for example, Klitmoller & Lauring, 2013), and communication strategies for dealing with problematic technology would appear to be relevant for a MetroFin training programme. Interestingly in the interview, Sam referred to his IT team as a:

> bunch of techies much more concerned with how systems work and how they can be improved than which location they work from.

This would suggest, as does the linguistic literature (see for example Jameson, 2007; Zaidman, 2001), that professional and other identities (for example, gender and socioeconomic status) can transcend national ones. This warrants further investigation in this context.

Interview 3. Instructional design manager – Melanie (onshore)

Melanie, an Australian, manages 60% of her team onshore and 40% in Bangalore. She strongly expressed the view that face-to-face time is essential as virtual teams start and continue to work together. However, she complained that due to cutbacks this no longer happens:

> We used to have a swap program between Bangalore and on-shore with monthly exchanges … this brought 8 Indians out here, but this has now been cut. We found once we had met our key team members face-to-face and had time to work and get to know each other, our projects went smoother and our teams seemed more productive.

This observation is in line with the business management research findings (see, for example, Gibson & Cohen, 2003). She went on to describe a specific MetroFin project in instructional design where she felt she had given clear instructions at a virtual planning meeting to the Bangalore team and got disappointing results; clearly communication had failed.

> I thought I had been crystal clear in my instructions and checked they'd understood but obviously when they said 'yes' they meant 'no'.

Losing face in the event of not understanding what a manager has said was reported in intercultural communication workplace studies in Asia as a common issue (see, for example, Scollon & Scollon, 2001). Melanie also highlighted in the interview that 'matrix reporting' was a 'shock to the system' onshore where managers appeared to have a particular discomfort with this new work order. She said:

> Unlike their colleagues off-shore, our guys (on-shore) are unfamiliar with managing multiple teams on multiple projects where the comfort of hierarchies and solid line accountabilities are now much more fluid and uncertain.

She further complained about the lack of knowledge sharing across the region and felt the 'values' of MetroFin relating to 'empowering' offshore colleagues and embracing 'multi-diversity' were not, in the main, being enacted in virtual team management behaviours onshore. Specific meeting behaviours relating to multi-tasking (e.g. answering emails when in the meeting) and putting themselves on mute during virtual meetings were also seen as problematic. She said:

> You have to work harder in the virtual space to make meetings work; you can't actually see your members and the goals of the meetings need to be clear; agendas, minutes, follow up action points are key … sloppy virtual meetings just don't work.

The difference in how on- and offshore teams were dealing with the changing strategy and management expectations in MetroFin revealed deep underlying tensions in the onshore and offshore work relationships.

Interview 4. Operational team manager and project development participant – Vivek, India (offshore)

Vivek, an Indian, is now an operational team manager in Bangalore but had previously worked onshore as part of a project team. He described MetroFin – Bangalore as an 'operational hub' while onshore is 'the financial service'. He said:

> In my team we focus on operational efficiency rather than the customer … and because of that difference it can lead to a different approach in setting our objectives … this is not made explicit and should be. I worked as part of a very collaborative team on-shore, but now that I am back in Bangalore the approach is very directive and top down … 'this is the way you do this' rather than 'what do you feel/think about the best way to do it?'. The team here has a lot to say about improvements but they don't get asked…The new regional strategy also means job losses on-shore and managers have smaller teams which they want to protect … so they just don't want to collaborate and cooperate that much.

The observation about feelings of onshore control and job protection resulting in a lack of collaboration with offshore colleagues obviously makes the published MetroFin values and vision statement difficult to implement. Vivek further went on to explain that his teams feel undervalued and disempowered when it comes to problem-solving, and the meetings are often nothing more than discussions between the onshore members who seem to have 'made up their minds'. He saw this as a possible threat to recent trends in offshoring development projects to Bangalore where knowledge-sharing and collaboration are critical. He further suggested:

> On-shore managers are very good at 'acculturalization' management, that is getting their teams to think and act on-shore, but this is not the point in VTM. No one group of managers should feel privileged in that role. I know a lot more about how to handle my different team members out of Bangalore … I've been doing it all my professional life. Maybe there is a great deal they can learn from us as 'global citizens' and used to communicating all over the place.

Vivek's statement reveals a deep resentment towards onshore control. He implies that onshore managers do not have the kind of offshore global mindsets typical of his colleagues in Asia where working across the region has been the norm for a long time. Power rather than cultural differentials appear to be at play here. Further research analyzing the texts of authentic virtual team meetings would perhaps reveal how the discourse reflects power differentials brought up for discussion in these interviews, however this is not the focus of this article.

Interview 5. Sales team manager and participant – Truc, Vietnam (offshore)

Truc had many complaints about the lack of onshore preparation for the virtual meetings she attended as part of the regional sales team, and questioned the need for so many meetings that were nothing more than 'information dumps' from onshore managers.

> I don't know why we have these weekly meetings as they don't really achieve anything more than finding out what is going on on-shore; we don't feel really included in these discussions nor do we get clear agendas and documentation in preparation for the meeting, nor minutes and action points.

Again there is a strong suggestion in this excerpt that the power and control resides onshore and the meetings are simply to provide information and direction rather than to collaborate and invite offshore participation. Truc also complained about the quality of the technology which she said made communication difficult. However, given the little value she placed on these meetings she was not prepared to invest locally (which is the onshore requirement) in technology upgrades as was the recommendation from the corporate IT group in MetroFin.

Whilst she did not complain about language breakdown, she felt teams onshore sometimes had difficulties understanding her colleagues' Vietnamese English and vice versa.

> I wouldn't say that there is a lot of communication breakdown but there are difficulties sometimes for us understanding some of the on-shore idioms and the pace of their talk, and they sometimes find our accent difficult.

Accents, as a location of communication breakdown in workplaces, are well-documented in a number of studies (see for example, Cowie & Murty, 2010; Sharma, 2005) and this comment would suggest that familiarizing virtual team participants and managers with different regional accents would be beneficial listening training. Time differences also appeared to impact these virtual meetings where she complained her onshore counterparts never really acknowledged the unsociable hours for many of these meetings. This warrants further investigation and would imply either ignorance or disrespect of offshore participants' contexts.

Interview 6. Offshore team meeting participant – Rajev, Indian (offshore)

Rajev reports into two regular virtual team meetings. As an IT engineer involved in a project developing new software and systems for MetroFin, his virtual team meeting experience appeared to be very different from his other virtual team meeting which involved reporting in on routine technology maintenance.

> The IT project is great most of the time and we communicate well; once we know the specification we can get on with things and there is a lot of knowledge exchange ... and we're expecting more work to come to Bangalore in the coming months because there is recognized expertise here. The other meeting is pretty much a waste of time ... I just go on mute and do my emails ... I don't understand why we have these meetings really ... it's a waste and I don't need to be there. In fact no one in the maintenance team says much ... it's like taking a roll call, listening and then taking orders.

Interestingly, Rajev's earlier observation reflects Sam's comments about the particular cohesiveness within the IT engineering team and sense of its members feeling valued contributors, and this is in stark contrast to Vivek's view and Sally's concern that offshore employees being seen as just 'grunt workers'. This warrants further investigation in terms of virtual team management and perhaps suggests that there are important differences in the types of virtual team meetings and the requirements to meet and their respective approaches and skills in management. It is of interest and relevance for this study if there are different communicative requirements depending on the nature of the meeting as Rajev seems to suggest. Paulus, Kohn, and Dzindolet (2011) found that the more complex and collaborative the meeting, the higher demand this put on team communication in comparison to routine type information dissemination type meetings. Further investigation, perhaps through a linguistic analysis of authentic virtual team meetings convened for different purposes, may illuminate this question.

Discussion

Whilst this study strongly suggests that further linguistic and critical discourse approaches to analyzing the authentic virtual team exchanges may reveal further underlying tensions, this paper has not set out specifically to provide that kind of analysis. As the research questions suggest, this study has been aimed at exploring the problems of virtual work team communication as expressed in the MetroFin TNA for the purpose of programme development.

Recurrent themes have emerged in this study, some of which could be categorized as root causes of problematic virtual team communication and others as symptoms. The causes relate to power differentials, misalignment around corporate values, professional identity struggles and fear of, and resistance to, offshoring. Without addressing these in the training support, the symptoms of poor technology quality, problematic leadership style, poor meeting skills and surface language use and cultural differences may simply mask the deeper issues. However, there appeared to be a reluctance within MetroFin to deal with the root causes evidenced in a key interview statement (see Interview 1) where Sally reported 'off-shoring as a euphemism for redundancies'. However, she said this should not be brought up in the training. The directive was therefore understood by the training company to be 'treat the symptoms, but not the causes'.

Given also that the training brief for delivery assigned only one day with no time for preparation or follow through, a question arises as to whether such an event would have any impact. This approach to corporate training is not unusual. Gaps in the way training solutions poorly reflect corporate vision and values are common (see for example, King, 2014). A Chief Executive Officer, whilst responsible for articulating the corporate vision, will rely on the executive team including the training department to achieve it. However:

> quite often learning professionals are approached by department managers to provide training that addresses a particular need, much like ordering a product. While fulfilling 'learning orders' can keep you busy, it does not provide a contextual understanding of how the request relates to the business plan and the CEO's vision. (King, 2014, p. 5)

MetroFin's training request appears to be little more than 'fulfilling the learning orders'. This is an important area for research in corporate training where impact does not fully reflect needs and is often not measured, despite heavy investment (Lockwood, 2002).

Another important issue that emerged from the TNA related to the use of English being used as the lingua franca in MetroFin. Offshore managers and participants who are second language speakers of English talked about disempowerment and identity problems when interacting virtually with onshore native speaker managers. Very few studies have explored the role of language in communication breakdown in this virtual setting and these may better explain the significant disparity in the way on- and offshore colleagues viewed 'silence' and 'overtalking'. It may well be the case that onshore managers are not aware of the kind of language they are using in their team meetings and therefore unaware of how this affects their team. This is a rich and important area of further research.

Conclusion

This study has illuminated some key areas for further research in virtual team communication. Findings contribute to an awareness-raising within the business context as to how English as a lingua franca is being used to facilitate or frustrate virtual team communication in a global setting. Without this perspective, the MetroFin training programme runs the risk of treating the surface symptoms as a 'learning order' exercise rather than dealing with the root causes related to identity, trust and empowerment in this new virtual work order.

Disclosure statement

No potential conflict of interest was reported by the author.

References

Belcher, D., & Lukkarila, L. (2011). Identity in the ESP context: Putting the learner front and center in needs analysis. In D. Belcher, A. Johns, & B. Paltridge (Eds.), *New directions in English for specific purposes research* (pp. 73–94). Ann Arbor, MI: The University of Michigan Press.

Blommaert, J., & Bulcaen, C. (2000). Critical discourse analysis. *Annual Review of Anthropology, 29*, 447–466. doi:10.1146/annurev.anthro.29.1.447

Cameron, D. (2000). *Good to talk? Living and working in a communication culture.* London: Sage.

Chutnik, M., & Grzesik, K. (2009). Leading a virtual intercultural team. Implications for virtual team leaders. *Journal of Intercultural Management, 1*(1), 82–90.

Cowie, C., & Murty, L. (2010). Researching and understanding accent shifts in Indian call centre agents. In G. Forey & J. Lockwood (Eds.), *Globalization, communication and the workplace: Talking across the world.* London: Continuum.

Daim, T. A., Reutiman, S., Hughes, B., Pathak, U., Bynum, W., & Bhatla, A (2012). Exploring the communication breakdown in global virtual teams. *International Journal of project Management, 30*, 199–212.

Darville, R. (1995). Literary experience, knowledge and power. In M. Campbell & A. Manicom (Eds.), *Knowledge, experience and ruling relations* (pp. 249–261). Toronto: University of Toronto Press.

Dekker, D. M., Rutte, C. G., & Van den Berg, P. T. (2008). Cultural differences in the perception of critical interaction behaviours in global virtual teams. *International Journal of Intercultural Relations, 32*, 441–452. doi:10.1016/j.ijintrel.2008.06.003

Fairclough, I., & Wodak, R. (1995). Critical discourse analysis. *The Critical Study of langauge*, 204–210.

Foley, G. (1994). Adult education and capitalist reorganization. *Studies in the Education of Adults, 26*(2), 121.

Forey, G., & Lockwood, J. (2007). 'I'd love to put someone in jail for this': An initial investigation of English needs in the business processing outsourcing (BPO) industry. *English for Specific Purposes, 26*, 308–326. doi:10.1016/j.esp.2006.09.005

Gee, J. (1994). New alignments and old literacies: From fast capitalism to the canon. *Australian Reading Association, 37*, 52.

Gee, J., Hull, G., & Lankshear, C. (1996). *The new work order: Behind the language of the new capitalism.* Sydney: Allen & Unwin.

Gibson, C., & Cohen, S. (Eds.). (2003). *Virtual teams that work: Creating condition for virtual team effectiveness* (pp. 69–76). San Francisco, CA: Jossey-Bass.

Harvey, D. (2005). *A brief history of neoliberalism.* Oxford: Oxford University Press.

Harzing, A.-W., Köster, K., & Magner, U. (2011). Babel in business: The language barrier and its solution in the HQ-subsidiary relationship. *Journal of World Business, 46*, 279–287. doi:10.1016/j.jwb.2010.07.005

Heller, M. (2003). Globalization, the new economy, and the commodification of language and identity. *Journal of Sociolinguistics, 7*, 473–492.

Heller, M. (2010). Language as a resource in the globalized new economy. In N. Coupland (Ed.), *The handbook of language and globalization* (pp. 349–365). Malden, MA: Blackwell.

Henderson, J. K. (2005). Language diversity in international management teams. *International Studies of Management and Organisation*, *35*(1), 66–82.

Hertel, G., Geister, S., & Konradt, U. (2005). Managing virtual teams: A review of current empirical research. *Human Resource Management Review*, *15*(1), 69–95. doi:10.1016/j.hrmr.2005.01.002

Hofstede, G. (1994). The business of international business is culture. *International Business Review*, *3*(1), 1–14. doi:10.1016/0969-5931(94)90011-6

Holden, N. (2002). *Cross-cultural management: A knowledge management perspective.* Harlow: Prentice Hall.

Iedema, R., & Sheeres, H., (2003). From doing work to talking work: Renegotiating knowing, doing, and identity. *Applied Linguistics*, *24*, 316–337. doi:10.1093/applin/24.3.316

Iedema, R. & Wodak, R. (1999). Introduction: Organizational discourses and practices. *Discourse and Society.* *10*(1), 5–19. doi:10.1177/0957926599010001001

Jackson, N. (2000). Writing up people at work: Investigations and workplace literacy. *Literacy and Numeracy Studies*, *10*(1–2), 5–22.

Jameson, D. A. (2007). Reconceptualizing cultural identity and its role in intercultural business communication. *Journal of Business Communication*, *44*, 199–235. doi:10.1177/0021943607301346

Janssens, M., & Brett, J. (2006). Cultural intelligence in global teams: A fusion model of collaboration. *Group & Organization Management*, *31*(1), 124–153.

Javenpaa, S., & Leidner, D. (1998). Communication and trust in global virtual teams. *Journal of Computer Mediated Communication*, *3*, 4.

Kayworth, T., & Leidner, D. (2002). Leadership effectiveness in global virtual teams. *Journal of Management Information Systems*, *18*(3), 7–40.

King, K. (2014). *White paper: A set of best practices for targeting, aligning and measuring learning.* Nashua, NH: Skillsoft.

Klitmøller, A., & Lauring, J. (2013). When global virtual teams share knowledge: Media richness, cultural difference and language commonality. *Journal of World Business*, *48*(3), 398–406. doi:10.1016/j.jwb.2012.07.023

Lockwood, J. (2002). *Language training and evaluation processes in Hong Kong workplaces* (Unpublished doctorate thesis). Pok Fu Lam: The University of Hong Kong.

NASSCOM. (2009). *The annual report of National Association of Software and Services Companies).* India.

Olsen, J., & Olsen, L. (2012). Virtual team trust: Task, communication and sequence. *Team Performance Management*, *18*, 256.

Park, J. S-Y. (2013). Metadiscursive regimes of diversity in a multinational corporation. *Language in Society*, *42*, 557–577. doi:10.1017/S0047404513000663

Paulus, P. B., Kohn, N., & Dzindolet, M. (2011) *Teams.* www.uts.edu/psychology/faculty/paulus/paulus.htm

Rhodes, C., Scheeres, H., & Iedema, R. (2008). Undecidability, identity and organisational Change. In C. R. Caldas-Coulthard & R. Iedema (Eds.), *Identity trouble: Critical discourse and contested identities.* London: Palgrave Macmillan.

RW CultureWizard. (2010). *The challenges of working in virtual teams* (Report). New York, NY.

Scollon, R., & Scollon, S. (2001). *Intercultural communication – A discourse approach.* London: Blackwell.

Sharma, D. (2005). Dialect stabilization and speaker awareness in non-native varieties of English. *Journal of Sociolinguistics*, *9*, 194–224.

Shenkar, O. (2011). Cultural distance revisited: Towards a more rigorous conceptualization and measurement of cultural differences. *Journal of International Business*, *43*, 1–11.

Walsh, M. (2011). *Leading remote teams is virtually the same.* USA: Forum. (www.forum.com).

Wodak, R. (1989). *Language. Power and ideology: Studies in political discourse.* Amsterdam: John Benjamins.

Zaidman, N. (2001). Cultural codes and language strategies in business communication: Interactions between Israeli and Indian business people. *Management Communication Quarterly*, *14*, 408–441.

Identities at odds: embedded and implicit language policing in the internationalized workplace

Spencer Hazel

Department of Culture and Identity, Roskilde University, Roskilde, Denmark

This study offers an interaction analytic account of how linguistic identities in internationalized workplaces in Denmark are indexed against members' institutional positions in particular interactional contexts. Where language policy may not be *explicitly* articulated between members, it is still *embedded* in how participants micro-manage their interactions and *implicit* in how members display orientations to deviance, in the case of encountering others in the workplace whose language repertoires or preferences do not meet with expectation pertaining to the institutional position they hold. The study uses recordings of naturally occurring interaction in different international workplace settings and argues for greater attention to be paid to the actual language-policy *practices* in international workplace settings, as an entry point into developing a more nuanced understanding of the practices through which professional identities are brought about, affirmed or contested, and the linguistic considerations that are implicated in this.

Dit artikel beschrijft een interactie-analytische studie over taal identiteiten in geïnternationaliseerd bedrijven en universiteiten in Denemarken. Het onderzoek keek naar hoe verschillende taal identiteiten vergeleken werden met werknemers' institutionele functies, tijdens werkactiviteiten uitgevoerd samen met anderen. Waar een officiële taalbeleid niet expliciet kan worden gearticuleerd tussen de verschillende gespreksdeelnemers, is het nog steeds ingebed in de manier waarop zij organiseren hun ontmoetingen, en het is impliciet in de manier waarop ze reageren op afwijkend gedrag, van leden die niet voldoen aan de verwachtingen met betrekking tot taal gebruik en hun situatie-specifieke identiteit als werknemer. De studie maakt gebruik van opnames van natuurlijke interacties (niet- uitgelokt of experimenteel) in verschillende werkplekken in internationale organisaties, en concludeert dat meer aandacht moet worden besteed aan hoe taalbeleid is geïnstantieerd in internationale werkplekken, en hoe taalvaardigheid is gekoppeld aan professionele identiteit.

Introduction

Workplaces around the world have increasingly come to be constituted as communities of transnationally mobile staff and clientele, and the resulting cultural and linguistic diversity to which this gives rise. One consequence is that members of these transient multilingual communities (Mortensen, 2013) need to coordinate dynamically fluctuating participation frameworks (Goffman, 1981; Goodwin, 1981, 2007) and their contingent language scenarios (Mortensen, 2010) as part and parcel of their ongoing daily workplace activities (e.g. Hazel & Mortensen, 2013; Torras, 2005). This in turn requires members to remain sensitive to a shifting bricolage of *linguistic identities* (Gafaranga, 2001) encountered at any given moment as they go about their work-related activities, in order to be able to respond appropriately, effectively and efficiently to each linguistic scenario as it arises. Consequently, a member's language competencies can become implicated in his or her institutional – and thereby also implicitly their professional – identity.

The current study offers an empirical, interaction analytic account of how linguistic identities are indexed against members' institutional positions in particular workplace interactional settings such as business meetings and university help desk service encounters. Drawing on Conversation Analysis (Goodwin & Heritage, 1990, hereafter CA) and Membership Categorization Analysis (Hester & Eglin, 1997, hereafter MCA), the study demonstrates how members topicalize linguistic identities that go against normative expectations, implicitly engaging in language policing at a praxeological level and treating members of the workplace community who do not meet with expectations regarding language repertoires as deviant or even sanctionable. The paper will argue for greater attention to be paid to the actual language-political *practices* in international workplace settings, as an entry point into developing a more nuanced understanding of the practices through which professional identities are brought about, affirmed and contested, and the linguistic considerations that are implicated in this. This would complement research strands that investigate language policy, ideology and attitudes through a focus on official documentation or by drawing on qualitative research methods such as focus groups and interviews.

A growing number of institutions have moved to adopt formal policies pertaining to language practices – including that at the level of language choice – in the workplace (e.g. Angouri & Miglbauer, 2014; Gunnarsson, 2014; Hultgren, 2014; Lønsmann, 2011; Neeley, 2013; Nekvapil & Nekula, 2006). Such explicit language policing may be introduced to respond to the changing demands that result from increased globalization, including the internationalized make-up of a particular institutional community, be it, for example, a company operating across borders or with greater numbers of migrant professionals, foreign-based clients or partners in other parts of the world, at popular tourist attractions or at particular institutional programmes within tertiary-level education. However, such language-policy strategies may not apply, or be appropriate, to all settings within a workplace community, or indeed reach all relevant parties. For example, in the case of a university seeking to develop an international profile, students, maintenance staff, canteen employees, language teachers and administrators may each have different levels of access, lines of communication or levels of investment in the organization's formal language policy. Furthermore, individual members may also hold entrenched ideological positions of their own pertaining to the relative value of the use of particular languages within a setting or to language requirements relating to institutional positions within a particular workforce. Hence, backroom language policies may not be implemented or adhered to across all settings within a workplace community, and this necessitates members to remain prescient to the dynamics of such transient multilingual settings (Goebel, 2010).

In linguistically dynamic environments where language choice is then *not* predetermined by formal institutional policy, e.g. relating to language use among technical support staff (Lønsmann, 2011) or in informal or liminal institutional settings (Hazel & Mortensen, 2013), selecting or negotiating a medium of interaction may become a relevant activity to which interlocutors need to attend (Auer, 1984; Torras, 1998). Within groups that enjoy a more or less stable membership, these practices can rely on prior experience and knowledge of other members' linguistic repertoires and preferences (Bonacina-Pugh, 2012; Spolsky, 2007). Members can draw on experience of interacting with particular colleagues, clients or partners, in order to select the appropriate language to use with them, or which bilingual mode (Gafaranga & Torras, 2001) to adopt. In addition, they may switch to a designated corporate language when engaged in particular types of activities, such as team meetings (Lønsmann, 2011) or student project group activities (Mortensen, 2010). Here, where language policy may not be *explicitly* discussed between members, it is still *embedded* in how participants micro-manage their interactions. Consequently, the locally determined language policy for the particular interactional setting can be located in how a medium of interaction is negotiated and/or enforced by members, without it being overtly topicalized in the talk. For example, Mortensen (2014) shows how locally established norms for language choice within student project groups are evidenced in how the members orient to the appropriateness of one or other language for engaging in particular activities, such as on-task or off-task talk. Elsewhere, in encounters where participants have no prior experience of interacting with one another, participants must also work together to alight upon the medium which best suits the parties involved and the institutionally oriented activities in which they are engaged (Heller, 1982; Torras, 1998). Especially at the incipient stage where people move from co-presence-in-space to being co-participants-in-interaction, we are able to distil from the sequential organization of social actions – including that at the level of language choice – who and what people are expected to be – institutionally, professionally – in these settings (see Hazel & Mortensen, 2014; Mortensen & Hazel, 2014).

Methodological approach

The line of research offered here builds on notions of the 'linguistic realisation of institutionality' (Heritage, 1997; Kurhila, 2006, p. 7). From this perspective, the institutionality of interaction is constituted through how participants' themselves attend to the setting and the particular *participation frameworks* (Goffman, 1981; also Goodwin, 1981, 2007) upon which an interaction is contingent, including how institutional identities are constituted in situ.

Social science has occasioned a number of lines of investigation characterized by a focus on situated social action and interaction observed in their natural everyday habitats. The methodological perspective applied in the current study has its origins in the American sociological approach to language and social interaction, known as Ethno-methodology (Garfinkel, 1967; henceforth EM). In EM, the study of human sociality is premised on an understanding that there are methods of which members of a society avail themselves in their understanding, production and navigation of their social world. It is the researcher's goal to explicate these *members' methods* for conducting social life (hence *Ethno-methodology*), rather than impose a priori theoretically derived categories, as is common in a majority of social scientific work. Social order is considered here an achievement by the participants, who rely on their common-sense knowledge of situated action in order to accomplish, in situ, orderliness in their conjoint social activities.

The EM approach has inspired a number of lines of research, most notably CA (Sacks, Schegloff, & Jefferson, 1974) and MCA (Hester & Eglin, 1997; Sacks, 1972). Both approaches take as a central concern that sociality must be understood from the viewpoint of the participants engaged in social life: CA in investigating the systematic practices oriented to by participants in the sequential organization of social action, and

MCA by explicating the procedures through which members associate particular activities or characteristics – predicates – with particular categories of people (Sacks, 1972). Such research explores

> the relevance of person categorization to the understanding and assessment of conduct, and the consequent importance of understanding how categories are made relevant, even if tacit, in ordinary conduct of interaction. (Schegloff, 2005, p. 474)

Sacks proposed that these membership categories are 'inference-rich' (Sacks, 1992, p. 40) with members displaying their understandings of particular characteristics that are accepted as common knowledge about members of the category (Sacks, 1979, p. 13).

By investigating the practices members themselves employ to display their understanding of ongoing activities between one another, a researcher is able to shed light on the very dynamic constitution of social order through members' own methods for social engagement. With CA and MCA using audio recordings and increasingly audiovisual recordings of – and artefacts stemming from – social engagement in its natural ecology, the research methodology offers powerful tools to unpack and describe the situated social processes involved in workplace organization.

Consequently, these lines of investigation have been strongly represented in applied research, highlighting the situated nature of social action, with important interaction analytic research being carried out in such institutional sites of engagement as business meetings (e.g. Markaki, Merlino, Mondada, & Oloff, 2010; Mondada, 2004), collaborative workplace activities (e.g. Murphy, 2005), health care (e.g. Brassac, Fixmer, Mondada, & Vinck, 2008; Heath, 2002; Koschmann, LeBaron, Goodwin, & Feltovich, 2011), public space milieu (e.g. Hindmarsh, Heath, Vom Lehn, & Cleverly, 2005; Mondada, 2009), educational and instructional settings (e.g. Goodwin, 1994; Greiffenhagen & Watson, 2009; Mori & Hasegawa, 2009; Mortensen & Hazel, 2011; Nishizaka, 2006) and public broadcast media (e.g. Raudaskoski, 2010).

The present study aims to contribute further to this field, investigating what implications the widespread internationalization of workplace settings has for the members, including the interactional competencies relevant to the navigation of such interactional settings. One salient area of internationalization relates to the impact on the participants with regard how a member's language competencies are implicated in their institutional – and thereby also their professional – identity. We turn now to build an empirical account of some such displays and to demonstrate how deviation from normative interactional patterns by members of the community can impact upon their status as member of their institutional category.

Data for the current study were collected by the author in internationalized workplace settings, including international university settings[1] (see Hazel, 2012), and international companies in Denmark.[2] Video-, and in some cases, audio-only recordings were produced using multiple recording devices for optimal coverage. Transcription conventions are based on those developed by Gail Jefferson (2004; further explanation provided in Appendix 1).

Language policing – situated language policies in practice

Spolsky (2004, 2007) differentiates between three levels of language policy: that found in language management (the formally agreed instruction and documentation), in beliefs (what people hold to be appropriate conduct) and in practice (what people actually *do*):

language practices, beliefs and management are not necessarily congruent. Each may reveal a different language policy. The way people speak, the way they think they should speak, and the way they think other people should speak may regularly differ. Looking at the language policy of established nations, one commonly finds major disparities between language policy laid down in the constitution and the actual practices in the society. Within social groups, it is common to find conflicting beliefs about the value of various language choices. One is therefore faced regularly with the question of which the real language policy is. (Spolsky, 2004, p. 217)

By this reasoning, social practices relating to language use are considered to constitute an actualization of a particular community's policies concerning appropriate conduct, including of course that at the level of language choice. Through such *practiced language policy* (Bonacina-Pugh, 2012), participants draw on regular patterns of language usage, with 'practice form[ing] a recognisable and analysable set of patterns' (Spolsky & Shohamy, 2000, p. 29). These in turn constitute interactional norms. As Bonacina-Pugh (2012, p. 219) writes:

> interactional norms are the implicit understanding that speakers have of what language (choice) act is appropriate or not in a given context. Speakers use these norms as "schemes" (Garfinkel, 1967) to interpret each others' language (choice) acts; that is, "a point of reference or action template for interpretation" (Seedhouse, 2004, p. 10).

Regularity, recognizable practices and underlying norms may point to relatively stable communities, where members rely on shared understandings, and members whose practices do not correlate with overall normative expectations may be interpreted by others in the community as somewhat deviant. Indeed, they may be treated as such also. These deviant cases can be identified through participants displaying an orientation to the particular conduct/act as requiring repair, or being marked in some way or other. By looking at the ways the participants treat these interactional moments, an analyst is able to identify the related normative expectations. Furthermore, they offer valuable insights into the ways in which members of a community are constituted as being deviant.

Embedded language policing

The following example is taken from a departmental meeting situated in an international company in Denmark, composed by a nationally heterogeneous workforce where transnational mobility is a common feature. The meeting has until this point been conducted in English, which here acts as a regularized lingua franca – for this type of activity – between the participants, who are from different European countries.[3] There are eight participants present, most of whom have at least some proficiency in Danish, and all are able to use English, albeit with differing levels of proficiency. The practiced language policy in evidence here – with English adopted as a corporate lingua franca – appears to be premised on how the team is constituted through members from different language backgrounds, and with new members joining and others leaving the team on occasion to work in other departments within this multinational company.

At the point of entry into this sequence, the Team Manager (ULLa) is talking with one of the team members (EMMa) about *work-at-home* days near the Easter break. As she does this, a third member of the team (ANNa) interjects with a comment.

EXAMPLE 1 SH-WP1 Ulla line manager; Emma and Anna — team members

```
10  ULL: yes i would say: (1.3) because we do have cover (0.5)
11       otherwise i'm not too eager→
12       er: that we are so little peo⌈ple⌉≋
13  EMM:                               ⌊mn ⌋
14  ULL: ≋in the office ⌈maybe at that time→⌉
15  ANN:                ⌊   ja fordi jeg   ⌋ måtte jo ik' få det→
                         yeah because I    wasn't allowed to get that
16       (3.0)
17  ULL: nej det var fordi du havde to dage
          no that was because you had two days
18       (0.7)
19  ANN: ↑ja→
          ↑yeah→
20       (0.4)
21  ANN: så jeg må ⌈gerne have en→⌉
          so I'm allowed to have one
22  ULL:           ⌊i den periode ⌋ (0.7)⌈altså jeg⌉ er ik' glad for det→
                     in that period       (0.7) so I'm not happy about it
23  ANN:                                 ⌊   xxx   ⌋
24       (0.3)
25  ANN: nej→ (0.2) ⌈men øh:⌉
          no   (0.2)  but er:
26  ULL:            ⌊i'm i'm⌋ not happy↗
27       harman has it because he's in norway↘
28       (0.9)
29       and he's working from from the oslo office↘
30       (0.6)
31       i'm not happy about having working from home in in those periods↗
32       but i am willing to get exceptions
33       but two days in that period is not accept⌈able⌉
34  ANN:                                          ⌊nej→⌋
                                                   no
35  ULL: and this was ⌈your initial point↘⌉
36  ANN:              ⌊but one was↘⌋
37       (0.7)
38  ULL: one is not accept⌈able⌉ but i'm willing to grant that er
39  ANN:                  ⌊ no ⌋
40  ULL: to gr⌈ant⌉ er permission
41  ANN:      ⌊mn⌋
```

We note in the example how Anna provides a critical comment to her line manager Ulla (line 15), where she raises an issue relating to her own request for *work-at-home* days, a decision where she feels she has been slighted. Importantly, we see how this interjection is treated as the voicing of a grievance by the manager Ulla, who in response provides an account for the decision (lines 17 and 22). This appears then to evidence a workplace culture where managers can be challenged by their subordinates and explicitly held to account for their decisions. Not only do we observe the challenge, but we also see that the manager orients to this as not necessarily a welcome trajectory but valid all the same. Although complaints make a variety of responsive turn types or action types relevant (Schegloff, 2005), for example, remedial actions, excuses, apologies and the like, here Ulla produces an account for her decision to only allow Anna a single extra *work-at-home* day. Although the complaint is thus not addressed in a remedial way, but instead rejected, the rejection is formatted as a dispreferred response (on preference organization, see Pomerantz, 1984): it is delayed, it includes an account for the decision and furthermore mitigates the rejection with a further account of how Ulla has already gone out of the way to make exceptions.

Pertinent to the study here, we note that the language chosen for providing the comment in line 17 is Danish, not English as in the rest of the meeting, and the side sequence that this occasions, is initially pursued in Danish. Auer (1984) has proposed that there is a normative preference in conversation for maintaining the same language across turns at talk (see also Gafaranga [2000] on same medium talk; Nevile & Wagner [2008]).

In this way, the choice of language used in a first pair part adjacency pair (e.g. a question) constrains the choice of language through which a second pair part (e.g. an answer) is produced. In the current sequence, this means that the unmarked choice for the manager here is to respond in Danish, which she does.

However, Ulla subsequently does initiate medium repair (Gafaranga, 2000), where she repeats her utterance initially produced in Danish ('jeg er ikke glad for det', line 22) subsequently in English ('I'm not happy', line 26). We see that this repair is initially resisted by Anna: her acceptance of the account in line 34 is still distinctly Danish ('nej'), but eventually she complies with the medium repair, displaying her understanding of the manager's account, which she formats both as an increment to Ulla's 'but two days in that period is not acceptable' (line 33), with her own 'but one was' (line 36), now in English.

We note then that in this interactional setting – a departmental team meeting – some challenges are legitimated, but at the level of language choice, Anna's opting for Danish is treated as unacceptable. Indeed, not only does the manager perform a dispreferred action in the form of an *other-initiated repair* (on preference organization and repair, see Jefferson, 1987; Schegloff, Jefferson, & Sacks, 1977) she formats the medium repair without any of the components that would normally mitigate for the dispreference of the action (these could be, e.g. delay, hesitation markers, inter- and intra-turn pauses, or an account for the repair). Robinson describes how the withholding of such formatting components 'tend[s] to have negative sociorelational implications' (2004, p. 320), but it can also act as a contextualization cue for inferring a particular range of social actions being performed, for example, teasing, arguing, some jocular activity, or producing a complaint. In this case, with such components withheld by Ulla, the repair appears formatted as an unequivocal, public rejection of Anna's language choice, and Anna is brought to book on the matter, in full view of her colleagues.

The example demonstrates how when members display language choice preferences that do not correlate with the prevailing *practiced language policy* (in the sense described by Spolsky and Shohamy [2000] and Bonacina-Pugh [2012]), they can be publicly sanctioned, with their language selection overruled. Indeed, even in workplace settings such as these where we observe a predominantly democratic organizational ideology being oriented to, where subordinates' personal opinion is not only accepted, but valued and encouraged, members of staff can have their choice of language overridden, regardless of the fact that it may be the *better* language through which to communicate with their interlocutor.[4] Of course, a manager who must operate with a fluctuating team of transnationally mobile employees, who each have different linguistic repertoires, career trajectories within the company and histories within the local setting, is faced with the issue of maintaining optimal lines of communication between team members. This includes transparency, where decisions are understood by all, not just those more closely connected. Ulla's *embedded language policing* here results in all team members being included as ratified overhearers (Goffman, 1981) to what is ostensibly a private complaint sequence between her and her subordinate.

Although this example is drawn from a *transient multilingual setting*, there is enough group stability for practices to become routinized, even within the ongoing changing membership of the team. Elsewhere, however, members face the necessity of having to enter into encounters with people they have never met previously. Here, participants must coordinate or negotiate language-policy practices on the spot, including at the level of appropriate language choice. As they do so, so we gain access to normative expectations relating to the matter. It is this that we turn to now.

Implicit language policing

Membership categories and their linguistic predicates

Parties entering into an interaction with a previously unacquainted person in a linguistically heterogeneous setting are faced with the member's concern of which language to opt for from the outset. A number of resources appear to facilitate them in settling on an operational medium for interaction. Some of these relate to membership categorization, through which they may project certain expectations relating to the language competencies and preferences of their incipient partners-in-interaction. Not all membership categories here are relevant. Gender, for example, sexual orientation or age group categories would be wholly irrelevant to the linguistic identities of the interlocutors-to-be.

However, there are membership categories – for example those pertaining to ethnic or racial background, geographic residence, or institutional identity – that appear to be used as a resource for discerning the probability for possible language preferences or competencies on the part of the unacquainted other. Someone with an East-Asian appearance may, for example, be judged less likely to have proficiency in Portuguese, than someone with Latin-American features. Regardless of the obvious margins of error that such categorization practices engender, people seek to reduce the levels of complexity when faced with social life in all its messy, diverse glory. By categorizing the members we encounter into social sub-categories of varying granularity, we draw on normative expectancies regarding such membership categories and the presumed characteristics and features associated with them (Antaki & Widdicombe, 1998).

In addition to the many 'transportable identities' (Zimmerman, 1998) described above, social identity constructs constituted in interaction may be drawn on to furnish participants with further cues regarding the appropriacy of a particular language choice for the setting. Here, identities are brought into being discursively, worked up as respective relational identities relevant to the interaction in which they are engaged (e.g. *parent, mechanic, nerd, punk, swinger*). As with the identity constructs described above, these membership categories too may engender particular associations, e.g. a particular dress code for a *punk*, a particular laissez-faire attitude for a *swinger*. It follows that such membership category predicates are useful tools, but only when the particular social identity is oriented to as being relevant to the business at hand.

As with the 'transportable identities', particular membership categories may also imply particular linguistic implications, including preferences for language choice in a particular setting, and linguistic repertoires and competencies. As way of illustration, consider the following extract, which serves to demonstrate how linguistic identities are implicated in certain social membership categories. Here, MARianne is standing behind the help desk counter at an International Office in a Danish university, when ANIta and BRIgitta approach.

Anita initiates her account for attending the help desk in English (lines 21 and 23). She does this immediately, without any preliminary request as to whether this is an appropriate choice. This displays a projection on her part that the member of staff is able to deal with the service encounter in English and that this language selection would be neither problematic, nor unexpected, for the given setting. For her part, the staff member triggers a switch to Danish once it becomes clear what is projected as the topic of the service. As soon as Anita announces that the students are interested in a study exchange abroad (line 24), she asks whether they are Danish speakers (line 26). This is not surprising, as the programme after which the students are enquiring is intended for

EXAMPLE 2 LTSH-day4-SE-1331 Marianne Staff; Anita and Brigitta -German students

```
18 ANI:  xx
19 MAR:  hej
20       (2.6)
21 ANI:  we have a (.) question
22 MAR:  yeah
23 ANI:  eh we we we like to ehm (0.3) go aboard and study aboard
24       eh and eh and with erasmus eh
25       (1.4)
26 MAR:  and you i snak- ta- i taler ikke dansk vel≈
         you talk- spe-you don't speak Danish do you
27 BRI:  ≈jo
         sure
28 ANI:  jo
         sure
29 BRI:  ja
         yes
30 ANI:  jo det kan vi også
         yeah we can do that too
31       (0.3)
32 MAR:  hvor- i er ikke fra dan- (.) fra: Danmark ⌈eller⌉
         where- you're not from Den- (.) fro:m Denmark or
33 BRI:                                    ⌊ xx ⌋ vi er fra tyskland
                                            xx  we are from germany
34       (0.8)
35 ANI:  men vi snakker dansk≈
         but we speak Danish
36 MAR:  ≈↑nå:: okay fint nok (.)
         ↑oh:: okay that's fine
37 MAR:  og i er fuldtidsstuderende ⌈her⌉ (.)
         and you're full-time students here
38 BRI:                             ⌊mmh⌋
39 MAR:  ⌈*↑okay⌉ (0.2) ja
          ↑okay (0.2) yes
         *STA produces smile
40 ANI:  ⌊mmh⌋
41       (0.6)
42 BRI:  øhm (0.6) ja vi vi vil øhm (0.2) ansøge (0.2)
         erm (0.6) yeah we we want to erm (0.2) apply (0.2)
43       på erasmus til øhm Madrid
         for erasmus to erm Madrid
```

full-degree students at the university, the overwhelming majority of which are Danish. Offering Anita and Brigitta the opportunity to conduct the encounter in Danish suggests that the normative expectation is that these encounters are conducted in the language 'of least resistance', at least on the part of the client (we return to this in the next section).

The staff member initially responds in English (line 26), though breaking off almost immediately and switching to the local language for the remainder of the turn, in which she asks whether they speak Danish. Interestingly, she projects her understanding that they *are* Danish speakers through the language choice in which she produces the question, namely Danish. The students confirm that they are able to speak Danish, which calls attention to their *capacity* to use of the language, rather than it being their *default*. This in turn prompts the staff member to offer a further candidate understanding that they are not from Denmark (line 32). Brigitta confirms this, in Danish, by self-categorizing herself and her partner as hailing from Germany.

We observe then how the staff member's initial categorization of the students as Danish occasions an extended insertion sequence (Schegloff, 1972) in which this misunderstanding is straightened out. In addition, the participants orient to the students' Danish proficiency as somewhat non-normative. Having first categorized them as Danish speakers, the staff member produces a change-of-state token (Heritage, 1984) with an upward pitch shift (↑nå::, translated as ↑oh::), indicating a shift in understanding, that they are not from Denmark after all. Subsequently, when Brigitta categorizes herself and Anita as being 'from Germany', Anita orients to their still being able to speak Danish as somewhat marked, through her use of the modifying phrase 'but we speak Danish'. It appears here that participants orient to the category 'international student' with a predicate 'non-Danish speaking' constituting the norm with 'Danish-speaking foreign students' representing a smaller subcategory. Indeed, the staff member's candidate formulation in line 37, proposing they are full-time students, may also reflect an understanding that *this* particular subcategory, the *full-time* student, would account for their Danish language proficiency, as opposed to other sub-categories of international students, such as *exchange* or *visiting* students. Although Anita has already set out that they would like to discuss studying abroad, which categorizes them as full-time students at the university, the staff member's response to Brigitta's confirmation of this line, 'okay' (line 39), is formatted as a change-of-state token (Heritage, 1984) with a marked upwards shift in pitch. This suggests that she has now been able to fully re-calibrate the categorization of the students, bringing the insertion sequence to a close. Anita subsequently reformulates her earlier turn in which she set out the reason for the visit, this time in Danish (lines 42 and 43).

The above analysis illustrates how membership categories such as 'international student', 'German', 'full-time student' and 'university international staff member' may be used by members to project the linguistic make-up of those they come into contact with. Where reality intervenes and expectations are uncorroborated, work is undertaken to re-calibrate the misalliance between expectation and actuality. In what follows, we will explore this further and demonstrate how such sequences of misalignment between institutional and linguistic identity may act to undermine the institutional position of a member of the community, by orienting to them as not type-fitting the institutional position relevant to the encounter. This, I will argue, is a form of *implicit language policing*, where members are treated as not conforming to their professional identities, on the basis of an absence of some or other expected linguistic resources.

Institutional identity and orientations to deviance in language repertoire

Although the public sanctioning of the sort observed in Example 1 may display the various power relations at play in dyadic engagements where there are formal divisions of labour and status, language policing can also be found in other participation frameworks, such as those described in the following examples, and where language preferences and competences are indexed against someone's institution-bound social identity. In the following analysis, we will start by introducing a particular recurrent practice for entering into a service encounter at a university International Office help desk (see also Mortensen & Hazel, 2014), before moving to discuss one of a collection of deviant cases.

Across all types of approach, a common pair of patterns for entering into the focused encounter is represented in the following transcripts, represented in examples 3–6.

In these examples, we note a canonical adjacency sequence of greeting tokens, here 'hi' or 'hej', a subsequent hesitation marker (e.g. 'erm' or 'øhm'), which acts as a pre-speech token indicating upcoming speakership, following which the *client* starts formulating the reason for the visit.

Although a Danish greeting 'hej' and an English 'hi' can sound distinctly different, to those unacquainted with Danish, they can sound very similar.[5] Furthermore, in these settings there is both a great deal of variation in how this greeting is vocalized. The upshot is that the linguistic code is at this stage ambiguous.[6] This linguistic ambiguity acts as a resource for negotiating the medium of interaction for the subsequent encounter. We note two patterns: the first involves the staff member (STA) producing the first greeting with the client (CLI) responding. In this pattern, the initial 'ambiguous' hej/hi greeting token is responded to with a similarly ambiguous return greeting from the client.

```
LTSH-day8-SE-1223 (Ex.3)

  01  STA:  hej/hi≈
  02  CLI:  ≈hej/hi
  03        (0.6)
  04  CLI:  øhm vi er tre der lige har
            fundet et udvekslingsophold
```

```
LTSH-day6-SE-1144 (Ex.4)

  01  STA:  hⸯi:/hej⸰
  02  CLI:  ⸰hi:/hejⸯ
  03        (1.2)
  04  CLI:  erm: I'm:: international student↗
```

```
Sub pattern 1

  01   STA:  1st greeting
  02   CLI:  2nd greeting
  03
  04   CLI:  topic initiation turn
```

```
LTSH-day8-SE-1123 (Ex.5)

  01  CLI: hej/hi
  02  STA: hej/hi
  03
  04  CLI: øh jeg har et spørgsmål
```

```
LTSH-day8-SE-1205 (Ex.6)

  01 CLI:  hej/hi
  02 STA:  hej/hi
  03       (0.9)
  04 CLI:  um I got a question I received this letter
```

```
Sub pattern 2

  01  CLI: 1st greeting
  02  STA: 2nd greeting
  03
  04  CLI: topic initiation turn
```

This allows for the client to respond in the same language and to proceed to the next turn where the medium becomes disambiguated, either as Danish as in the first example or as English as in the second. The second pattern has the first greeting produced by the client, with the member of staff producing the return greeting. Here, the staff member is in the position to treat the first greeting (produced by the client) as *either* Danish or English. The client is then in the position to treat this return greeting as either Danish or English and to proceed to formulate the next turn in that medium of interaction.

The above patterns for entering into a service encounter at this International Office help desk evidence a particular organization of affording *the client the right* to select one of a number of languages to serve as medium for interaction, here Danish or English. It is always the client who is afforded the turn where the language becomes disambiguated. This in turn demonstrates categorization work carried out by the participants, who at this incipient stage of their focused encounter are able to display within their turn organization an institutional orientation, with an asymmetrical distribution of interactional rights and obligations. Secondly, these membership categories are linked with particular category-bound associations relating to language repertoires. Particularly, the category 'International Office staff member' is oriented to as having the linguistic arsenal to deal with a client in whichever language the client selects (from the collection consisting of Danish and English).

Routinized practices such as those described here pass off in an unmarked – *seen-but-unnoticed* – fashion, as has been described for normatively appropriate social conduct in general (Garfinkel, 1967). Analyses of cases that deviate from the regular interactional patterns can provide us with a useful second level of analysis. These instances provide us with further insight into what normative expectations are present, according to which parties orient themselves in the particular setting at hand. Deviant cases can be identified through participants displaying an orientation to the particular conduct/action requiring repair, or being marked in some way or other. By looking at the ways the participants treat these interactional moments, an analyst can get at the underlying norms (see Hutchby & Wooffit, 1998, for discussion of deviant case analysis).

In the current data-set, there are a number of these deviant cases, where the step-wise move into this business-at-hand is momentarily suspended along the same lines as discussed in Example 2. Here, we will discuss one of the instances where it is the staff member whose language repertoire becomes a topic requiring attention prior to the service encounter proceeding. In this excerpt, a client approaches the help desk counter and he and the staff member enter into an encounter. However, the meeting hits trouble when the staff member initiates medium repair (Gafaranga, 2000) from Danish to English.

We note the canonical opening sequence described earlier (lines 17–19). Following this pattern the client is again in the position to treat the second greeting, produced by the

`Example 7 LTSH-day4-1201 Tom staff; Kaj client`

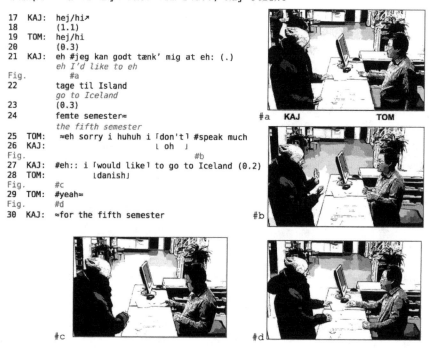

```
17  KAJ:  hej/hiↄ
18        (1.1)
19  TOM:  hej/hi
20        (0.3)
21  KAJ:  eh #jeg kan godt tænk' mig at eh: (.)
            eh I'd like to eh
Fig.        #a
22          tage til Island
            go to Iceland
23        (0.3)
24          femte semester≈                        #a  KAJ        TOM
            the fifth semester
25  TOM:    ≈eh sorry i huhuh i ⌈don't⌉ #speak much
26  KAJ:                         ⌊ oh ⌋
Fig.                                    #b
27  KAJ:  #eh:: i ⌈would like⌉ to go to Iceland (0.2)
28  TOM:          ⌊danish⌋
Fig.      #c
29  TOM:  #yeah≈
Fig.      #d
30  KAJ:  ≈for the fifth semester                  #b
```

staff member in response to his own, as being in either English or Danish. He subsequently embarks on formulating the topic of the enquiry, selecting Danish to do so. At the point in which we normally observe a 'continuer' token on the part of the staff member, here the staff member occasions a suspension of the unfolding multi-unit turn. He offers an apology for not being able to speak Danish, formatted with laughter tokens (lines 25 and 28). This apology acts as what Schegloff (2005) has described as a retro-acting object, prompting a search for possible 'complainable' conduct located in the prior talk. As soon as the clerk's choice of English is identifiable ('sorry I huhuh', line 25), and the trouble source thus recognizable, the apology is downplayed by the client. This is a preferred next action to an apology (Robinson, 2004). Here the client moves his hands from the counter and brings them up to chest height (Figure b) in a demonstrative gesture of disputing the relevance of the apologizing – either by a 'warding off' of the apology or producing this as an apologetic gesture in its own right, acknowledging the mis-categorizing of the staff member as a Danish speaker. Whichever reading one takes, the gesture acts to attenuate the staff member's transgression (Robinson, 2004), although not without locating the 'complainable', which is here the clerk's inability to conduct the encounter in Danish. The client subsequently restarts his turn, this time in English.

The participants here negotiate an explicit repair of the medium of interaction (Gafaranga, 2000), but what is more, it is produced in a dispreferred format (Pomerantz, 1984; Schegloff et al., 1977): it is delayed, disfluent, includes hesitation markers, with an explicit apology and account for the repair initiation on the part of the staff member. These formatting components appear to orient to an understanding of the staff member's Danish language proficiency being a cause of interactional trouble, and hence being a valid expectation on the part of a client.

The lack of Danish is thus arguably treated as a relevant deficiency on the part of his membership in the category relating to his institutional position. The staff member is oriented to by both parties as not type-fitting the membership category relating to his institutional identity, with Danish being *accountably absent*. This indicates that not being able to speak in the client's preferred language is a sensitive issue which touches on what Garfinkel (1964, p. 225) refers to as the moral order:

> A society's members encounter and know the moral order as perceivedly normal courses of action - familiar scenes of everyday affairs, the world of daily life known in common with others and with others taken for granted.

Breaches in the everyday normality or affairs attract attention, result in anxiety, moral and psychological evaluations even, and can threaten the status of the breacher, in this case the member of staff.

Schegloff (2005, p. 452) has argued that the 'complainability of some form of conduct can be contingent on the identity of the agents and the recipients of the conduct—identities often grounded in category memberships', and that this can be seen to be oriented to, even in the absence of an explicit complaint. The upshot of perturbations such as that featured in the above example is that the member of staff is oriented to by *both* the client *and* the staff member himself as deviating from the normative expectations pertaining to the membership category 'International Office staff member', at least with regard his linguistic identity. Of course, this is not treated *explicitly* as problematic on the part of those who come into contact with him: it is *implicit* in the way expectations are displayed as requiring recalibration. With each occasion potentially flagging up the misalignment between the institutional position that he holds and his linguistic repertoire, these repair sequences may then act to undermine his institutional identity and confidence as a fully *competent* member of staff, indeed potentially bringing about a marginalization of particular members of the workplace community. This supports findings documented elsewhere by survey-based studies such as those by Ehrenreich (2010) and Neeley (2013).

Coda: adopting strategies for avoiding explicit medium repair

Elsewhere (Hazel, in press), I have described a number of strategies (not always successful) that this particular member of staff has adopted, which serve to circumvent the type of interactional trouble analyzed here, and micro-manage the entry into the encounter. First there is the *pre-emptive strike*, where he avoids the greeting sequence altogether and opens the interaction with a turn that is clearly, unambiguously English. This exploits the preference for same language across turns (Auer, 1984; Gafaranga, 2000; Nevile & Wagner, 2008), constraining the language choice of his co-participant. Second, he is seen drawing on resources in the environment, his receptive language competence in Danish or a related language and his understanding of the range of topics common to the service requests in order to respond to clients' opening turns, while in the process performing embedded medium repair (Gafaranga, 2010) from Danish to English. The adoption of such strategies would appear to indicate a disposition to avoid such situations where his linguistic identity is indexed against his institutional membership category, with the potentially negative ramifications for his professional identity.

We note that in order to avoid a topicalizing of the staff member's 'deficient' language repertoire in this way, he or she is able to draw on a range of resources to micro-manage the trajectory into the service encounter. Doing so allows for the staff member to forestall the adoption of a 'problematic' language as medium of interaction, or alternatively to prompt the client to switch to the staff member's preferred medium. Furthermore, this is done without occasioning an explicit language negotiation sequence, where the staff member's language competencies are flagged up as being at odds with normative expectation.

The analyses presented here demonstrate how language repertoires, preferences, and competencies are indexed against members' institutional roles. Where these linguistic identities do not meet with normative expectations regarding a particular institutional position, this may be flagged by the parties as deviant, and business that needs attending to for the interaction to proceed. These sequences display many hallmarks of being dispreferred: they are disfluent, delayed and require of the 'deviant' member to provide an account for the non-compliance with normative expectations. This perceived deviance may in turn act to unintentionally compromise the institutional identities of particular members of the community, leading to potential marginalization.

Discussion and conclusion

We opened with a discussion of how language repertoires and competencies, in sum one's linguistic identity, are indexed against particular membership categories, including those related to professional or institutional identities. The subsequent analyses focused on workplace settings constituted by linguistically diverse populations of staff and clients, where language selection is oriented to as a members' issue. For example, a particular category-bound predicate associated with the institutional status of team members in an international company in Denmark is the unproblematic, confident use of English during workplace meetings, regardless of the personal preferences or competences of the team members to do so. Elsewhere, in a Danish university setting, international students are expected to *lack* proficiency in the local language, while staff at the International Office help desk are expected to be at least bilingual in Danish and English, regardless of their institutional role within the organization. Where this is not the case, as in the examples offered here, participants display an orientation to this *non-observance* (Spolsky & Shohamy, 2000), treating the members as deviating from normative expectations relating to their membership category, and therefore not conforming to their respective institutional identities. As a consequence, workplace members' linguistic identities are indexed as *other-than-the norm*, suggesting that this otherness in fact works as a process of implicit evaluation within particular communities of practice. In the same way a member of staff can be held accountable for being unable to accommodate the line manager or the client in terms of carrying out their job, or addressing the particular issue that has prompted a service encounter, the staff member can also be held morally accountable for what language repertoire is available for carrying out the tasks.

The overriding theme for the Special Issue is a critical exploration of how working in highly interconnected and multicultural workplace communities shapes language and sociocultural practices and offers a set of discussions of the methodological challenges and opportunities that these transient settings offer the field of language and intercultural communication. The current paper has sought to demonstrate how empirical accounts of situated language practice can enhance our understanding of how language policy, language ideology and language attitudes play out in the field, with consequences for the institutional or professional identities of the members in these communities. The particular *emic* perspective developed through CA- and MCA-inspired analyses is especially beneficial here, as it allows for researchers to develop empirically grounded accounts of the ways in which members in the workplace communities produce social order in situ, through the micro-managed social practices evidenced in interaction, including sequential organizational practices of turn-taking, repair strategies, accounting practices and orientations to deviance.

Although discursive approaches to the analysis of institutional and professional identities have gained in momentum in the last few years, studies of identities as they emerge in the carrying out of everyday work practices, especially those studies using recordings of 'real-life' encounters, are still very much in the minority (Bargiela-Chiappini, 2011). The corrective offered here and in similar work elsewhere (e.g. Day, 1994; Markaki et al., 2010) does not seek to underplay the insights generated by the types of study that investigate the interplay of linguistic and professional identities within international workplace settings, which have been conducted using other methodological tools, such as quantitative survey reports (e.g. Harzing & Pudelko, 2013), qualitative survey tools (e.g. Ehrenreich, 2010; Mahili, 2014; Neeley, 2013), ethnographic observation or mixed-method approaches that combine ethnographic fieldwork with survey tools (e.g. Lauring, 2008; Lønsmann, 2014). Rather, interaction analytic accounts such as the one presented here aim to contribute to this field of scholarship, by offering insight into the moment-by-moment enactment of social order, including at the level of identity negotiation.

I will discuss this with two examples. First, interaction analytic research can offer additional nuance to studies in the field of transnational mobility. For example, where a recent critique by Canagarajah (2013) has sought to offer greater granularity to the sociolinguistics of globalization as represented by Blommaert and colleagues (e.g. Blommaert, 2010; Collins, Baynham, & Slembrouck, 2009), which he argues employs too blunt a conceptualization of *scalarity* to be able to account for the agency of migrant workers as they re-negotiate their linguistic identities within their new, translocal sociolinguistic environments, his own study draws on interview data with migrants, which is still some distance removed from the settings themselves (a point acknowledged by himself). More immediate scrutiny of the interactions in which people are involved, as featured in the current study, affords both of these lines of research a window into how such agency is constituted, contested, negotiated and resolved between the parties to these encounters in situ. Hence, we are able to develop a different level of insight: that of how participants display *between one another* their respective understanding of what norms, expectations, rights and obligations are deemed relevant for *this* moment, in *this* activity, in *this* setting with respect to language and indexicality. Consequently, we are in the position to build up a fuller, more fine-grained account of the fleeting moments where identity work is being occasioned, where people place one another within a matrix of social order; practices which would be difficult to explicate through even the most detailed accounts elicited through survey tools such as interviews. Where Canagarajah's study, and those aforementioned studies such as Neeley (2013) and Ehrenreich (2010) can report on some *outcomes* of workplace internationalization on members' experiences of how this impacts on their position, self-esteem and perceived agency within their workplace communities, interaction analytic investigations can shed light on the very *processes* from which these accounts result.

Second, this line of research continues to add to theoretical work on discursive identities, and more broadly on theorizing identity. Looking at the internationalized work setting, Lauring (2008), for example, explores how L1 differences may impact on the formation of in-group social identities among workplace members. Here, he critiques Social Identity Theory (e.g. Tajfel, 1982) with what he perceives as its linear link between language and identity, criticizing this conceptualization as too deterministic and static and arguing for a more dynamic consideration of language use as a means for strategic self-representation in the transnational workplace. In transient multilingual settings and communities such as those featured in the current study, we can explore this further, and show how it is not necessarily the L1 background that becomes the relevant object within institutional activities, but a member's available language arsenal, language preferences and competences; in sum, their linguistic identity and how this accommodates whichever institutional identity is oriented to as relevant to that encounter. It is the linguistic resources that a member is able to mobilize that is here the relevant *object of identification* (Lauring, 2008) with relation to one's institutional category, rather than this or that language, or the particular (L1 or L2) status of the language to the user.

With an increasing number of institutional settings becoming internationalized, the findings presented here have important implications for workplaces characterized by transnational mobility. Increasing an awareness of social practices that link professional identities with other social identity constructs such as ethnicity, nationality or in this case linguistic identity, can (1) prepare the ground for avoiding the potential pitfalls of group fragmentation, anxiety, alienation and isolation experienced by particular members of the workplace community (e.g. Deneire, 2008); (2) promote greater mutual accommodation between divergent normative expectations and (3) promote further understanding of the longer term impact that such deviance marking may have on a member's upward social mobility within the workplace. The shifting sands of the increasingly transnational workplace settings that have recently become so commonplace across the globe offer both practitioner and researcher an opportunity to reconsider sedimented understandings of community membership and belonging, social identity formation and workplace practices, and explore afresh the dynamic processes involved in the constitution of workplace – and other types of – communities.

Notes

1. These data were collected as part of the Research Centre for Cultural and Linguistic Practices in the International University.
2. Carried out as part of the LINGCORP Research project.
3. Prior to the formal proceedings of the meeting commencing, as well as during breaks in the meetings, participants use other languages also.
4. Interestingly, Anna, who appears to be insisting on a right to use Danish with her Danish manager, is not herself a Dane, but is from Sweden (albeit someone who has lived in Denmark a number of years), and appears therefore to be claiming the right to use a different L2 than English.
5. A reviewer of the current article has pointed out that if these greeting tokens are produced with rising intonation, it is likely to be heard as a Danish *hej* rather than an English *hi*. This would definitely be the case for many settings. However, the data from this setting do not seem to bear this out, as there is a great deal of variation in how the L2 users of both English and Danish produce these tokens, including at the level of intonation contour. Participants are unable, then, to treat this as a reliable marker for the use of *hej* or *hi*.

6. See Woolard (1999) and Torras (1998) for discussion of bivalent utterances, tokens that could be heard as being from either one language or another, such as the Catalan and Spanish 'hola'.

Disclosure statement

No potential conflict of interest was reported by the author.

References

Angouri, J., & Miglbauer, M. (2014). "And then we summarise in English for the others": The lived experience of the multilingual workplace. *Multilingua*, *33*(1–2), 147–172.
Antaki, C., & Widdicombe, S. (1998). *Identities in talk*. London: Sage.
Auer, P. (1984). *Bilingual conversation*. Amsterdam: Benjamins.
Bargiela-Chiappini, F. (2011). Foreword. In J. Angouri & M. Marra (Eds.), *Constructing identities at work* (pp. xiii–xi). Basingstoke: Palgrave Macmillan.
Blommaert, J. (2010). *The sociolinguistics of globalization*. Cambridge: Cambridge University Press.
Bonacina-Pugh, F. (2012). Researching 'practiced language policies': Insights from conversation analysis. *Language Policy*, *11*, 213–234.
Brassac, C., Fixmer, P., Mondada, L., & Vinck, D. (2008). Interweaving objects, gestures, and talk in context. *Mind, Culture, and Activity*, *15*(3), 208–233.
Canagarajah, S. (2013).Agency and power in intercultural communication: negotiating English in translocal spaces. *Language and Intercultural Communication*, *13*(2), 202–224. doi:10.1080/14708477.2013.770867
Collins, J., Baynham, M., & Slembrouck, S. (Eds.). (2009). *Globalization and language in contact: Scale, migration, and communicative practices*. London: Continuum.
Day, D. (1994). Tang's dilemma and other problems: Ethnification processes at some multicultural workplaces. *Pragmatics*, *4*(3), 315–336.
Deneire, M. (2008). English in the French workplace: Realism and anxieties. *World Englishes*, *27*(2), 181–195. doi:10.1111/j.1467-971X.2008.00551.x
Ehrenreich, S. (2010). English as a business lingua franca in a German Multinational corporation: Meeting the challenge. *Journal of Business Communication*, *47*, 408–431. doi:10.1177/0021943610377303
Gafaranga, J. (2000). Medium repair vs. other-language repair: Telling the medium of a bilingual conversation. *International Journal of Bilingualism*, *4*, 327–350.
Gafaranga, J. (2001). Linguistic identities in talk-in-interaction: Order in bilingual conversation. *Journal of Pragmatics*, *33*, 1901–1925. doi:10.1016/S0378-2166(01)00008-X
Gafaranga, J. (2010). Medium request: Talking language shift into being. *Language in Society*, *39*(2), 241–270. doi:10.1017/S0047404510000047
Gafaranga, J., & Torras, M.-C. (2001). Language versus medium in the study of bilingual conversation. *International Journal of Bilingualism*, *5*(2), 195–219. doi:10.1177/13670069010050020401
Garfinkel, H. (1964). Studies of the routine grounds of everyday activities. *Social Problems*, *11*(3), 225–250. doi:10.2307/798722
Garfinkel, H. (1967). *Studies in ethnomethodology*. Englewood Cliffs, NJ: Prentice-Hall.
Goebel, Z. (2010). Identity and social conduct in a transient multilingual setting. *Language in Society*, *39*(2), 203–240. doi:10.1017/S0047404510000059
Goffman, E. (1981). *Forms of talk*. Oxford: Blackwell.
Goodwin, C. (1981). *Conversational organization: Interaction between speakers and hearers*. New York: Academic Press.

Goodwin, C. (1994). Professional vision. *American Anthropologist, 96*, 606–633. doi:10.1525/aa.1994.96.3.02a00100

Goodwin, C. (2007). Participation, stance and affect in the organization of activities. *Discourse & Society, 18* (1), 53–73. doi:10.1177/0957926507069457

Goodwin, C., & Heritage, J. (1990). Conversation analysis. *Annual Review of Anthropology, 19*(1), 283–307. doi:10.1146/annurev.an.19.100190.001435

Greiffenhagen, C., & Watson, R. (2009). Visual repairables: Analysing the work of repair in human-computer interaction. *Visual Communication, 8*(1), 65–90. doi:10.1177/1470357208099148

Gunnarsson, B.-L. (2014). Multilingualism in European workplaces. *Multilingua, 33*(1–2), 11–33.

Harzing, A.-W., & Pudelko, M. (2013). Language competencies, policies and practices in multinational corporations: a comprehensive review and comparison of Anglophone, Asian, Continental European and Nordic MNCs. *Journal of World Business, 48*(1), 87–97. doi:10.10 16/j.jwb.2012.06.011

Hazel, S. (2012). *Interactional competence in the institutional setting of the international university* (Unpublished doctoral thesis). Roskilde University, Roskilde.

Hazel, S. (in press). Institutional identity negotiations in multilingual workplace settings. In Lubie Alatriste (Ed.), *Discourse studies in diverse settings: Dissemination and application*. Clevedon: Multilingual Matters.

Hazel, S., & Mortensen, J. (2013). Kitchen talk – Exploring linguistic practices in liminal institutional interactions in a multilingual university setting. In H. Haberland, D. Lønsmann, & B. Preisler (Eds.), *Language alternation, language choice and language encounter in international tertiary education* (pp. 3–30). Dordrecht: Springer.

Hazel, S., & Mortensen, K. (2014). Embodying the institution – Multimodal practices in developing interaction in study counselling meetings. *Journal of Pragmatics, 65*, 10–29.

Heath, C. (2002). Demonstrative suffering: The gestural (re)embodiment of symptoms. *Journal of Communication, 52*, 597–616. doi:10.1111/j.1460-2466.2002.tb02564.x

Heller, M. (1982). Negotiation of language choice in Montreal. In J. Gumperz (Ed.), *Language and social identity* (pp. 108–118). Cambridge: Cambridge University Press.

Heritage, J. (1984). A change-of-state token and aspects of its sequential placement. In J. M. Atkinson & J. Heritage (Eds.), *Structures of social action: Studies in conversation analysis* (pp. 299–345). Cambridge: Cambridge University Press.

Heritage, J. (1997). Conversation analysis and institutional talk. In D. Silverman (Ed.), *Qualitative research: Theory, method and practice* (pp. 161–182). Thousand Oaks, CA: Sage.

Hester, S., & Eglin, P. (1997). Membership categorization analysis: An introduction. In S. Hester & P. Eglin (Eds.), *Culture in action: Studies in membership categorization analysis* (pp. 1–23). Washington, DC: International Institute for Ethnomethodology and Conversation Analysis & University Press of America.

Hindmarsh, J., Heath, C., Vom Lehn, D., & Cleverly, J. (2005). Creating assemblies in public environments: Social interaction, interactive exhibits and CSCW. *Computer Supported Cooperative Work (CSCW), 14*(1), 1–41. doi:10.1007/s10606-004-1814-8

Hultgren, A. K. (2014). Whose parallel lingualism? Overt and covert ideologies in Danish university language policies. *Multilingua, 33*(1-2), 61–87.

Hutchby, I., & Wooffit, R. (1998). *Conversation analysis*. Cambridge: Polity Press.

Jefferson, G. (1987). On exposed and embedded correction in conversation. In G. Button & J. Lee (Eds.), *Talk and social organisation* (pp. 86–100). Clevedon: Multilingual Matters.

Jefferson, G. (2004). Glossary of transcript symbols with an introduction. In G. Lerner (Ed.), *Conversation analysis. Studies from the first generation* (pp. 13–32). Amsterdam: John Benjamins.

Koschmann, T., LeBaron, C., Goodwin, C., & Feltovich, P. (2011). "Can you see the cystic artery yet?" A simple matter of trust. *Journal of Pragmatics, 43*(2), 521–541. doi:10.1016/j.pragma.2009.09.009

Kurhila, S. (2006). *Second language interaction*. Amsterdam: Benjamins.

Lauring, J. (2008). Rethinking social identity theory in international encounters: Language use as a negotiated object for identity making. *International Journal of Cross Cultural Management, 8*(3), 343–361. doi:10.1177/1470595808096673

Lønsmann, D. (2011). *English as a corporate language. Language choice and language ideologies in an international company in Denmark* (Unpublished PhD thesis). Roskilde University, Roskilde.

Lønsmann, D. (2014). Linguistic diversity in the international workplace: Language ideologies and processes of exclusion. *Multilingua 33*(1-2), 89–116.

Mahili, I. (2014). 'It's pretty simple and in Greek...': Global and local languages in the Greek corporate setting. *Multilingua, 33*(1-2), 117–146.

Markaki, V., Merlino, S., Mondada, L., & Oloff, F. (2010). Laughter in professional meetings: The organization of an emergent ethnic joke. *Journal of Pragmatics, 42*, 1526–1542. doi:10.1016/j.pragma.2010.01.013

MacWhinney, B., & Wagner, J. (2010). Transcribing, searching and data sharing: The CLAN software and the TalkBank data repository. *Gespraechsforschung, 11*, 154–173.

Mondada, L. (2004). Ways of "doing being plurilingual" in international work meetings. In R. Gardner & J. Wagner (Eds.), *Second language conversations* (pp. 27–60). London: Continuum.

Mondada, L. (2009). Emergent focused interactions in public places: A systematic analysis of the multimodal achievement of a common interactional space. *Journal of Pragmatics, 41*, 1977–1997. doi:10.1016/j.pragma.2008.09.019

Mori, J., & Hasegawa, A. (2009). Doing being a foreign language learner in a classroom: Embodiment of cognitive states as social events. *IRAL – International Review of Applied Linguistics in Language Teaching, 47*(1), 65–94.

Mortensen, J. (2010). *Epistemic stance marking in the use of English as a lingua franca* (Unpublished doctoral thesis). Roskilde: Roskilde University.

Mortensen, J. (2013). Notes on the use of English as a lingua franca as an object of study. *Journal of English as a Lingua Franca, 2*(1), 25–46.

Mortensen, K. (2014). Language policy from below: Language choice in student project groups in a multilingual university setting. *Journal of Multilingual and Multicultural Development, 35*(4), 425–442. doi:10.1080/01434632.2013.874438

Mortensen, K., & Hazel, S. (2011). Initiating round robins in the L2 classroom–preliminary observations. *Novitas-ROYAL (Research on Youth and Language), 5*(1), 55–70.

Mortensen, K., & Hazel S. (2014). Moving into interaction—Social practices for initiating encounters at a help desk. *Journal of Pragmatics, 62*, 46–67. doi:10.1016/j.pragma.2013.11.009

Murphy, K. M. (2005). Collaborative imagining: The interactive use of gestures, talk, and graphic representation in architectural practice. *Semiotica, 156*, 113–145.

Neeley, T. B. (2013). Language matters: Status loss and achieved status distinctions in global organizations. *Organization Science, 24*(2), 476–497. doi:10.1287/orsc.1120.0739

Nekvapil, J., & Nekula, M. (2006). On language management in multinational companies in the Czech Republic. *Current Issues in Language Planning, 7*(2–3), 307–327. doi:10.2167/cilp100.0

Nevile, M., & Wagner, J. (2008). Managing languages and participation in a multilingual group examination. In H. Haberland, J. Mortensen, A. Fabricius, B. Preisler, K. Risager & S. Kjærbeck (Eds.), *Higher education in the global village* (pp. 149–175). Roskilde: Roskilde Universitetscenter.

Nishizaka, A. (2006). What to learn: The embodied structure of the environment. *Research on Language & Social Interaction, 39*(2), 119–154. doi:10.1207/s15327973rlsi3902_1

Pomerantz, A. (1984). Agreeing and disagreeing with assessments: Some features of preferred/dispreferred turn shapes. In J. M. Atkinson & J. Heritage (Eds.), *Structures of social action: Studies in conversation analysis* (pp. 57–101). Cambridge: Cambridge University Press.

Raudaskoski, P. (2010). "Hi father", "Hi mother": A multimodal analysis of a significant, identity changing phone call mediated on TV. *Journal of Pragmatics, 42*(2), 426–442. doi:10.1016/j.pragma.2009.06.016

Robinson, J. D. (2004). The sequential organization of "explicit" apologies in naturally occurring English. *Research on Language & Social Interaction, 37*(3): 291–330. doi:10.1207/s15327973rlsi3703_2

Sacks, H. (1972). An initial investigation of the usability of conversational data for doing sociology. In D. Sudnow (Ed.), *Studies in social interaction* (pp. 31–74). New York: Free Press.

Sacks, H. (1979). Hotrodder: A revolutionary category. In G. Psathas (Ed.), *Sociocultural dimensions of language use* (pp. 7–14). New York: Irvington.

Sacks, H. (1992). *Lectures on conversation*. Gail Jefferson (Ed.). Oxford: Blackwell.

Sacks, H., Schegloff, E. A., & Jefferson, G. (1974). A simplest systematics for the organization of turn-taking for conversation. *Language, 50*, 696–735.

Schegloff, E. A. (1972). Sequencing in conversational openings. In J. J. Gumperz & D. Hymes (Eds.), *Directions in sociolinguistics* (pp. 346–380). New York: Holt, Rinehart and Winston.

Schegloff, E. A. (2005). On complainability. *Social Problems*, *52*, 449–476. doi:10.1525/sp.2005.52.4.449

Schegloff, E. A., Jefferson, G., & Sacks, H. (1977). The preference for self-correction in the organisation of repair in conversation. Reproduced by G. Psathas (Ed.), *Interactional competence* (pp. 31–62). Washington, DC: International Institute for Ethnomethodology and Conversation Analysis.

Seedhouse, P. (2004). *The interactional architecture of the language classroom: A conversation analysis perspective*. Malden, MA: Blackwell.

Spolsky, B. (2004). *Language policy*. Cambridge: Cambridge University Press.

Spolsky, B. (2007). Towards a theory of language policy. *Working Papers in Educational Linguistics*, *22*(1), 1–14.

Spolsky, B., & Shohamy, E. (2000). Language practice, language ideology, and language policy. In R. D. Lambert & E. Shohamy (Eds.), *Language policy and pedagogy: Essays in honour of A. Ronald Walton* (pp. 1–41). Amsterdam: Benjamins.

Tajfel, H. (1982). Social psychology of intergroup relations. *Annual Review of Psychology*, *33*(1), 1–39. doi:10.1146/annurev.ps.33.020182.000245

Torras, M.-C. (1998). *Catalan, Castilian or both? Code negotiation in bilingual service encounters* (Working Paper No. 96). Lancaster: Center for Language in Social Life. University of Lancaster.

Torras, M.-C. (2005). Social identity and language choice in bilingual service talk. In K. Richards & P. Seedhouse (Eds.), *Applying conversation analysis* (pp. 107–123). Basingstoke: Palgrave Macmillan.

Woolard, K. A. (1999). Strategies of simultaneity and bivalency in bilingual communication. *Journal of Linguistic Anthropology*, *8*, 3–29.

Zimmerman, D. H. (1998). Identity, context and interaction. In C. Antaki & S. Widdicombe (Eds.), *Identities in talk* (pp. 87–106). London: Sage.

Appendix 1. Transcription conventions

Identifier	TEA:
Pause	(0.2)
Overlap markers top	⌈ ⌉
Overlap markers bottom	⌊ ⌋
Intonation: rising	↗
continuing	→
falling	↘
Pitch shift	↑
Latched turns	≈
Smiley voice	☺
Inbreath	·hhhh
Stress	now
Accelerated speech	Δand youΔ
Translation	*In italics*

The transcription conventions are based on those developed by Gail Jefferson (e.g. 2004). Some are used in modified form for use in the CLAN software tool (MacWhinney & Wagner, 2010).

International city branding as intercultural discourse: workplace, development, and globalization

Shi-xu

Centre for Contemporary Chinese Discourse Studies, Zhejiang University, Zhejiang, China

Although the communicative dimension of urban development has caught the imagination of urban studies scholars, the cultural, and intercultural, nature of this discourse has received less attention than it deserves. As a case study and illustration of urban development workplace discourse from out of a Chinese/Asian/developing-world context, the present article examines the properties, problems, and potentials of the global branding practice of Hangzhou, a renowned tourist and ancient capital city on the east coastal region of China. First, after critiquing tendencies in relevant communication approaches, the paper outlines a holistic, cultural concept of urban branding of the developing world – as a culturally saturated, development-oriented, workplace discourse. Then, based on ethnographic data collected from a plethora of sites and sources (the municipality, trade association, the Internet, interviews, newspapers, street posters, museums, and historical records), the paper studies, qualitatively and quantitatively, a variety of interlocking international branding practices (municipal management, expos, festivals, exhibitions, international tours, websites, foreign language use, award-winning, etc.). In conclusion, the paper draws implications for future research and practice on urban development and branding in the developing world.

摘要：虽然已有城市学者从交际语言的角度对城市发展问题进行了研究，但这种话语的文化特性、跨文化特性尚未得到足够的发掘。本文以杭州这一中国东部沿海地区的著名旅游城市与古都为例，进行城市发展话语的研究，探索在中国/亚洲/发展中国家这一大语境背景下，杭州在城市品牌全球化建设过程中表现出的特征、问题及潜力。首先，在对现流行的主流研究方式提出批评之后，本文第一次从整体视角阐述了发展中国家城市品牌的国际营销概念——一种具有文化性和发展指向性的工作场所话语。其次，本文聚焦城市品牌国际化建设、传播、接受的实践活动，采用民族志式的多渠道数据采集方法（涉及市政府、商业组织、互联网、采访、报纸、街头海报、博物馆、历史记录等），从质性和量性的角度就包括市政管理、博览会、传统节日推广、展览、国际旅游、网站、外语使用情况等在内的各种活动进行综合分析和评价。最后，本文就发展中国家的城市发展和城市品牌建设问题，对未来的研究与实践提出了建议。

Problems and aims

Urban development is one of the basic conditions and central goals of the developing world. It is propelled by globalization and accomplished through a variety of forms of cultural-communicative practice. The present study enquires into a special and important dimension of urban development of the developing world, namely, city branding to the international community, or international city branding for short.

Extant research has largely concentrated on Western-world and 'World' cities (Amin, Massey, & Thrift, 2000; Beaverstock, Smith, & Taylor, 1999; Ley, 1995) and models used there are often assumed to be universal. As a partial consequence, the integral, cultural and intercultural, nature of international city branding discourse (CBD) has not received the attention it deserves. It will be necessary and urgent then to take the international branding of developing world cities seriously.

The field of city branding research is fragmented. Generally speaking, there is a tendency to polarize the social cultural aspect and the economic or technical aspect of city development and brand promotion; there is especially a lack of sufficient attention to the former (Lees, 2004; Williams, 2010). This is reflected, for example, in the lack of clear and explicit notions of discourse/communication in urban studies (Lees, 2004, p. 101, 104). The division, and consequently confusion, are caused in great measure by differences and disparities in social scientific perspectives, i.e., perspectives that involve not only philosophical and theoretical foundations, but also research interests (Lucarelli & Berg, 2011).

In the present study, I shall take a holistic and cultural-political stance and take developing world city branding as a form of *cultural discourse*. Here, 'discourse,' interchangeable with 'communication,' refers, quite briefly, to social events or activities in which people communicate through linguistic and nonlinguistic means with one another in given historical and cultural contexts. Because human communication differs between cultures, to wit, in terms of goals, values, concepts, strategies, etc., and more importantly, is characterized by competing cultural relations and representations, I shall use the epithet 'cultural,' hence, cultural discourse.

As a case study and illustration of Asian/Developing-World urban development, accordingly, I shall focus on the city branding of Hangzhou for the international community; Hangzhou is an ancient capital and tourist city on the east coastal region of China. My aim is to identify and characterize some of the properties, problems, and potentials of urban development discourse of the developing world. This means that I shall be studying the elements, strategies, difficulties, challenges and opportunities involved in the international, more precisely, intercultural, discursive (co-)construction of Hangzhou's image and identity. I shall at the same time be evaluating the city branding practices in terms of their effects and outcomes for (urban) development, as is the central and most important objective of Chinese/Asian/Developing-World societies.

As data for city branding research, one might take up an individual event or activity. But this way would lead only to partial or even misleading answers. For, city branding takes place in varied forms and as such can have different characteristics in different cases. So I choose instead to observe a variety of branding practices that occur at different social and semiotic levels. Thus, different kinds of topics ranging from efforts by the municipality, mega-events to trade-oriented activities, on the one hand, and varied forms of data such as interviews, actual practice and secondary documentation, on the other hand, are used here. This 'big-data' method, as it were, will allow one to access a wide spectrum of activities, such that not only the overall international branding situation of Hangzhou, but also the particular branding practices involving leisure, the landscape, food, drink, use of new media, etc., will come into purview.

To make sense of, account for, and weigh up such a diversity of materials, one might take a singular, say linguistic, or social, or managerial, perspective and examine one dimension of the data on the part of the municipality or a business (enterprise) or some civil organization. But such a fragmented approach could lead to bias and consequently ineffectual or counterproductive conclusions. So I shall instead resort to multiple and multifaceted – historical and intercultural – ways of approaching the collected data. More specifically, I shall take a cultural discourse studies perspective in looking at the different types of branding practice in the forms of first- and second-hand data and insider- and outsider-perspectives. That means that I shall examine each of them in terms of the various (interlocking) components of a (n inter)cultural communicative event, the interconnections between these types of practice and, where possible, in contrast to cities in nondeveloping-world societies.

CBD is central to a host of city planning, marketing, and management goals: demography, population, the environment, business, tourism, talents, resources, and domestic and international investment. It can have important implications for the well-being of the residents, visitors, and tourists of a city. More generally, it can impact directly on the social cultural development of a city and further afield (e.g., social inclusion and harmony and cultural diversity). When seen as an internationally and interculturally oriented discourse, it can have an impact on not just the city itself but also the world at large. Considered from the point of view of workplace discourse, it constitutes the working lives and so the livelihood of a city.

Thus, by exploring the cultural and intercultural nature of CBD, especially from a developing-world/Asian/Chinese perspective, we may expect to achieve a better understanding of not only the specific cultural characteristics and relations involved but also the complexities of the discourse of urban development in general and of city branding in particular. Further, by looking at the Chinese city's international branding discourse as workplace communication, more particularly, we may gain insights into the conditions, dimensions, and possibilities of the workplace in relation to urban development in the Asian/developing world more generally.

Discourses of urban development and branding

City branding is a crucial and effective tool for urban development; from another perspective, because it can serve as a guide for urban development, it is also a constitutive part of it. Research on the topic, which has spanned over more than three decades, is internationally recognized and continues to grow (Lucarelli & Berg, 2011; see also Kavaratzis, 2004, Keller, 2012; Lees, 2004, Wilson, 1996, Zukin & Greenberg, 1998). What is particularly noteworthy is that there is an increasing recognition of, and attention to, the discursive dimension of city branding (e.g., Lees, 2004; Sevcik, 2011).

Let us first attempt to carve out the theoretical and methodological frameworks that will be employed in this study. On the whole and at the outset, it may be said that the literature suggests that CBD studies is a nascent, promising, and important field. On this we may quote Lees (2004, p. 101):

> The impact of the discursive turn on urban research (both political economic and cultural political urban research) is growing as more and more researchers seek to integrate the study of language and culture into urban geographical analysis. (For a variety of examples, see Amin et al., 2000; Beauregard, 1993; Imrie & Raco, 2003; Ley, 1995; McCann, 2004; Mitchell, 1996; Rutheiser, 1996; Slater, 2002; Wilson, 1996; Zukin & Greenberg, 1998)

Further, recent literature has recognized that city branding is not separable from other aspects or dimensions of the social practice of city promotion; it is created, conveyed, and understood – constituted – in and through discourse/communication. City branding and discourse are thus dialectically integrated, hence, CBD. Okano and Samson (2010, p. 12) point to this integral and dialectic condition of cultural discourse when they suggest:

> Culture is something that individuals or groups 'create,' or alternatively something that such individuals or groups 'receive.' In other words, in order to trace the development of culture, it is necessary to consider the mutual relations between the three parties, the 'creator,' the 'cultural property,' and the 'recipients,' and they cannot be discussed separately from the conditions of the society that gave them birth [...] The forms of communication between the 'creator' subject and the 'receiver' subject are important.

Building on work such as these, let me formulate in what follows a discursively and culturally more explicit theoretical scaffolding. To start with, city branding is understood in this study as the communicative or discursive practice of constructing, marketing, and understanding the image, identity and, arguably, 'face,' of a city for the sake of increasing recognition and prestige and ultimately success, as well as self-affirmation, in the context of intensified local and global urban competition or for competitiveness for short, hence, CBD for short.[1]

Second, CBD is created out of the process of globalization, on the one hand, and urbanization, on the other hand. Here arises the need to distinguish one city from others to further enhance prestige. Ultimately, it is done in order to survive and succeed in today's increasingly competitive national and international contexts. The notion of city branding comes antecedently from that of corporate (product) branding; but from the present perspective, the city is neither a product or a corporation, nor a nation, and so the branding must take on its own characteristics. In contrast to the product/corporation, the city is more of a multiplex, dynamic, and above all living entity; in contrast to the nation, it is less political and smaller in size but has more to do with everyday livelihood.

Third, CBD has varied stakeholders, who range from the municipality, the businesses, the state, the residents, and the visitors. City branding is a consequence of how stakeholders speak of branding. In this respect, it may be added that people as stakeholders may not just create city brands but also be affected by the life changes brought about by the brands they create. From another perspective, CBD is not limited to the productive side; the receptive/responsive/evaluative side is also crucially important, which may come in forms of impression, perception, reputation, and arguably expectation – by residents/citizens, tourists/visitors, businesses, and governments. This leads to another central issue. CBD has specific audiences: domestic/local and international/global. In the present study, I am concerned with the international audience, who may range from tourists, visitors, to government and business organizations.

Fourth, the practice of CBD may be achieved through a diversity of interrelated semiotic forms, strategies, and mediums, including notably (1) channels of communication, (2) signs, (3) genres of communication, and (4) contents of communication. Thus, in terms of content, CBD can vary depending on the perspectives, principles, and conditions of a city in question: a city may be branded as geographic space, governed and inhabited settlement, or quintessential feature(s) of the place, for example Lucarelli and Berg (2011). This implies that virtually anything of city life can be the object of urban branding; we may think of such interrelated cultural resources as: history, heritage (e.g., festivals and cuisine), customs (e.g., tea drinking), monument, iconic building, landscape, celebrities, heroes, art and design (e.g., clothing). As signs, we may refer to the language, graphics, architecture, art (e.g., music and painting), personage that are mobilized; as genres, we may think of logos, slogans, brochures, advertisements, documents (e.g., positioning statements and mission statement), speeches, photos, expos, tourism, and mega-events. In terms of strategies, CBD may be produced (and thus understood) in implicit/indirect or explicit/direct ways. As channels, we may think of radio, TV, the Internet, newspapers, magazines, film, posters, billboards, museum, word-of-mouth, international travel, etc.

Fifth, and very importantly, CBD has a 'workplace' dimension; much of workplace discourse is done in, and by, organizations, municipals, entrepreneurial endeavors, and civil organizations, and so each is subject to particular ethical requirements. Workplace discourse has been studied in terms of its formal features (of linguistic genres), settings (e.g., medical and legal), social interaction (e.g., conversation and intercultural communication), and contents (e.g., small talk and humor), from different disciplinary perspectives (e.g., linguistics and social theory), and through a diversity of approaches (e.g., ethnography and discourse analysis) (see Gunnarsson, 2009; Holmes, 2011; Koester, 2010). However, this line of research has been conducted mainly within Western societies and special professions, on preferred aspects of language (e.g., linguistic texts) and over preferred topics (e.g., politeness, power, and conflict resolution). From the perspective taken in this study, CBD is not simply about text or talk at work or about conversational interaction in work settings. It involves much more: it is a workplace discourse that has a wide public mandate, is achieved through a nexus of communicative elements and processes, and exerts broad societal, cultural, and global impact; therefore, it is important to assess if and how the workplace discourse of city branding contributes to local social and cultural development.

Sixth, CBD is *culturally* differentiated in terms of, for instance, historical conditions (e.g., the context of late-modern Third World urbanization in global setting), representations, power relations, goals, and principles of interaction. Consequently, it is culturally competing. It may be stressed, too, that, as a cultural phenomenon, CBD is dynamic through time: it may go through culturally variable stages and paths of development (Gold & Gold, 2004; Hajer, 1995; Jensen, 2007; Mommas, 2002). Western branded, and well-known, cities are considerably larger in number than those in the rest of the world. Their branding is facilitated by a great variety of advantages, including centers of world economy and geographical locations.

Last, but by no means the least, Chinese CBD is characterized by its culture-specific condition of history, on the one hand, and its profound concern with social economic development, on the other hand. Therefore, our analysis must take the *development condition in the global context* seriously and adopt the social economic development as the most important criterion of assessment (Shi-xu, 2014).

The methodology of city branding research

In a binary and universalistic way of thinking about, and investigating into, urban communication, researchers normally focus on a singular event, or more typically, the textual form of a singular event, and appraise it from a culturally 'neutral' stance (e.g., Flowerdew, 2004). But the problem here is that one urban event is often interconnected with many others, as well as with local and global culture and history; the textual form is inseparable from interpretation and response, and other textual forms. What is deemed as, for example, 'manipulative' or 'undemocratic,' from the 'universal' point of view, may, from a local cultural and historical perspective, be a key aspect of something more complex.

From our methodological perspective (Shi-xu, in press), then, we must approach our object of study holistically, dialectically, and cultural-politically. This means that we must examine and evaluate CBD comprehensively, historically, and (inter)culturally, drawing on not only objective evidence (i.e., first-, second-hand, and background data) but also subjective experience (i.e., the researcher's own personal knowledge and cultural-political stance).

Our specific methods concern two interconnected stages of research: data collection and data interpretation. With regard to the former stage – i.e., one in which data are searched, selected, and structured – the following three strategies apply. First, the researcher should choose as an object of investigation concrete, actual practices: major events, expos, fairs, businesses, architecture, landscape, intangible heritages, etc., which are oriented toward the international community. Second, the researcher should seek information concerning the agents, the intent/form, the use of channels and symbols, historical process and international relations on the part of productive side of city branding. In that connection, attention should be paid to information on relevant international impact or response. Third, the researcher should try to obtain information through direct observation (e.g., mega-events, exhibitions, and forums) and secondary sources (e.g., the Internet, journalism, documentation, and interviews).

With regard to the latter ('reading') stage, the practices of city is studied from the point of view of (inter)cultural discourse – that is, as a set of interrelated categories of the intercultural communicative event/activity: (1) communicative agents, (2) intent/form/relation, (3) mediums, (4) purposes/effects, (5) historical processes, and (6) intercultural representations and relations. Here multidisciplinary concepts, methods, and standards must be applied depending on the nature of phenomena under scrutiny and the purpose of the research project. Further, intracultural and intercultural comparisons are made where possible. For example, Hangzhou's international cuisine branding may be compared with its tea branding, or Hangzhou's international city branding with that of Paris, but all with a view to better understanding Hangzhou's case.

I begin the analysis with background information because it functions here as a guide for collecting and understanding the focal data. The background is divided into five dimensions. First, Hangzhou, the capital city of Zhejiang Province, is a historical and tourist city situated in one of the most developed, eastern coastal regions of China, the Yangtze Delta. It has a territory of 16,596 km^2 (the inner city is 430 km^2) and a population of over 5 million people. The city has had double-digit gross domestic product growth for the past 10 or so years and has enjoyed high-level development, particularly in the past few years as evidenced in social, cultural, economic, municipal, and environmental survey statistics.[2] Second, the city has one of the country's most valued and internationally renowned lakes and many historical sites dating back to the Qin Dynasty over 2200 years ago. Third, it applied for UNESCO world heritage status in 1999 and succeeded in 2011; during this period, it embarked on a 10-year long 'Comprehensive Development Plan' for that purpose, at least in part. Along with the UNESCO bid, the city has been pursuing internationalization in the context of accelerated globalization. Fourth, Hangzhou has historically been given numerous designations, official and otherwise. In 1958, for instance, Hangzhou Municipal Construction Bureau positioned the city as 'comprehensive city of heavy industry.' In 2000, Hangzhou branded itself as 'Paradise Silicon Valley,' and attracted investors like Huawei, Zhifubao, and Wangyi. Last, but by no means the least, in August 2006, the Municipality of Hangzhou put together an expert group of artists, men of letters, sociologists, and city planners and launched a call for the selection of a city brand for Hangzhou. Over 2000 people from 20 some provinces of China put forward 4620 items of proposals. Following a complex process of standard-setting, expert evaluation, and public voting, the brand

生活品质之城 [the City of Quality Life] was chosen. What is historically interesting and significant is that against the former centralizing tradition in national development, when decisions were made at the top, this brand 'from the bottom' was formally adopted at the 10th Congress of the CCP Hangzhou Committee (February 2007), and endorsed a few days later at the 11th Congress in the report: *The CCP Hangzhou Committee's Decision on maintaining and developing a harmonious society and the City of Quality-Life* (施旭 2008). 生活品质之城, or the City of Quality Life, is understood to mean the standard levels of quality life in five domains: economic life, cultural life, political life, social life, and environmental life (杭州市政府 2007; 黄宇亮、王竹 2006). These domains of life are also recreated in 12 different brand combinations:

> 东方休闲之都，品质生活之城 (Eastern leisure capital, quality-life city);
> 天堂硅谷，品质生活 (Silicon paradise, quality life);
> 品质生活，中国茶都 (Quality life, tea capital of China);
> 文化名城，品质杭州 (Town of culture, Hangzhou of quality)

The focal point in the present study is this official city brand. As indicated before, our analysis examines the international branding (communicating, marketing, and interpreting) of Hangzhou. Here it may be noted that while the brand's meaning, development, and communication are well documented, it is unclear who the intended audience is – whether for local, national, and international recipients; as a result, no specification of how the branding practices might be differentiated exists.

In order to examine Hangzhou's international branding, I have chosen a series of relevant phenomena that operate at different semiotic levels. Specifically, I focus on the city's international branding as a whole, thus at the highest meaningful level, on the one hand, and on the other hand, I look at a number of particular activities and events that contribute to and are constitutive of the city's international branding, namely, the World Leisure Expo, the West Lake International Expo, the Longjing Tea branding, and Hangzhou culinary branding. By investigating a range of workplace sites and practices of international city branding at different levels, I hope to reveal the current conditions, possibilities, and problems of the city's international branding.

With respect to the diversity of phenomena under investigation, I have opted to draw from a range of data, including interviews with key agents, actual branding practices, and secondary documentation and journalism. In so doing, I hope to yield deep insights into the properties of Hangzhou's city-brand promotion to the international community.

Analysis and assessment

The branding practices in question will be studied each as cultural discourse, thus in terms of the communicative agent, intent/form/relation, and media and outcomes from historical and intercultural perspectives. As these practices are interrelated and mutually complimentary, comparisons are made to highlight their merits and their demerits. In that connection, particular attention will also be paid to the shared dimension of international city branding (e.g., the use of the Internet for city branding). Because city branding practices must be understood as embedded in a particular historical and intercultural juncture, attempts will also be made to account for them accordingly.

Municipal management

In order to provide an overview of the management of the city's brand from an insider's perspective or 'from behind the scene,' an approximately 85-minute, in-depth interview with the director of the Centre for Research and Evaluation on Life Quality of Hangzhou was conducted by the present author, together with three students (7 March 2014). The director was informed at the outset of the interview that our purpose was to understand the nature, content, and strategies of the work involved in Hangzhou's city branding for the international community, and more particularly, the difficulties, challenges, and experiences related to the city's international branding.

From a cultural discourse point of view, several noteworthy features exist in the city-brand managerial language. First, this city is one of the few places in China, and perhaps in the world, that has a municipal-level task force, composed of several offices, that is specifically charged with the city's perennial brand management. Second, the city has an officially designated brand, as indicated above; in addition, the state government has an extra, semantically different, brand for it ('one-base-and-four-centers').[3] Third, under the auspices of this task force, a number of regular, international mega-events are organized in the city, such as the World Leisure Expo, the West Lake Expo, and the International Comics and Cartoons Festival. Fourth, such events, sometimes organized in conjunction with one another, are jointly sponsored by the municipality, businesses, the media, etc., and attended by people from all walks of life including foreigners, notably in the form of a so-called experiencing day (when 'quality-life' may be experienced). Fifth, the city's official brand seems to be semantically indistinct or vague, though this may be associated with various life-quality designations (see the ones of past 10 years in Table 1). Sixth, the set of organizations in charge of the city's brand development has a collective website (http://www.wehangzhou.cn/), but it is all in Chinese. Last, the making of the Hangzhou brand is presented with 'cultural' difficulties when compared with other well-known, Western cities, like New York, Paris, or Berlin. That is, although Hangzhou is financially capable of brand construction, it lacks the soft power or technical know-how to carry the task out. As he puts it,

I feel the difference lies not so much in the economic conditions. These years China develops very fast. In terms of infrastructure, would you say there is much difference between Shanghai and New York? Scarcely any. Perhaps the level of modernization is even higher than that of well-known cities of developed countries. In respect of economic foundation, I think the biggest difference lies rather in the respect of culture, soft power specifically. Take for example our cultural industry. Hangzhou pays a lot of attention to this these years. We have been trying to build the capital of cartoon and animation and we integrate this into the system of Hangzhou's city-brand. We made a point of enabling interconnection and interaction of trade brands and the city's general brand. At that time it was a major aspect of (brands') interaction. But if you compared Hangzhou and Britain regarding development of the cultural creative industry, there is still a large distance. We are still paying more attention to such things as hardware, value of production, quantities, etc. But in the respect of cultural import and influence, or high-level artistic design, we still lag greatly behind. [我觉得这个差异更多的不是在它的经济基础，这两年我们国家发展也很快，就像从硬件方面来说，你说上海和纽约有很大的差别吗？基本上没什么差别，可能有些现代化的程度还高于一些发达国家的著名城市，在经济支撑这方面上，我觉得最大的差异就是在文化，这个软的方面。我举个例子讲，比如我们的文化产业，杭州这几年也是非常重视的，我们一直在打造动漫之都，我们也是把它纳入到城市品牌系统里面的。我们当时提到了一个行业品牌和城市整体品牌的联动，互动，当时这也是互动很重要的一方面，但是你看我们杭州的文创业的发展和英国的文创业的发展，它的差别就非常大，我们更多的还是注重一些硬性的东西，产值啊，数量啊，但在文化内涵的渗透方面，高端艺术的设计方面还很欠缺。]

168

In this part of the interview, it is clear that the director is contrasting the Chinese city with other Western developed cities (e.g., 'New York,' cities of 'Britain,' and 'well-known cities of developed countries'); the director stresses in particular the deficiency in what he calls the 'soft,' 'cultural' side of city branding in Hangzhou and in China by suggesting that the latter seeks what is not desirable but lacks in what is desirable (see the last sentence of the quote).

World expos

Within the city's branding framework as indicated above, Hangzhou has held two sets of major, serial international expos: the World Leisure Expo and the West Lake Expo; both are organized in line with, and as part of, Hangzhou's city branding. In the history of the World Leisure Expo, the first one was held in Brisbane, Australia, in 1988. Since then, the exposition was held every two or three years around the world. In 2006, the World

Table 1. Awards/plaques conferred on Hangzhou.

Year	Titles and awarding organizations
2001	'Habitat Scroll of Honour Award' by United Nations Centre for Human Settlements (habitat), UNCHS (http://cn.unhabitat.org/content.asp?typeid=19&catid=490&id=3156#Hangzhou)
2002	The International Award for live-able communities by LivCom Management Company (http://www.livcomawards.com/previous-winners/2006-index.htm)
2002	'International Garden City' by International Federation of Parks and Recreation Administration (http://www.hicenter.cn/facts_11.asp)
2003–2008	'Best Investment Environment Cities of China' by the World Bank (2003, 2004, 2005, 2006, 2007, 2008) (http://zjnews.zjol.com.cn/05zjnews/system/2007/09/11/008786891.shtml; http://www.hicenter.cn/facts_11.asp)
2006	'Oriental Leisure Capital' by the World Leisure Organization (http://www.hangzhou.com.cn/20060801/ca1218356.htm)
2006	'The Best Tourism City of China' by the United Nations World Tourism Organization and National TourismAdministration (http://www.hicenter.cn/facts_11.asp)
2007	'China's best tourist city' by the National Tourism Administration and the United Nations World Tourism Organization (http://www.china.org.cn/archive/2007-02/10/content_1199624.htm)
2007	'Medaille d'Or' by Fédération internationale du tourisme (FIT) (http://www.federationinternationaledutourisme.eu/distinctions-en-chine.htm)
2004–2009	'the Best Commercial Cities in Mainland of China' by *Forbes* (http://eng.hangzhou.gov.cn/main/zpd/English/AboutHangZhou/T326241.shtml)
2011	'Creativity Demonstration' by the organizing committee of International Forum on Cultural Industry (http://en.hangzhou.com.cn/News/content/2011-08/03/content_3829959.htm)
2011	'World Heritage Site' by UNESCO World Heritage Centre (http://en.gotohz.com/whyhangzhou/wlh/#sthash.euuYlZ1Q.eYD7oRC5.dpbs)
2012	'UNESCO Creative Cities Network City of Crafts & Folk Art' by UNESCO (http://news.ifeng.com/gundong/detail_2012_05/18/14620127_0.shtml)

Leisure Organization (WLO) decided that the World Leisure Expo would be held every five years and that Hangzhou would be the permanent venue for it. In 2006 and 2011, Hangzhou played the host and was awarded 'the Oriental Capital of Leisure' for the first event. Consistent with Hangzhou's official city-brand 生活品质之城 (City of Quality Life), which came into being in 2007, the World Leisure Expo 2011 (September 17 to November 18), sponsored by World Leisure Organization and Hangzhou Municipal People's Government, adopted the theme of 'Leisure – Enhancing the Quality of Life.' For the Expo of 2011, the official website (en.wl-expo.com) and video (http://v.hoolo.tv/video-10039.html) illustrate the type of promotional materials and news reports associated with the event.

Let us take a look at the Expo of 2011 (from September 17 to November 18) in particular. From a cultural discursive point of view, a number of features may be noted. First, there is sizable international participation: 80 cities, 37 million visitors, and 50 enterprises from China and abroad. Second, under the theme of 'Leisure: Enhancing the Quality of Life,' the Expo of 2011 was composed of a variety of organized communicative events: a summit meeting, conferences, and forums. Third, the Expo is rendered present in various forms of texts (ads, news reports, special columns, and publications), as well as artifacts (e.g., souvenirs) and conducted through different channels (i.e., website and online videos) and in a number of international venues (e.g. international convention centers) and scores of spaces (i.e. routes, and sites of leisure activities). More broadly, it is featured in a host of activities and events (e.g., Cultural Creative Industry Expo, International Tea Conference, and Tea Product Fair). Finally, the Expo has had a trade turnover of ca. 22.6 billion RMB, foreign investment of ca US$1.1 billion and domestic investment of 13.4 billion RMB.

The West Lake Expo is another serial mega-event that is directly linked with the city's branding. The very first event was held in 1929; a successful international fair for some time. But the expo did not resume until seven decades later in 2000. It may be noted that the logo is an expression of the characteristics and aspiration of Hangzhou: water, leisure, vegetation, etc.

For the sake of understanding better the current state of the expo, let us compare the last one, the 15th, with the second. The latter, which lasted for 22 days, attracted 5 million visitors from home and abroad, held a score of professional exhibitions with 2500 exhibitors coming over 30 countries and regions. The trade volume amounts to nearly 7 billion RMB, domestic investment to 13.73 billion RMB, and foreign investment to 311 million US$.

The most recent 15th Expo, initiated and funded (with at least 17 million RMB) by the Hangzhou Government and executed by the Office of Hangzhou West Lake Expo Organizing Committee, lasted 29 days (12 October–9 November 2013) under the theme of 'Innovative EXPO, beautiful Hangzhou.' It has an official website: http://www.xh-expo.com/ (other relevant sites include: http://www.xh-expo.com/481/2013/09/16208.html). Sponsored by over 15 companies, the Expo is comprised of 50 events (fairs, conferences, exhibitions, and other activities), including major international events such as follows:

- The International West Lake Tourism Festival
- Hangzhou International Art and Culture Festival
- Hangzhou International Trail Walker Conference
- International Conference on Sensor in the Internet of Things
- World Top 500 Enterprises Roundtable Conference

The expo attracts about 8 million visitors from home and abroad; 50 different countries and regions are represented. The exhibitions and fairs are mainly held in internationally oriented venues (e.g., the White Horse Lake International Convention and Exhibition Center, Hangzhou Peace International Exhibition and Conference Center, and Zhejiang World Trade International Exhibition Center); 23% of the spaces are allocated to foreign exhibitors. CCTV, local newspapers (e.g., special column in 《都市快报》), radio, local TV station, street posters, museums, conferences, and websites (e.g., *youku* and *sohu*) are used in the promotion; visits to the official website reach 5 million. What is particularly noteworthy is that cooperation between international media outlets is achieved and about 100 domestic and foreign media outlets produce 3500 reports. Different foreign languages are used (e.g., the guideposts in Prince Bay Park (太子湾公园): four in addition to Chinese (English, French, Japanese, and Korean). The mega-event generated a total trade volume of RMB 15.7 billion, domestic investment of RMB 15.2 billion, and foreign investment of US$1 billion.[4]

Tea exhibitions

Tea is another topic around which Hangzhou has done much in its CBD for the international community; i.e., Hangzhou has presented a range of interconnected activities and artifacts for its international brand promotion. In 2011, *Longjing* tea of Hangzhou became part of city's share in the UNESCO world heritage list.[5] It has since become internationally known. Historically, however, *Longjing* tea was exported even before the Opium War (1840), though China was blocked from tea selling following the war by the British that supported India's tea trade.

There are a number of features to be noted from a cultural discourse point of view in the city's current international attempts at branding its tea, thereby branding itself as the city of quality life.[6] First, international events designed to brand the tea from Hangzhou are of relatively recent occurrence. It was only in 2005 that the first West Lake International Tea Culture Expo took place, and since then, it has been held once every year, around the time of the year's first tea-picking; similarly, it was in 2010 that the International Expo of Hangzhou's Well-known Teas, together with the First Contemporary Chinese Tea Culture Festival, was held in the city and has since been organized once every year. Second, the city's (as well as particular prefectures') government, on the one hand, and the nation's international tea (culture) research organizations (e.g., China International Tea Research Association) on the other, are major players as hosts and organizers behind the few international tea fairs and festivals held in Hangzhou. What is also remarkable is that for one day every year 'all countrymen drink tea'; the very first event was held on 20 April 2009. Third, the tea-promotional activities are often enriched and enhanced by being organized in connection with the city's other trade brands such as leisure and cuisine, as part of other mega-events such as the World Expo, or in accompaniment with other activities or artifacts such as tourism, dancing, and landscape. Moreover, the organizers often invite various media to participate in and report on the events. In the mediational aspect, it may be noted, too, that there is an online video: http://www.cnteaexpo.com/czqy.html and official websites on tea promotion: http://www.hangzhou.gov.cn/main/zwdt/ztzj/cwhjs/index.shtml and http://www.hangzhou.com.cn/cbhtbbd/index.htm; nevertheless, neither site has an English language page. In terms of spacial communication, Hangzhou has a few noteworthy architectural venues for tea producing, making and drinking; e.g., the Tea Museum of China (中国茶叶博物馆),[7] the Home of Tea-drinking (茶人之家) and the International Village of Tea-drinking (国际茶人村). Fourth, in terms of intents and purposes of such events, it is clear that they are held with a view to contributing to the city's reputation as the capital of tea, but more broadly to the city's overarching brand, namely, the city of quality life, and more particularly for a period of time prior 2011 to the city's bid for UNESCO world heritage listing. However, it should be pointed out that, although many events are crowned with international designations, there seems little explicit effort at reaching out to the international community and *Longjing* tea is still largely unknown internationally.[8] The tea-experiencing exchanges seem to have involved only some Japanese and Koreans. The tea industry does not seem to have organized any tea-promotional event overseas, let alone having any tea establishments abroad, unlike the Hangzhou cuisine trade, to which we now turn.

Traveling cuisine

Yet another topic and form of international city branding is found in the ways Hangzhou promotes its local cuisine. Supported by the municipal government, the city's food catering association has traveled regularly to foreign countries to promote the city's cuisine. In order to get an insider's view on this, the present author, together with three of his students, conducted an interview with the former secretary and two representatives from the Hangzhou Association of Restaurants (www.hzms.org). Prior to the interview, the association was informed about the research project; subsequently, one of the representatives provided a written statement (by email), answering a few general questions regarding the association's international efforts. During the interview, the questions proceeded from the nature and function of the association, its international activities, ways of distinguishing the local cuisine style, to difficulties involved in its international outreach.

A few observations may be made based on the spoken interview as well as the written one. The association represents about 20,000 large and medium restaurants in Hangzhou, accounting for about 60% of the total number. Since 2008, international food festivals are regularly held every year in the city under the auspices of the municipality, often within mega-events like the World Leisure Expo. If one is held abroad, it is usually at the invitation of a local restaurant association and normally one country per year is chosen as a destination. The places they mentioned as having visited are Spain, France, Austria, Singapore, and the USA (i.e., the UN). It may also be mentioned that the city participates in food festivals in other Chinese cities as well. The cuisine is presented as specifically of Hangzhou, with names to do with features of the city, but adapted to local customs if appropriate (like 'Pork of *Dongpo* (poet)' or 'Vinegar fish of West Lake' made of local fish with less bones). It appears that the association is well aware of the purposes of the international promotion of Hangzhou cuisine as the best method: namely, to make the city better known (also as 'capital of fine food'), to attract more visitors and tourists, and to help increase the revenue of the city, as well as of the restaurants themselves. Finally, at the question of why the city fails to establish its own restaurants abroad, the interviewees make it clear that it is next to impossible because the procedures in the West are too complex and Chinese practitioners are used to depending on networks and cannot deal with Western restrictive measures (i.e. 'too many permits required'). On the whole, it may be argued that the range of communication and exchange is rather small (one country per year), while the number of foreigners reached is unknown, that there is a lack of verbal communication whether in the form of brochures or books, and that there is obvious and serious need to establish local outlets of Hangzhou cuisine in foreign countries (also considering that foreign culinary outlets are everywhere in this city).

The Internet and international languages

As part of our discourse research, attention should be directed at the ways in which the city's international brand and branding are mediated as well – for example, the languages used and channels of communication drawn upon. A general search was conducted on the use of 'quality-of-life'-related websites hosted by Hangzhou, and it is found that a number of institutions have Internet sites using the English language and a few using other foreign languages. These organizations may be classified into three categories: (1) city-government offices and organizations under its administration, (2) provincial-government-administered institutions (Hangzhou is the capital of Zhejiang Province), and (3) state-owned enterprises. The first group has by far more websites; in parenthesis, few relevant trade associations would have a website with an English language page (e.g., Association of Performing Art: http://www.hzyyyxh.com/; Restaurants and Hotels Guild: www.hzms.org). The information of the three groups is given in the order of the owner, the website, and the foreign languages used; from the name of the owner it will be possible to appreciate the nature of the site in question[9]:

Municipal offices and organizations under its administration

Municipal Government Portal: http://www.hangzhou.gov.cn/ (English);
Information Office: http://www.hicenter.cn (English);
Tourism Committee: http://www.gotohz.com/ (English, Japanese, Korean and German);
Landscape and Heritage Site Administrative Committee: http://xhsy.hzwestlake.gov.cn/index.aspx (English);
Liangzhu Heritage Site Committee: http://www.lzsite.gov.cn/ (English, Japanese, Korean, Spanish, German);
Bureau of Gardens and Heritages: http://www.hzwestlake.gov.cn/ (English, Japanese, Korean);
World Leisure Expo: http://www.wl-expo.com/ (English);
West Lake International Expo: http://www.xh-expo.com/ (English);
Southern-Song Imperial Kiln Museum: http://www.ssikiln.com/newEbiz1/EbizPortalFG/portal/html/index.html (English);
Comprehensive Canal Protection Committee: http://www.grandcanal.com.cn/ (English, Japanese, Korean);
China Tea Museum: http://www.teamuseum.cn/default.aspx (English, Japanese);
Hangzhou History Museum: http://www.hzmuseum.com/ (English);
China Silk Museum: http://www.chinasilkmuseum.com/ (English);
Lingying Temple: http://www.lingyinsi.org/ (English, Japanese);
Hangzhou Daily: http://www.hangzhou.com.cn/ (Japanese, Korean).

Provincial-government-supported institutions based in Hangzhou

Zhejiang Art Gallery: http://www.zjam.org.cn/ (English);
Zhejiang Symphony Orchestra: http://www.zjso.org/index.asp (English);
China Cartoons and Animation Festival: http://www.cicaf.com/ (English).

State-owned enterprises

Grand Opera House Limited: http://www.hzdjy.com/index.php (English);
Olympic and International Expo Center: http://www.hzoiec.com/ (English).

From the list of websites above, it may be seen that the city's administrative organizations open to the international community quite a large number of information platforms in connection with the promotion of the city, including its brand. Moreover, in addition to the English language, many of the sites use other foreign languages, reaching out to a wider international community. If we look at the contents of the websites, then some further features may be of note. While a few sites provide Chinese culture-specific information as characteristic of Hangzhou, e.g., on legendary sites and local food and drink (http://www.hicenter.cn/facts_33.asp), some sites have more or less the same information and moreover the information is rather general, i.e., Hangzhou is described as distinguishable neither in China nor in the world:

> Hangzhou, capital of Zhejiang Province, has been one of China's most renowned and prosperous cities for much of the last 1000 years. Located in the Yangtze River Delta, Hangzhou is well known for its beautiful natural scenery, the West Lake being its most renowned location. Ranked among the most competitive cities and also named the Happiest City in China for five consecutive years, Hangzhou has a reputation for outstanding quality of life that attracts people of different ages and lifestyles to visit, live, work, and learn. Hangzhou citizens take great pride in their city and value it as an urban habitat designed for great living. (http://www.chinadaily.com.cn/m/hangzhou/e/2009–08/12/content_8561615.htm)

The last issue regarding the medium of communication concerns translation, i.e., translation of the brand name. The Chinese '生活品质之城' has been commonly translated into English as 'City of Quality Life.' From the productive point of view, the question is how Hangzhou may best represent, promote, and market what such a translation may render to the international community. From the point of view of brand reception, the question is how this name itself may be perceived and understood. While surveys of some sorts may be conducted, from the present point of view it may be arguable that the English phrase could sound too vague or broad to ring true or realistic and consequently could prove difficult to effectively market the brand. A similar example of possibly dubious meaning of translation may be: 'there is heaven above, Hangzhou and Suzhou below' (http://www.chinadaily.com.cn/m/hangzhou/e/2007-11/07/content_8551481.htm).

International recognitions

As argued in the beginning, branding has both productive and receptive sides. How Hangzhou's brand of quality life is understood and responded to by the international community, professional and ordinary, should be part of our research. Earlier, I have indicated, where possible, the role of the international target community in the branding practices examined and the extent and manner of its participation. Here, it may be noted that Hangzhou has won a number of international recognitions in the form of awards and plaques in the past decade and a half (see Table 1).

However, it is realized that much more comprehensive research would be needed in order to ascertain the nature and extent of the international uptake of Hangzhou's brand as the city of quality of life. For instance, research attention may be directed to what aspect, if any, of Hangzhou is explicitly present in the global village, how people (visitors or otherwise) understand it, and where Hangzhou's brand has affected their lives in any way.

Conclusion

In the study of Asian/Third World urban development in general and of international city branding in particular, I have chosen to focus on the case of the Chinese coastal historical, thriving tourist city of Hangzhou. The project was motivated partly by the understanding that city branding is a new and crucial part of urban development workplace discourse and partly by the observation that Third World cities have been disproportionately understudied. My particular purpose has then been to identify, analyze, explain, as well as assess Hangzhou's international CBD as a developing-world case in terms of its properties, problems, and potentials. To that end, I have sketched out a cultural-discursive, 'workplace' account of city branding and sought, accordingly, to obtain a variety of data across a range of settings and examine them from historical and intercultural perspectives. In the remainder of this paper, I shall offer a synthesis and overall assessment based on the respective analyses so far.

First, it is through a public campaign that the city of Hangzhou adopts and acquires an official brand, to wit, the City of Quality Life, and that the city has specific municipal offices to oversee, implement, and monitor the brand's communication, management, and development, internationally as well as nationally. Although this is a rare case not only just in the Chinese context but also in the world at large, such a proactive city-campaign may prove to be an effective strategy for less well-known, Third-World cities, such as the one in question, in the fast-globalizing age. Second, in addition to the municipality, businesses, and civil organizations, large numbers of citizens, as well as foreigners, actively participate in the all-year-round branding events, via, e.g., the so-called experiencing day. So, through mega-events, ordinary people can become city-brand makers and communicators at that, too. In this sense, workplace discourse extends to the public domain, contributing directly and effectively to urban, sociocultural development. Third, the city-brand of Hangzhou is articulated to the international community in and through a diversity of explicitly promotional practices both at the general and all-encompassing level (e.g., the World Leisure Expo and the West Lake Expo) and across a good number of trades (e.g., the industries of tea, cuisine, fashion, high-tech, and e-commerce). Worthy of note here is that different levels and types of branding practice are coordinated and integrated; this way, greater effect may be expected. Such multifacetedness and interconnection of branding practices seem particularly necessary for a relatively vague and polysemic city-brand such as Hangzhou's. Fourth, Hangzhou's branding practices draw on a variety of media available and possible logos, websites, videos, posters, brochures, etc.; relevant organizations at different levels use the English language as well as other international languages on their websites. Such broad use of communicative mediums will enhance international accessibility. (Of course, by the same token, it could be suggested that still more foreign languages, whether European, Asian, Latin American, or African, as well as still more internationally oriented specialist websites (pages), be established, say on the city's cuisine, tea-houses, and fashion.) Furthermore, as the case of the city's culinary trade shows, it is possible for relevant trade representatives and firms to go physically abroad in order to make known and promote their trade brand and thereby their city brand. Finally, as our case demonstrates, branding practices can be coupled with not just economic gains as in the form of domestic and foreign investment but also various international distinctions.

In conclusion, it must be mentioned that the present study reveals shortcomings, constraints, and potentials with regard to the internationalization of the city's brand as well. To start with, unlike the brands of London as a 'financial center,' Sydney as 'city of the opera house,' or Hong Kong as 'Asia's world city,' Hangzhou's brand of 'city of quality life' may sound rather abstract. Consequently, it would be doubly challenging to

175

mobilize wide-ranging, domain-specific branding activities (such as the 'day of all citizens drinking tea' and 'fine food festival'). Moreover, there seems rarely any attempt to go abroad to brand the city (except for the culinary and tourism trades). Related to this, too, there does not seem to be an explicit distinction made in the branding for the international markets. Given the numerous foreign firm outlets spread out in Hangzhou (say shops, restaurants, and cafes), there is both a long way to go and great potentials. For this an insider view has been that the difficulty of reaching out to the international community and having a strong impact lies in the Chinese cultural conditions and conventions; this means that cultural creativity is called for to make an international breakthrough. In addition, although an impressive variety of mediums of communication has been employed, one can see that still other tools and channels may be resorted to in the workplace discourse, e.g., the Quick Response (QR) code, APPs, in order to maximize international branding.

Acknowledgements

Support for the present research by the Humanities and Social Sciences Fund of the Ministry of Education [grant no.11YJA740075] is gratefully acknowledged. Gratitude is expressed also to the participants of my course, Cultural Discourse Studies, as well as my research assistant Xie Xiuting, at Zhejiang University, who helped collect much of the data used here. Meticulous comments and incisive suggestions by the anonymous reviewers and the guest-editors are greatly appreciated.

Disclosure statement

No potential conflict of interest was reported by the author.

Notes

1. City branding is often defined too broadly or too vague; the following is not untypical: 'the purposeful symbolic embodiment of all information connected to a city in order to create associations and expectations around it' (Lucarelli & Berg, 2011, p. 21).
2. Relevant information may be found at: http://data.stats.gov.cn/workspace/index?a=q&type=global&dbcode=csnd&m=csnd&dimension=zb&code=A0101&region=330100&time=2012, 2012. See also 季靖, 陈静 2008, 《杭州》课题组 2008, 邹身城 2006.
3. http://hzfzw.hz.gov.cn/jjhz/myjs/201205/t20120507_315759.html.
4. See: http://www.xh-expo.com/zt/15th/xhexpobm/.
5. See http://whc.unesco.org/en/news/767/: 'The World Heritage Committee has inscribed the West Lake Cultural Landscape of Hangzhou, comprising the West Lake and the hills surrounding its three sides, on UNESCO's World Heritage List.' At the first West Lake International Tea Expo held in 2005, Hangzhou was awarded the plaque '中国茶都' (China's Capital of Tea).
6. Reference information may be found at: http://hznews.hangzhou.com.cn/chengshi/content/2013-03/27/content_4667544_2.htm (with English page); http://lxs.cncn.com/70786-news-show-68859.html.
7. It has *web page*s in English and Japanese: http://www.teamuseum.cn/default.aspx.
8. Some other related websites in English: www.teavivre.com; TravelChinaGuide.com; en.gotohz.com (of Hangzhou).
9. It may be pointed out, though, that some websites concerning key aspects of the 'quality life' of Hangzhou are in Chinese only (e.g., Landscape and heritage site administrative committee: http://xhsy.hzwestlake.gov.cn/index.aspx; Xiling Seal Engraver's Society: http://www.xlys1904.com/; West Lake Museum: http://www.westlakemuseum.com/).

References

Amin, A., Massey, D., & Thrift, N. (2000). *Cities for the many not the few*. Bristol: The Policy Press.

Beaverstock, J. V., Smith, R. G., & Taylor, P. J. (1999). A roster of world cities. *Cities*, *16*, 445–458. doi:10.1016/S0264-2751(99)00042-6

Beauregard, R. A. (1993). *Voices of decline: The postwar fate of US cities*. Oxford: Blackwell.

Flowerdew, J. (2004). The discursive construction of a world-class city. *Discourse & Society*, *15*, 579–605. doi:10.1177/0957926504045033

Gold, J. R., & Gold, M. M. (2004). *Cities of culture*. Surrey: Ashgate.

Gunnarsson, B. L. (2009). Discourse in organizations and workplaces. In L. Wei & V. Cook (Eds.), *Contemporary applied linguistics: Linguistics for the real world* (pp. 122–141). London: Continuum International.

Hajer, M. A. (1995). *The politics of environmental discourse*. Oxford: Oxford University Press.

Holmes, J. (2011). Discourse in the workplace. In K. Hyland & B. Paltridge (Eds.), *Continuum companion to discourse analysis* (pp. 185–198). London: Continuum.

Imrie, R., & Raco, M. (Eds.). (2003). *Urban renaissance? New labour, community and urban policy*. Bristol: Policy Press.

Jensen, O. B. (2007). Culture stories: Understanding cultural urban branding. *Planning Theory*, *6*, 211–236. doi:10.1177/1473095207082032

Kavaratzis, M. (2004). From city marketing to city branding: Towards a theoretical framework for developing city brands. *Place Branding*, *1*(1), 58–73.

Keller, K. L. (2012). *Strategic brand management* (4th ed.). Edinburgh: Pearson Education.

Koester, A. (2010). *Workplace discourse*. London: Continuum.

Lees, L. (2004). Urban geography discourse analysis and urban research. *Progress in Human Geography*, *28*(1), 101–107. doi:10.1191/0309132504ph473pr

Ley, D. (1995). Between Europe and Asia: The case of the missing sequoias. *Ecumene*, *2*, 185–210.

Lucarelli, A., & Berg, P. O. (2011). City branding: A state-of-the-art review of the research domain. *Journal of Place Management and Development*, *4*(1), 9–27. doi:10.1108/17538331111117133

McCann, E. (2004). Best places: Inter-urban competition, quality of life, and popular media discourses. *Urban Studies*, *41*(10), 1909–1929.

Mitchell, K. (1996). Visions of Vancouver: Ideology, democracy, and the future of urban development. *Urban Geography*, *17*, 478–501. doi:10.2747/0272-3638.17.6.478

Mommas, H. (2002). City branding: The necessity of socio-cultural goals. In T. Hauben, M. Vermeulen, & V. Patteeuw (Eds.), *City branding: Image building and building images* (pp. 32–48). Rotterdam: NAI Uitgevers.

Okano, H., & Samson, D. (2010). Cultural urban branding and creative cities: A theoretical framework for promoting creativity in the public spaces. *Cities*, *27*, 10–15.

Rutheiser, C. (1996). *Imagineering Atlanta*. London: Verso.

Sevcik, T. (2011). Strategic urban narratives: Beyond conventional city branding. *Development*, *54*, 343–344. doi:10.1057/dev.2011.59

Shi-xu. (2014). *Chinese discourse studies*. Basingstoke: Macmillan.

Shi-xu. (in press). Cultural discourse studies. In K. Tracy, C. Ilie, & T. Sandel (Eds.), *International Encyclopaedia of language and social interaction*. Malden, MA: Wiley-Blackwell.

Slater, T. (2002). Looking at the 'North American City' through the lens of gentrification discourse. *Urban Geography*, *23*(2), 131–153.

Williams, K. (2010). Sustainable cities: Research and practice challenges. *International Journal of Urban Sustainable Development*, *1*(1), 128–133.

Wilson, W. J. (1996). *When work disappears: The world of the new urban poor*. New York: Knopf.

Zukin, S., & M. Greenberg. (1998). From Coney Island to Las Vegas in the urban imaginary: Discursive practices of growth and decline. *Urban Affairs Review 33*(5), 627–654.

References in Chinese

季靖, 陈静 (2008) 。传播与城市品牌塑造 – – 以杭州, 上海为例。《消费导刊》, 21, 16-17。

杭州市政府 (2007) 。杭州"生活品质之城"城市品牌表述系统 (要点) 。《杭州通讯 (生活品质版) 》, (1) , 20-21。

《杭州》课题组 (2008) 。《杭州》。北京：当代中国出版社。

黄宇亮, 王竹 (2006) 。杭州城市识别系统的诠释与实践。《华中建筑》, 24 (8) 。

施旭 (2008) 。从话语研究的视角看城市发展。《文化艺术研究》, 3, 32-43。

邹身城 (2006) 。从研究城市个性特征出发, 探讨杭州的发展定位。中国城市发展网 http://chinacity.org.cn。

Index

INDEX